FACING
FACE

FACING
FACE

SKYLER RAYE

CITI OF
BOOKS

CITIOFBOOKS, INC.
3736 Eubank NE Suite A1
Albuquerque, NM 87111-3579
www.citiofbooks.com
Hotline: 1 (877) 389-2759
Fax: 1 (505) 930-7244

Ordering Information:
Quantity sales. Special discounts are available on quantity purchases by corporations, associations, and others. For details, contact the publisher at the address above.

Printed in the United States of America.

ISBN-13:	Softcover	979-8-89391-326-2
	eBook	979-8-89391-327-9

Library of Congress Control Number: 2024918991

TABLE OF CONTENTS

PREFACE

Writing was my escape. It was the only part of me that acknowledged my brokenness. Little did I know, I was beginning to face face.

After my fall . . . I got a Humpty Dumpty figurine from a close friend. This, unbeknownst to me, was more like a curse than a gift. As I usually try to be optimistic, I saw only the best in all the king's men. Further down the road, that friend, among others, would no longer be in my life. Nobody was trying to put me back together again. In fact, it was just the opposite. I felt what was left of my life was, piece by piece, being torn apart.

After my fall . . . life as I knew it completely crumbled, leaving nothing but horrendous feelings of pain and intense emotions. I still had, thank goodness, my constant companion Buckley, my black-as-night standard poodle, as well as my passion for plants. And through it all, I kept writing. Writing was my escape. Having my diary published was never a consideration, until my friend Donna suggested it to me. I was honest. It was dark, honest, and raw. Had I not had a brain injury, I never would have agreed to Donna making this a published book.

This book is not intended to make anyone look good or bad (just in case, most names have been changed to protect the guilty). It's not intended to make you feel sorry for, or like or dislike me. In fact, I'm sure there will be times when you'll think I'm stupid, funny, crazy, all of the above and just plain glad you're not in my shoes. Anyway, come to find out the face I needed to face was mine. This helped me do just that. If it will give someone else hope, all the better.

SKYLER'S ACKNOWLEDGEMENTS

Thank you, God, for being my constant, for your love, and for giving me new grace. I am so appreciative of all you've done in my life, and look forward to what you have in store for my future.

Thank you, Diana, for believing in and showing me your boundless love, especially at the most unlovable period of my life. I'm so grateful for you. I'm pretty sure if you had not put all my journals and notes together for Donna, this book would never have been written. I love you every day of my life.

Donna . . . although I knew you before my accident, we became friends afterward. Thank you for your perseverance in getting this book done. But most of all, thank you for your friendship. Although I've wished it didn't exist 99% of the time, I'm glad you made it happen. I like me more because I faced faced.

Aunt Hazel, Aunt Marlene, Marge and Jim . . . words can never tell you how much I love and appreciate you, and all your encouragement and prayers through the toughest times of my life.

Of course, my wonderful dog Buckley Sir Rocko . . . you were the greatest canine ever. I knew from the beginning you were special. Thanks for loving me when I didn't love myself or think anyone else did. Your loyalty was amazing.

Mom. Although I really do not want you to read this book, or at least parts of it, I do want you to know that I am so thankful to have you as my mom. I know for a fact you prayed for me daily. I am thankful to have the opportunity to get to know you and you me. We've had some misperceptions of one another, but I do know you love me. Thanks for all you've done.

Yanna, I don't know where, or if, I would be without you. You played such a huge part in keeping me alive. I'll always be grateful to you for allowing Buckley to come with me to our sessions, and for when you came to my house. You truly are an asset to your profession, and I can never thank you enough for your help during my journey back to being a whole person.

Rich, Patti, Linda, and Paul . . . thank you for doing what God asked of you and starting City of Refuge.

Logan, my friend, thank you for all the help with getting my artwork together and on the cover.

INTRO

The place to start is the beginning of the end of me. What you are about to encounter are excerpts from journals and art therapy I amazingly had the presence of mind to keep through years of turbulence. I was often in a blizzard of vertigo while writing, so this book might seem a bit unbalanced. Sometimes the sub-plots got way too thick. It's just the way it was. I now believe I wrote in attempt to bail myself out of things I couldn't deal with. The "me" I knew was taken away. What was left?

Anything can happen, as I have learned. Along my journey I discovered it's not so much what happens to you in this life, but rather how you react to it. I have learned, through bitter lessons, the value of life. It nearly killed me.

The words of a lady, Kathryn Collman, I saw on Sunday morning TV when I was very young stayed with me all these years. She spoke about believing in miracles. Know what? I do. In many ways, I am one. We all are.

The following pages will divulge some unbelievably dark times for me. But darkness can be a place where the unknown can turn into opportunity. I believe a person can discover his or her true strength when crawling upon the depths of rock bottom. It is then we must ask: are we dying to live or are we living to die?

CHAPTER ONE
TAKE ONE

First question: Where to start?

There are so many places.

Last question: Where to end?

I have had the luxury of getting to know myself.

GETTING BUSY GIVING UP

CHAPTER ONE
TAKE TWO

Does it seem to you, like it does to me, that there are not many times when we are fully in charge of our lives? As children, most of us anyway, we clearly are not. As adolescents trying to fit in, we defiantly attempt to be. We lose it a bit when playing the dating game. To some of you, this may sound familiar: "I don't care. We can do what you want to do." As the relationship ages, it often turns into, "You never do what I want to do, but it seems I'm always doing what you want to do." Hmmm. Is it just me?

In any case, it is all too often we allow others to call the shots and let them be more in charge of us than we are. It's like letting an extra play the leading role in the movie of our life. It seems to me it would be a much better story if everyone played themselves.

CHAPTER ONE
TAKE THREE

This is it. It's time for Facing Face.

I thought I lost my life in 2001. Could have been 1999. 2003 is a very good candidate. No, for sure it had to be 2005. Was it just odd years? It's hard to say, because, unfortunately, I have so many experiences to choose from.

Since 2001, I have been on a terribly long, dark journey that nearly had me sunk for good. The culprit most responsible for leading me down that hell-hole was prescription drugs. You know, the legal pills that get peddled by the gazillions to the hopeful millions on a daily basis. I must admit, I've indulged in the illegal ones as well. But it was the legal ones, given to me by physicians who were supposed to be taking care of me, that sent me on this unbelievable, endless nightmare. I lost everything. Of all the things I lost, I missed my mind the most.

CHAPTER ONE
TAKE FOUR

Should I take things in chronological or catastrophic order? Don't worry, I won't make you read through the how I got screwed-up because of my parents chapter. Well, maybe a little. I grew up during the sixties and seventies in the part of the country most famous for housing nine nuclear reactors whose plutonium was used in a new-fangled bomb against Japan, Tri-Cities, Washington.

As a child I often played with my imaginary friends. They always told me how important I was and how much they needed me. I didn't get that from anyone else.

When I was around the age of ten, my dad decided to be a rancher. He moved our house, yes, our house, out to this land he bought. Our new life was quite different from the suburban life we lived. We were now ranchers, and my two brothers and I were true ranch-hands. Every day we had to move these huge sprinkler lines for the farm, including before and after school. This often involved getting rid of big rocks and thistles. We had a few Chevy trucks, which I managed to drive before I could completely see out the windshield or reach the pedals.

Until I hit college, I thought all girls lived like me, driving tractors and trucks, bucking hay, working right along with the boys. Dad's motto for me was: "Work like a man, but sit like a lady." I think that caused issues in my life. There were many times I was mad I was born a girl. Mostly because of the answer I got from my parents to questions like,

"Why do my brothers get to stay out later than me?" and, "Why do I have to set the sprinklers and do the dishes and my brothers don't?" Yep, you can guess the answer.

I planned the whole thing as a child. Who I would be and how I would matter to so many people. See, my problem was I didn't think I was important

unless someone else thought so. I was only as good as I was told. There were times I was so big, but most times I was so small.

I won't make you read too much about the time in 1996 when my beloved dog of 16 years, Benson, died in my arms with the tune from Jeopardy in the background. The answer is: long legged, bald-butted antique dog. Who was Benson Maynard Smith? It had been a toss up as to who would die first: my Dad or my dog. Benson won that race by almost a year.

I won't go into much detail about the time I had neurosurgery in 1997 as a result of a boogie board blowout. I'll just say it was yet another experience that taught me one of life's valuable lessons the hard way: don't mix Mai Tai's and boogie boards.

I can't leave out my good friend, Paulette Davis, lead singer in the band Paulette & Power. She was a social worker by day, blues diva by night. Once I had the opportunity to accompany her and the band to the Monterey Blues Festival, where she performed and even dedicated a song to me, "Payback is a Mother For Ya. Paulette died in a head-on car crash in 1998.

CHAPTER ONE
TAKE FIVE

In one of my previous lives, during those wild and crazy Reagan eighties, I was an auto parts runner by day, coke dealer by day and night. That was a lucrative time. I would go into nice restaurants and, through waitresses, trade matchboxes of coke for cash. A week pulling in ten grand was not unusual.

One Friday night, after getting paid, I made my last auto parts delivery. I had to wait for this customer to sign for the parts, and, unfortunately for me, he was working underneath a car. My pager went off and wouldn't you know, it was one of my top waitresses with a rush order. Like I said, it was Friday night, I just got paid, and if that wasn't cause enough for wanting to get out of there, now I had another delivery to make. My customer was still under this car. All I could see were his feet sticking out. I must say, he had good taste in boots. Impatient, I wound up kicking his well-dressed foot. That got his attention! And I found myself staring at two of the most beautiful blue eyes I'd ever seen.

I soon learned more about Pete, the man behind those stunning eyes. As he became a good customer, I learned he also had a tough childhood. We got better acquainted over tequilas and chips soaked in salsa. Cuervo Gold, that was important. At some point, when it became obvious he was more than ready to get into my jeans, I had to tell him I happened to have a girlfriend. He didn't care. We wound up quitting coke together, and being best buddies. Inevitably, much later in our relationship, the attraction became too tough to fight. I guess we were "friends with benefits" way before its popularity. Our friendship and sexual relationship were just that, and it would continue for years. I really did love him, and he loved me. Of that love I am sure.

Another thing Pete and I shared was our dream of being independent. I had started a thriving business, The Plant Pleasers Inc., where I can be creative with nature, my real passion. Pete was a successful stunt car driver, as well as a transportation coordinator in film productions. Life was good for both of us.

For relaxation, Pete would go off every year to Mexico and drive in the Baja 500. In the summer of 1999, as the world was gearing up for Y2K, it was something as simple as a few screws (literally) that kept him no more than three miles from the finish line. Of all things, his motor fell out on that hot, dusty road. It was three hours before the next car breezed by to take his place in the winner's circle. His ego was still bruised when I chided him about it.

"It wasn't a simple fix, Sherri!" he proclaimed.

"Three hours!" I exclaimed. "Now, I ask, are or are you not an auto mechanic?"

My parents loved Pete. My mother thought that he was the son-in-law of her dreams. Until the three of us watched this movie together. During one scene, when Father Somebody or other was saying a prayer, Pete said, "God is just a crutch for a lot of people." Well, my holier-than-thou religious mother was ready to call the wedding off.

The last time Pete and I went to my folks' place was when my father sold the ranch. My mother didn't even know he was thinking about it until two weeks before moving day. Needless to say, it was not the most pleasant of visits. Dad took Pete aside and gave him one of his prized possessions. "I want you to have this here gun from now on," he told Pete. "Don't reckon I'll get much target practice in at the mobile home park."

"I would hope not," Pete replied as he accepted the gun. The gun I saw as a child, always hanging in Dad's holster draped over the recliner.

Pete was the one who got me into films. Not on the screen, silly, behind the scenes. I started my film career in the glamorous world of transportation. But I quickly found my way into the wonderful world of plants, or greens as it's called in the biz. Some of the films we worked on include ones you may have actually heard of: Practical Magic, Bandits, and Men of Honor.

Three weeks before the premier Pete and I were to attend for Men of Honor . . . I shudder as I remember the message on my answering machine telling me of his tragic death in a head-on car crash with a semi-truck. What a shock, and loss, to those of us who loved him. GOD I MISS HIM.

I cannot share my fond memories of Pete without telling you about Darren also. Pete introduced us, and we became fast friends. I was the first bisexual person Darren ever met (that he knew of). Yet Darren asked me out. And asked me out. Again and again. I tried to let him down easily at first, but then I had to get rough. When he bluntly asked why the two of us consenting adults couldn't at least have sex together, I had to tell him, "Darren, you couldn't handle it." Truth be told, I was the one who couldn't handle my emotions.

I really did care for him. I have to say, I admired his physique. He was so strong and muscular I called him "Bam Bam." I couldn't bring myself to ever really respect him though. Mostly because he didn't respect himself. He had trouble with alcohol that he'd never admit to.

Darren gave me the closest semblance to the one thing I really wanted: a sense of family. One of his two daughters, Chris, was the most beautiful little five year old I'd ever seen. Chris reminded me of myself to me at times. Aside from her long dark hair, which I had at her age, she had the same inquisitive, yet painful, look on her face. It didn't take long for me to become her fill in mom. Darren, romantic that he was N'T, told me on the phone he was falling in love with me. I realized I couldn't be with him. I mean, he could barely handle our friendship. Sometimes I think how easy it could have been, the four of us playing house together. Family. I tried for as long as I could, but it wasn't the right role for me.

And that decision was not made lightly. I can't tell you how many times I had to endure this beautiful child expounding, for what seemed like hours and hours, good reasons why I should marry her father. I recognized another common trait Chris and I shared: solving problems in our head before they happen. I finally realized you can't possibly have all problems figured out before they happen. What a waste of time!

Speaking of problems, someone else became me, and my finances became a living nightmare. The !@#* took my briefcase, which had my full name and identity in numbers: social security, bank accounts, passport, and date of birth. And let me tell you, this new me was spending money like it was going out of style. Looked like I was having a great time. Never caught the !@#*.

While I was trying to minimize the damage to my personal credit rating and bank accounts, I trusted my accountant to take care of my business finances. Strange, but true. So imagine my surprise when I learned that my accountant wanted to start a new business and her financial capital was generously provided via my business bank account. Because I had been, go ahead, fill in the blank:_____(trusting, stupid, irresponsible, nuts, all of the above) and signed over a power of attorney to her to sign business checks for me, she wound up taking over $100,000.

Now I don't want you to think things were all bad. You-know-what happens, right? At least Plant Pleasers was a blooming success. In addition to having my regular customers, I did landscape design work for several award winning residential and commercial land developments. I also worked on several movie productions that chose to film in Portland.

My dating life was busy until a world-class tap dancer wanted me to go out on a date with her. She was in her 20's, while I was 37, She was beautiful on the outside, but I really wasn't interested. Finally, I gave in when she never left after the 1st date. The only thing she taught me was how to tap dance. I did a mean shim sham, shimmy.

I took her to Hawaii, which means I have to introduce BonMom to you. Years earlier, on my way home from Japan, I stopped at the Big Island to meet up with my good friend Candy and her husband. While at a luau with Candy we met BonMom, who thought I was K.D. Lang. We hit it off immediately. BonMom lived there six months out of the year. She took me snorkeling for the first time the same day she said she wanted adopt me. She played a huge part in my life, though I don't see her as much as I used to. I don't do anything like I used to.

My trip with Lizzie was another in a series of trips to Hawaii I had taken with former girlfriends who all claimed their love for me and matrimonial intentions. In front of BonMom. So this time, BonMom, with her keen sense of humor, announces to me, at a dinner with a group of upper crust ladies, "You know, I am an ordained minister. And, as it happens, I really like your friend. What would you say if I marry the two of you? I have an opening at two o'clock on Thursday."

"What did you say?" I asked, stunned.

"You heard me. I can marry the two of you."

I could have fallen down except for the fact that I was sitting at this huge banquet table. I flashed back to writing vows to my first love, which seemed like a hundred years ago. Did I want to write them to Lizzie? More importantly, I wanted to know, will there be another? We tied the knot on December 9, 1999, although it was tied loosely, and thank God was not legal.

CHAPTER TWO
ABOUT FACE

Early in 2001, my union rep called me to work in the greens department for the production company filming *The Hunted* starring Tommy Lee Jones and Benicio Del Toro. I reported for work as instructed at the construction warehouse at 6 a.m. It was about 9:20 when, finally, Harry, the "lead greens" arrived. Let's just say Harry liked tipping the bottle.

Later that day I spoke with a friend I knew from previous productions, who was a driver for my department. He casually mentioned a conversation he had with Harry, who questioned my ability. "Don't worry," my friend assured me, "it's not just you. Harry doesn't like women working in the greens department as a general principle. He knows you have a great reputation with several movies under your belt, and your own company doing the same kinds of things in the real world."

"I can hold my own," I confidently stated.

By the end of my second day on the job, Harry said he was going to make me the "on-set greens" when the production company started filming next week. This was okay with me, as it meant a pay increase. I was the only "greens" person working for Harry the first week. I recommended hiring another union guy I knew from the set of *Bandits*, Mark, who lived in Idaho. I hired Mark and his brother after *Bandits* wrapped, as the production company hired my business the Plant Pleasers Incorporated to do the restoration at film sites.

April 6, 2001, was an unusually warm, beautiful day. I was working on a shoot in a downtown Portland plaza. Harry returned to the set after spending time at the nearest bar. He was not a happy drunk. All he would do was yell at me. He bellowed just as good, or bad, as my dad.

As "on-set greens" I got the call to the camera, and was told to get rid of a hard angle. After looking through the camera, I instantly knew it was the white top of a bus stop.

The camera was at the top of these brick stairs facing a park. As I turned around to go back down the stairs, a cable dropped, my right foot got tangled in it, and I completely lost my balance. In spite of desperate attempts to regain it, and two crew members trying to catch me, I fell backwards approximately four feet to six feet down the stairs onto my head.

Within that split second, as I was falling, I was 12 again, back at the ranch. I'm on top of a huge semi-flatbed boom truck. My brothers brought the freshly baled hay to our dad, who hooked the bale using the boom control and sent the bales up to me so I could unhook and stack them. Dad accidentally hit the wrong lever, and the boom hit me in the side of my head, sending me flying about 20' down. Flat on the dirt, all I could see were his boots running toward me as he was cussing at me.

Years later, before he died, Dad asked me, "Remember that time I almost killed you?" And I knew that was his way of saying he was glad he didn't.

BOOM! The greatest impact to the brick surface was made with the center of the back of my head.

A split second. Think about this. If the cable had fallen a second earlier, or a second later, you probably wouldn't be reading this book. It's amazing how much life can change in just a split second. I know there are many of you who know exactly what I'm talking about.

Someone from catering kindly helped me to the on-set medic. Of course the cover-their-asses necessary piles of paperwork were filled out. Surprisingly, we wrapped early that day, which was okay with me.

At 4 a.m. the next morning, I amazed the Teamster who picked me up to go to the next location up on Mt. Hood. The guys on-set were also amazed that I showed up. As if I could even consider not working.

We spent about a week up there. I worked every day bundled up in my parka with not one inch of skin showing, let alone my swollen head. My workload was pretty easy, and I had the help of many caring union brothers and sisters. The guys that saw me fall took good care of me, always asking if I was okay.

Back in Portland, on the morning of April 19, 2001, I reported for work as usual. The medic, a friend I worked with on other productions, had been keeping a close eye on me. He informed me that he called for a chiropractor to come there to see me. My head looked like a huge lopsided watermelon, the kind you could enter in the county fair. The medic was sure my injuries required more than the aspirins I was gulping down.

I was asked by the Locations Manager to come up with two large front yard shrubs. Which I went ahead and got, 'cause, like the snail mailman, I always deliver. About an hour after I returned with the prized shrubs, the chiropractor, Dr. Simpson, showed up. I asked him to adjust me (as if it were that simple). After just a glimpse at me he could only say, "You'll have to come in for extensive testing." I read the look of amazement in his eyes as if he had said, "Dead girl walking."

"You made a house call to tell me that? What I need is some relief! There's gotta be something you can do, isn't there? Can't you pop it or something?" I begged.

"We need to get you to my office where I can do a more thorough exam," he told me as he handed me his card. "Come at eight tomorrow." And with that he left.

After wrap that day Harry approached me with more good news. "Don't bother reporting in tomorrow," he growled.

"What? Why not?" I questioned.

"Got a two week hiatus. Not enough work. So long."

Now, wait a minute. Think about this, I told myself. I busted my butt on this job, from trimming trees in the snow on Mt. Hood to finding and digging up several front yard shrubs by the side of the freeway. Aside from the fact that I'd been in the union for some time, and the fact that I was first hire, and the fact that I was local hire, not to mention my vast experience and natural talents, I was out of work while Mark, the guy I recommended from Idaho, was still working. This didn't seem quite fair. Actually, it seemed like discrimination to me.

But, alas, I had other things to occupy myself with. My unrelenting, unending, unnerving pain. Needless to say, I was now free to make it to the chiropractor's. Great.

When I saw Dr. Simpson again he suggested I have some x-rays taken since I was in excruciating pain every time I moved my head and/ or shoulder. This made working for Plant Pleasers not quite so pleasing for me. But I had obligations to my customers, and I did my very best bailing to at least keep the business afloat.

Two weeks had now passed. I called Harry to ask if it was time for me to come back to work. "No," he grumbled, "don't bother showing up."

"Well, what's up with that? Isn't the woods scene scheduled to shoot this week?" I still had some brain power left.

"No work, forget it!" he shouted.

"You know," I calmly said, "I understand Mark is still working."

At that point he screamed at me something like this is why he doesn't like working with women 'cause they think they can do anything. He then hung up. At that point I called my union rep to file a grievance. He heard I'd been laid off. He would check into it and get back to me.

I heard nothing back from him. But I did hear about my x-ray, CAT scan, and MRI results. They showed that my brain had actually shifted. My fall had blown out the only two good discs I had left in my neck. The injuries to my head and shoulders and in between would keep me from working, among other things. I found myself falling and puking a lot, which didn't help.

The union rep called and talked to Lizzie, who told him about my injuries. His response was that I couldn't have a workers comp claim and file a grievance at the same time. I guess it's one per customer. Okay, I thought, I'll get better and be back at work soon. Let's go for the grievance.

A friend thought I could sue and win millions, so she connected me with her attorney friend. We spoke briefly and I was advised to go ahead with both the grievance and claim. Which I did.

In the meantime, my pain persisted and often persevered, but I couldn't let it control me. It went contrary to the basic core value I have, which is that I will do my damnedest to bail out the boat before I let it go down. There is no other option.

At my next visit with him, Dr. Simpson referred me to my new personal physician, Dr. Pilsner. "I know I can help you, and I know she'll refer you back," he told me with certainty. And I was happy because she was a naturopathic doctor.

When I saw Dr. Pilsner I emphatically told her, "I only want natural meds. I want nothing to do with narcotics. Please. I already have brain damage, and don't need any narcotics to help confuse me even more."

The good doctor first wanted to get my neurosurgical records, and did indeed send me back to Dr. Simpson. He did try, on several occasions, to adjust me (tough job, I know), which hurt more than I was hurting. He then referred me to someone else for massage therapy and added an acupuncturist. You should have seen the acupuncturist's reaction to the needles popping out after he inserted them. He'd put one in, then another, and the first one would pop out as would the next and so on. He told me, "I think acupuncture not good for you."

Every treatment I underwent served only to increase my level of pain. I now had almost no feeling in either arm and was in pain to the point of constant nausea. It was so unbearable that I could barely hold onto the bail bucket. I was at the point where I made the first of what turned out to be too many emergency room trips. I saw Dr. Pilsner there and just broke down and cried.

At that point even Dr. Pilsner knew we needed a different plan of attack. No more visits to Dr. Simpson and his associates (yes!). We were now going to put my life back in the hands of my prior neurosurgeon, Dr. Bower. He had performed major neurosurgery on me just a few years earlier to fix the boogie board accident. So I figured he could fix me again. On June 11, Dr. Bower's sage advice was, "I'm not the guy for you this time. A shunt might help, but that's your decision to make."

I had begun to recover some feeling in both my arms (whew!) when I saw Dr. Pilsner again. "Now what?" I less-than-enthusiastically asked.

"Physical therapy could help," she replied. "Until then, any treatment we do could further aggravate your injuries. I want you to take this happy pill and some other meds."

This "happy pill" did NOT live up to its name. Instead, the "happy pill" turned out to be Effexor, and combined with the other non-natural med she gave me, Xanax, equaled more like crazy than happy. I thought "just say no" would work, but come to find out my trusted naturopathic doctor was more of a pusher than most drug dealers I've known. At the time, I didn't really pay much attention to what the prescriptions were so much as what they could do to help me. And I had my little mouseketeer on my case to take the meds as prescribed. This path took me from crazy to really insane.

I scheduled an appointment with my new physical therapist for the very end of June, after she could review my medical records. Three days prior to my appointment I received a letter from the union rep stating I had no grounds for a grievance. Ouch. Good thing I had physical therapy coming up. It was the one thing in my life I looked forward to.

MY JOURNAL

8/7/01 ~

12:10 a.m.

Dear God,

Please send guidance. I wouldn't mind if you sent it along with financial comfort and friends. Friendly ones, good and honest. Home. Family. Please.

Thank you.

S

CHAPTER THREE
EXTREME LUCK

Years ago, a palm reader told me that I have extreme luck. I smiled broadly, until her finger waved in my face, saying, "Oh, not always a good thing. This luck can go either way."

I had to admit I could no longer tend to Plant Pleasers in the manner I prided myself in. Toward the end of August, I negotiated a deal to sell it to this lady for the fair price of $250,000. We were going to finalize it after her trip to Greece in September.

Early in September, my cousin Kenny and his friend from Idaho came to work for Plant Pleasers. I really appreciated their help and let them stay at my house. One morning we were up early to go over the day's schedule. Just like every morning, Katie Couric was on my TV. (I liked waking up with you every morning, Katie.) I glanced at the TV and saw an airplane fly into the World Trade Center. Kenny saw it also, and we just stared, unable to speak. It was an unbelievable event unfolding right before our eyes. As our eyes were fixated on the screen in horror, we witnessed people jumping out of this humungous skyscraper. It was raw. I was raw. It was the darkest sunny day ever.

Oh my God. I am so lucky to be alive. Extremely.

When the lady returned from Greece, she backed out of the sale due to the uncertain economy (welcome to my world).

In mid-October, my realtor friend tried to help by listing my house for me, since I could no longer make the payments. As I only owed approximately $30,000, and it was worth over $350,000, you'd think that I'd have helped instead of sabotaging her efforts. I did NOT want to move and lose my home. So, I took the sale fliers in front of the house and used them as kindling in my fireplace. When she called to tell me she was bringing over potential buyers, I didn't scurry to straighten up the house like most people would. I got ready by removing my front curtains and replacing them with a sheet I burned holes in. When they arrived my friend was smart enough to know not to go any further. She could tell something was not quite right, and she was pretty sure it was me.

As potential buyers approached my door, I would make sure they overheard me disguising my voice as two or three different people, shouting, "Where are my needles?"

"I told you I don't use them. I snort my drugs! Maybe it was one of those hookers you brought over."

"I need heroin fast!"

Needless to say, they hastily hurried off.

My birthday is December 31st. Always had a hell of a birthday party. All I really wanted for my birthday was for this year to end. At least I got that much.

I am physically unable to sustain the devotion and passion I lovingly gave to Plant Pleasers. I printed out this letter to mail to my clients:

Dear *Whichever Valued Customer You Are,*

Due to an injury I sustained I have been unable to work. So as of December 31, 2001 The Plant Pleasers Inc. will be no more. Thank you for your business throughout the years. It truly has been a pleasure working with you and pleasing your plants.

Sincerely,
Sherri Smith

To sum up, 2001 was not a good year, I'm sorry to say. Not for families who lost their loved ones on Sept. 11th. And not for me. It was the year of my fall which begat my fall. 2001 left me with a traumatic brain injury, post concussion syndrome, vertigo, bulges in my neck, a huge bump on my head, and last, but definitely not least, chronic pain. I was considered permanently partially disabled and, let's not forget, unemployed. What followed closely was anxiety disorder and severe depression.

2002 started out with a positive, sort of. I met a kid on an elevator at my attorney's building. We were going down, mind you. His t-shirt proudly stated: "LEAF IT TO US." I said okay, and made this boy's New Year very happy. I gave him a HUGE discount on Plant Pleasers. It was a good move for him and, most importantly, for the plants. He took the option of making payments, and only had to pay for the clients that stayed with him. The business was appraised at over $250,000. Over a two year period I got about $250 a month from him.

3/14/02 ~

Sometime after midnight

I was taken to an emergency room due to an inability to stop throwing up. That and the mother-of-all-mothers of a migraine, which made my head feel like it was going to blow off. I was having an anxiety attack, and the room couldn't stop spinning. They gave me meds for the nausea, and suggested I see a doctor on staff for pressure point manipulation. Oh yeah, I was also told a yoga class would be good for me. Then they sent me on my way.

Due to the incredible pain, my balance was way off (though some might say I was always unbalanced), and I'd often wind up on the ground. It was all related to months of ingesting too many meds, the prescribed ones, some of which should NOT have been mixed (thanks, Doc). I was really losing it, as evidenced by that insane argument I had with Lizzie. Well, not the argument so much. It was what happened next.

I went downstairs to my shop. The pain was so intense that I simply decided to cut it off. In my mind, as I headed toward my shiny new chop saw, it made sense that if I cut off my arm I would no longer be in this pain. My eyes were closed (I hate the sight of blood), and my arm was on the table. I heard Lizzie scream. As I turned around, I saw blood coming from her face. I quickly looked down to see that, yes, my arm was still attached. Curiously, I wondered why she was bleeding. Then I realized what happened. She walked in right as I was pulling the chop saw down to my arm and pulled the plug, literally. The saw was designed to stop on a dime, and I can testify that it did. The power cord was pulled with such force that it came back to hit her in the face, which required stitches on her upper lip.

My old friend Gary happened to stop by minutes after this happened. He looked confused as Lizzie told him I was about to seriously cut off my arm while her face was bleeding. He told me to sit down, stay there, and told his dog to watch me. He took Lizzie to the emergency room.

In the light of the next day, Lizzie called Dr. Pilsner and told her what happened. Yes, the same good doctor who was giving me Effexor, Xanax, Celexa, PLUS others (Baclofen, Zoloft, Zyprexa, Neurontin). Lizzie told me the doc wanted me to go and commit myself to the psych ward. She put the phone to my ear, and Dr. Pilsner threatened, "If you don't go in and commit yourself, I will send an ambulance over to forcefully take and commit you." She said if I went voluntarily I could leave when I wanted.

I cried, asking, "Why do I have to go to the psych ward?" She answered by saying, "I'm not equipped to deal with the psychiatric drugs you're taking." Whoa. Now, let me remind you, I agreed to see this doctor because she was a naturopath. As far as I knew, I was supposed to be on meds made from tree bark and plants. What psychiatric drugs??

You know, looking back, I have no doubt I would never have been admitted to the mental ward had I not taken the "psychiatric drugs" she prescribed and Lizzie filled. And with that wonderful vision called hindsight, I understood this ordeal was as bad as or worse than the stupid fall.

I went and checked myself in. I soon found out that leaving was no longer my call. While in the hospital, desperately wanting to talk with someone normal who cared for me, I called home and was happy to hear Lizzie's voice.

"Hi! What are you doing?" I asked.

"Packing," she answered. It was like someone hit me in the stomach. She continued, saying, "I still love you, but I'm tired of it all."

My head was pounding faster than my heart. I was trying to find a way to swallow this. It was like swallowing a handful of nails. "Lizzie, please, don't do this!" I cried. "Doesn't the fact I am locked up in the mental ward and came in here voluntarily say anything to you? I can't believe you are locking me up in this shithole and then leaving!" I was stunned that she chose this particular time to move out. She was going to leave Buckley alone! And me! How could this be happening?

According to Lizzie, "This injury is affecting more lives than just the injured." She then proceeded to give me her list of complaints. Okay, so her lip did require stitches while keeping me from cutting off my arm. That's legit, I admit. She couldn't live any more being worried and stressed out over me while at work. Basically, she was afraid to leave me alone. She got tired of not being able to get enough sleep, since I could only sleep an average of forty-five minutes at one time and three hours total in a twenty-four hour period. She wasn't a nurse. Bottom line was, she couldn't handle my pain.

"No one but me sees you this way," she whined. "And those few who have visited can obviously not handle seeing you so . . . down, and in such pain and feeling so helpless. The hardest part is that it's been close to a year since you fell, and your pain, along with everything else, is much worse."

It was nearly a year since my fall. She didn't want to live with me either. So, I kind of understood why she left. But I was still mad as hell at her for not being honest and, let's face it, the timing really sucked.

I thought this really must be the bottom. I'm now in water over my head.

But I'm frantically bailing.

CHAPTER FOUR
THE GREAT ESCAPE

Two days after I was admitted, I left against medical advice (a.m.a. for those of us in the know). Now, this is not as easy as you might think. The nurses told me it was their moral obligation to not let me go. I promised I'd be right back. I just needed to take care of my dog.

I surmised interaction would be the key to my escape. I had to become part of a family. (Now, this was easy for me, as I've done it many times. The problem was keeping them.) There was this lady, Luisa, whose husband beat her and her kids, and she went crazy, or so they say. Whether they pulled her out of the situation to protect her or others, it was the right thing to do. So here it is. Visitation hour. Luisa's family is here. I knew I had to be cool. I only knew a little bit of Spanish, but I knew enough. A smile and a nod can get you a long way in life. Here I go.

Luisa's family included about eight or nine black-haired people. I took off my hat and semi-straightened my thick black head of hair. "Can I hold your baby?" I asked. "Bonita, bonita," I said as I hoped I was holding a girl. I did this as Luisa went to ask the nurse to let her family leave. I walked with them to the locked door. They looked at me curiously and proceeded to take their baby back. As the door beeped, the nurse shepherded them out as I was strategically standing front and center. I pushed the door and walked really, really fast. I knew this hospital well, and headed for the stairs. I ran down, still in pajamas mind you, hoping I wouldn't trip on them. I made it through the main lobby shouting, "Call me a cab! Call me a cab!" Once outside I thought, "What great service!" because there was a cab sitting right there.

Freedom was here at last. And somewhere in Portland is a Middle Eastern cab driver who will never be the same. He came to the hospital, I thought, to pick me up. As I jumped into the cab, I looked back to see if anyone was following. I'm not sure who was more surprised: me, the cab driver, or the lady I just about sat on. I was more than happy to help scoop up her things and get her out.

"This is an emergency. Quick, get me to Cora and sixty-ninth," I demanded as I directed him the fastest way home. Poor guy unwittingly took me, not saying a word. He was probably thinking he didn't have much choice and that I actually had money to pay the fare. Well, I had no money, or keys, since they were inside my home. Bub, a very good long-time friend, told me earlier that day she left $100 in my mail slot, which I planned to use to pay the driver.

"Stay here," I told the confused cab driver as I got out when we reached home. "I'll be right back with your money." I tried the front door. Locked. The bedroom window. Locked. As I walked around to the back, my mind was racing as I tried to decide which window to break. Bingo! The kitchen window was unlocked! But, alas, there was no money. There was not even a phone to be found in my home that Lizzie had done a good job of ransacking. I went back out to the cab driver. As I grabbed his cell phone I asked, "Can I borrow that?" He was speechless.

I called a friend that lived close by. "Stella, is that you? I need a big favor. I just took a cab home and have no money. Would you loan me fifteen dollars?"

Without hesitation, she said, "Sure." "Great! Thank you so much!"

I handed the cabbie the phone. "She will tell you where to go to get the money. Nice tip also."

Inside my house it felt strangely unfamiliar. Marks on the walls where pictures had once hung. Empty boxes scattered around. It felt alone. I really thought Lizzie was the one who wouldn't leave. I certainly did not expect she would leave in such a cowardly way.

I mean, it was just days earlier she and her mother were consoling me, telling me they were my family and would never leave. (I think her mom had a crush on me and meant it. After all, we were closer in age.)

In my head I hear the song "Here I Go Again" by Whitesnake. I am wondering if I really am so unbalanced.

Everyone has a hard time seeing any of the characteristics of the Sherri they knew. It's still Me. I knew what I needed to do. I had to convince everyone I was done with the mental ward and was going to stay home.

I needed to get the attention off me, so I thought I would pay tribute to those still there.

TO ALL THAT TOUCHED MY LIFE

Steve: Great minds think alike, but probably too much. Your words were the first sane ones I heard, which was reassuring since I had hoped more like me existed. (I still think you're not crazy.)

To the Carens: Thanks for the smiles and tears and sharing your colorful crayons.

Chrissy: I really admired what a warm fun person I felt you to be . . . I know the word fun seems a little out of place considering where we were but, hey, it's my letter.

I know my time there was short, but well spent. I wish it could have been longer. I want to thank you for the things I learned from you. We are all the same when we hit bottom. There are no expectations of each other. Nothing to lose by laying it all on the line. No one knew me before, so there would be no comparing. I have nothing left to give but me. No friends were bought.

To all the wonderful nurses (and you know who you are) who gave me the balance I needed, both by helping me in my weakest moments and yet treating me with respect (mostly by allowing me to give that suppository to myself even if I later found out there was a camera in my room).

I received so many things there I am now out using. Everyone in there, get all the ammunition you can. It comes in very handy.

Thank you again everyone for helping plant the seeds of self worth and hope in me.

To the nurses who tried to talk me into staying, I did tell the truth when I said I would not hurt myself. You made me think before I left. Not only did I not hurt myself, but I ended up having a peaceful two hour bath, then laughed at my dog who showed me how happy he was to have me home.

Maybe the best part of being home was falling asleep in front of the fireplace with my faithful Buckley. I have to say that my dog kept me from killing myself. I knew no one could love him like I do.

CHAPTER FIVE
WALKING INTO THE INFERNO

3/17/02 ~

St. Patrick's Day

Do you know why you shouldn't iron your four-leaf clover?

You would be pressing your luck.

I know it was my choice during early adulthood to put most of myself into my career rather than pursue a "family." That was my calling, if you will, my passion, my true love. Now, at the age of 42, I have neither.

I've prided myself on being a go-getter. It's just the keeping part I have a problem with. But I can't go get what I know any more, and I don't know what there is for me to get.

A friend convinced me to go back to the mental ward again. IT TOOK HER SIX HOURS TO CONVINCE ME THOUGH. She took me herself, not trusting I would turn myself in if left on my own. Well, she had a point.

This time it truly is the bottom. They put a hold on me. I don't remember much about it. "It" pushed me even harder and faster down the intense spiral of darkness. The way I look at it, take a high (pardon the pun) energy person such as myself, injure her so she will never again get to the end of day without pain and medication and their effects—the energy has to go somewhere. It turns into nervousness and anxiety. Which keeps the spiral spiraling.

I'm sorry to report I found out just how much they frowned on those that choose the a.m.a. route.

This day I was, according to my hospital records, manic. Very, very, manic. I'm not sure this is the right emergency room. What's up with the green reclining chairs in every room? And why is there a cop outside my room? My questions were answered in one sentence. "We are placing a Multnomah County hold on you," said the hospital social worker, quite matter-of-factly. It was at this point I realized that Nurse Ratchet is alive and well and living in Multnomah County. I was held in what's called "double lockdown." What that means is that they put you down deep in the basement and keep you so drugged that you pretty much just sleep most of the time.

There is one thing that I remember all too well. I called my oldest brother, who lives within a few hours drive. He's a preacher. "Mick, this is your sister . . . I am scared. I am in the hospital in the mental unit . . . double lockdown "

I broke down crying.

Before I could say another word, he said, "Sis, my wife and I feel you have a chip on your shoulder and do not want us around."

Whoa—this was not anything close to what I thought he'd say. My mind's now racing, passing through all the times I have gone to his house. I'd drop everything and drive the 400 miles there. I even paid for me and Mom to go see him and his family in Japan.

He never came to see me unless he was in Portland doing something else. Such as running a race and needing a shower, or guest speaking at a church. I frequently went to see him and his family.

This hurt me, and would continue to do so for years to come. Everyone loves me everyone loves to hate me. Maybe the truth is no one is even thinking of me. That is the worst.

And the absolute most awful, horrid, worst of it all: I was tied to my bed and abused by an intern. I know this happened, and it pushed me into the lowest of lowest places that exist.

After what felt like about a million years I was discharged. Here's where having a family member step in to advocate for me would have been nice. Someone to make sure I was actually getting the right treatment. I was released with no follow-up, but with a week's worth of about 15-20 different meds, including a new one, Depakote. This is given usually to prevent seizures or for seriously manic episodes of bipolar. My diagnosis was bipolar and possible personality disorder. My doctor there retired that same day.

3/23/02 ~

I'm keeping myself busy with things that don't require sharp objects. A couple of months earlier I brought home a headstone engraved by Gary. It said: REST IN PEACE. What I added to the stone was, sadly, a natural fit:

1988—2001

THE PLANT PLEASERS, INC.

I truly did not want to see people, or more likely, I didn't want people to see me. So I put a "Do Not Disturb—Sleeping" sign on my front door and never went out. It would have been nice to have family support. I hadn't ever asked for help from my family, the kind of help where money is not involved, only their presence . . . a hug. Dad was gone. My mother lives in Jerusalem, and my brother Joe lives on the east coast. Mick is a good preacher from what I hear. He travels the world helping people. Except me.

It was incomprehensible that, out of all the "families" that have opened their arms to me throughout the years, I would have picked Lizzie and her mom and think they would be there for me during this time in my life. Poor judgment . . . bad gamble.

I collected some of the very few things she left and boxed them away. I sat down and wrote her a letter. I just wanted her to know she could have had me for a friend. I would have gladly moved her out and set her up. I really mean it when I say things like "I love you." I am pretty sure love means "I want your happiness over mine." Why can't we be friends?

I continued to keep myself busy winding up the last few business things I could. But I felt myself spiraling deeper into a tunnel of blackness . . .

3/24/02 ~

My shoulder hurts . . . my head . . . my heart. Gilda and Jeffrey (my substitute parental units who live across the street) visit. The friend that convinced me to go in came over and brought some of my stuff she had from when I re-admitted.

My pal Bub called. God, are you there? I want to belong.

I don't think I can get through this, and I wonder if I need to be back at the mental ward. They say I am bipolar and manic. I say I am extreme and energetic.

The down time is dark.

I have not heard from any of my family. WHAT IS WRONG WITH ME??????

I wonder if I even want to know. I feel it is too late to matter. Why won't someone catch me??

Gotta keep bailing.

I just ran across the card my mom sent with $100. It made me cry.

I guess I never realized how far down my fall would take me . . . I could have swore I hit the bottom more than once, but then I continue to race downwards through this BLACK TUNNEL . . . thank God for those pinholes that allow some light for me to see there is some of me left. When in the blackness of depression, even a pinhole is huge. I dare not look away from this pinhole, lest I never find it again.

Okay, let's get down to what really hurts the most.

Ever since I stood out by the mailbox waiting for the school bus, singing songs in praise of Jesus, I prayed that some day I would have a family, a happy family. Love. Support. I mean, really, isn't that what most people want? Because, as many of you may know, the alternative can sure have its down side.

Alright. So I haven't exactly helped myself in that area. I could say I have done just about everything one could do to prevent it. Having gay relationships certainly isn't helpful. Relationships. Each one ends and I put up another brick on my wall. I no longer trust the wall.

I am still in shock over the fact that Lizzie moved out. It feels like salt in a huge open sore. I had no idea she would do this. What the hell is going on inside her head? Or in her life? I don't think I can swallow all of this and all the pills.

Another sleepless night. The Academy Awards were on last night. A year ago I was working with people on The Hunted who've won these awards.

I don't know if my body is capable to feel the stuff I need to deal with. Like, how could I have been so blind with Lizzie? What kind of person can lock their lover up and just up and move out???? Really. Am I crazy or is that slightly inhumane?

3/31/02 ~

Easter Sunday

Now is especially when the family thing really hurts. I have had the pleasure to spend holidays with so many families. At least when I had a girlfriend, my own family was established. Or so I thought.

Used to be I could always count on Pete. Or Darren. What a story he is. Anyway, Lizzie called this morning. I knew she'd be doing something with her family. Come on Lizzie, let's face this. I'll make it easy for you. There is nothing more than a friendship here for us. Walk with your head held high with what you know and always low enough so not to trip on anything.

Honestly. Has anything changed here?

I called my brother Joe this morning. I want Mom's number in Jerusalem. Joe told me I really let go verbally at Mick last week on the phone at the mental ward.

I told him I knew I had a chemical imbalance, and thought Dad did as well. I told him it was very hard to be so much like Dad. I wanted to get my head right, or get it right in my head.

I couldn't blame him for not being here for me, nor can I blame anyone but myself. The thing is, it doesn't matter who is right or who is wrong, *I am still very much alone*

With the pain. The pain never leaves. Sometimes it will let up to a dull burning pain. Other times it will feel like there is a burn from the right back of my head all over the shoulders, though it's mostly on the right side.

Oh God, help me. I am so sick of the pain. Really, really, I am.

There. I have my pain, my dog, my obligations, and now I will add to the list. My search for who I am—or maybe compiling all the various me's over the years to become 100%. Sometimes I really hate that optimistic side of me. SHUT UP SHUT UP!

What I really feel sucks. I realize what I want but don't have I may never have . . .

A FAMILY.

P.S. dEAR gOD,

THANK YOU FOR RISING UP FROM THE DEAD ON THIS DAY LONG AGO.

Families are the people who are there without you having to call. Friends are people who say after the fact "You should have called."

My stomach is so sick all the time. I'm having difficulty even keeping the meds down. My arm hurts all the time. It isn't a case of do I or don't I hurt. It is how much it hurts.

There is always a level of pain. I started the day off at a level of seven to eight. The more I use meds the more aware I am of an increase in the pain department. I wonder if the pain will ever go completely, even for a little while. I am afraid to do anything that could be potentially dangerous for me. I can never know for certain when the dizziness will strike or when I will get those muscle cramps that make my entire arm pull up in a very freaky way. Never knowing what's going to happen to me, and trying not to do anything stupid (which is hard all by itself).

Sherri, you are not the smartest tool in the shed, but you are the strongest.

Or should I say, you are the least likely to show weakness.

Did I get out of the mental ward too early? At least I slept there. I hope I can grasp onto something real. Without gambling away my heart. I have always said, "Don't gamble what you cannot afford to lose."

It's the kind of day I would have been most happy working in the yard.

Any yard. Instead, I was trapped.

4/1/02 ~

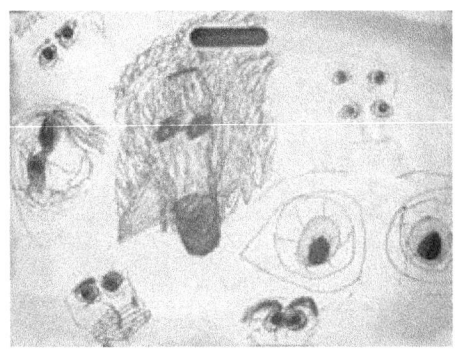

Art Therapy Class April Fool's Day

4/10/02 ~

The days passed slowly; nights passed even slower. I continued to see the wonderful doctor who: a) prescribed me all these pills in the first place, and had me admitted. Why? you may ask. Good question. Okay, I'll tell you: she got me into spatial dynamics therapy and that actually seemed to help the most. I was told I had post concussion syndrome and vertigo. I was receiving cranial pressure after being tested for and diagnosed with vertigo (great movie, lousy condition). That test was insane. I was then also prescribed Valium for my vertigo, Neurontin, another med developed for epilepsy and given for certain nerve pain, Zoloft, and some shot in the butt.

My head and heart are heavy. I've got to learn this time what it is

I need to know, and who I really am. I've gotten heavy again. That is something within my control. I am starting to focus enough that I am going to do something about it.

I am lonely. But, now that I think about it, it also seems I was lonely at times when I was with my "loves." I have a few friends that check on me now and then. But they are friends, not family. No one wants to be my family. Thank God for my loyal dog.

So, now, to make sure you're still with me, I will recap events. Okay, here we go:

Lost several "loved ones"

I was injured

Can't work at the business I've built up over fifteen years

Lost my business

Workers comp is really incomprehensible

Gained tons of weight

My girlfriend moved out on me while I'm committed in a mental ward Committed to hellhole in a different mental ward

Can't rely on my brother/family

Going to have to file bankruptcy I was told I was crazy

No one is there for me

Anyway, at this point I figure things have got to be looking up by now.

Don't you think?

4/17/02 ~

Something unusual happened, which is not unusual for me. It seems that there are steps that need to be taken to be discharged from a mental ward. "They" say stopping these prescribed drugs is more dangerous than taking too many of them. I got discharged without them scheduling a follow-up visit with a doctor to take over my treatment, and was out of the meds they gave me. (Dr. Pilsner and I have an unspoken understanding that she will not prescribe anything more for me.)

Gilda, my concerned neighbor, called my personal insurance to find a psychiatrist. I do not understand pills. I am afraid to take them and I am afraid not to.

The insurance agent found an outpatient clinic for me. I called, and, thank goodness, someone did a wonderful job of saving my life just by doing her job. I have an appointment for an "evaluation."

After being evaluated it was decided I would start partial hospital day therapy. The first part is usually only a five day program. After three days in the program I met with psychiatrist Dr. Nina Patterson. She decided that the best thing for me was to go back to inpatient and get my meds squared away, as she was changing them. This way she could study my records, and with new meds she wanted someone to keep on eye on me. Something about keeping me safe from myself, I think. So I won't say I willingly went, but I was escorted to inpatient.

During my stay this time I just tried to get through it. This time somehow I found it more humorous, particularly since last time was lock-down and very un-humorous. The cast of characters was pretty amusing, and they kept me pretty drugged up. Every time I saw a nurse he or she shot me with something or other.

I met a girl named Molly. She was new to the ward, sitting by the nurse's station waiting for a room. I thought she looked familiar, so I said, "Hello," and we talked a little. I realized I had seen her earlier in ER. She didn't have the awesome insurance I have, and she was held in the ER all that time, told there were not any available beds.

I stayed about five days and didn't hatch any escape plans. They let me out with many new prescriptions they thought I'd be safe with, and signed me up for day treatment.

CHAPTER SIX
CRAZY SCHOOL, ROUND ONE

4/22/02 ~

Providence's assessment of me:

"Partial Hospital Psychiatric Evaluation

Mental Status Exam: This is a well-groomed woman who appeared a little bit older than her stated age. She was cooperative. Her speech was fluent. She was depressed. Her affect was tearful. She complains of some symptoms consistent with anxiety and possible panic type symptoms. There is no evidence of any thought disorder. She did report that she can't remember much of her recent hospitalization. She appeared to be alert and oriented. She denied any auditory or visual hallucinations. There is no evidence of paranoia in the interview. She denies homicide ideation but reports daily suicidal ideation. She denies having any intent or plan. She did have a recent gesture whereby she tried to cut off her arm with a saw but was stopped by a friend.

Assessment: This . . . 42 year-old woman . . . had multiple losses recently. She presents multiple symptoms of depression including depressed mood, mood swings, and sleep disturbance . . . She does have symptoms of major depression complicated by chronic pain and some limited coping skills.

Diagnosis:

Axis 1—1.Major Depressive Disorder, severe, without psychotic features

2. Bipolar Disorder, depressed phase
3. R/O Generalized Anxiety Disorder

Axis II—Deferred

Axis III—Chronic Pain Syndrome

Axis IV—Stressors are severe"

So, I begin "partial hospital stay" Monday through Friday, 9 a.m. to 3 p.m., with several therapists and different groups.

5/02 ~

Art Therapy

5/27/02 ~

Memorial Day

I have a lot of people to remember. Pete. Pamela. Dad. Benson (okay, he was a dog but close to a people). You guys know I'm thinking of you. I also can't help thinking about all my other losses. Relationships. One after the next. Kind of like my sleepless nights. Not because I had to and not because I wanted to, not because I kissed the girl behind the magazine. Just do. Bad habits. I saw bumper stickers today that read: "Families are Forever" and "Don't Postpone Joy."

I have some friends that come by, like one of my exes now married to a guy, and Gary and his wife. I thank them, as I'm sure it was not pleasant for them. I mostly find projects around the house to do whether they need it or not.

I talked with my ex about another bad habit—the pot. "I know it isn't a good thing to do while I'm on as much medication as I am on."

"What are you taking?" she asked.

"Oh, what aren't I taking? I'm on Depakote, Baclofen, Zoloft, Zyprexa, Neurontin . . . those are the ones I can remember anyway." I am so confused. Is it the meds or is it the meds with pot? Anyway, there is a problem. I do admit I smoke too much. And my dilemma is that if I am honest with the docs about the pot I'm pretty sure they would want me to go inpatient. That is, unquestionably, not what I want to happen. So I am going to try to cut down and stop. There. I am the one that matters.

The days run into one another like a train running off the tracks. I am all alone sitting here in my house wondering when things will get better. The pain is awful. An old friend came over the other night. She told me, "The reason you yearn for a relationship is that God put the yearning for a relationship in you. So, maybe you should have a relationship with Him."

Okay. I will try to do two things at once. I know, pretty tricky. I will stop my bad habit of smoking pot and try a new habit and talk to God. I mean, I am stripped down to bare bones here. I am desperate and ready to do what works. No more losses.

I saw Molly at crazy school outpatient day treatment. I hardly recognized her, she looked so much better. She told me it was just the make-up that creates the magic.

So she's now my co-inpatient, co-outpatient, co-make-up buying friend. She suggested I try to say I have had a lot of "changes" in my life instead of losses. I will try to do what I should. Keep bailing, one bucket at a time.

6/7/02 ~

During my daze at crazy school, one of the seven full-time therapists there was shaking his head back and forth as if in disbelief when I told him my story. He said something to me he probably wasn't supposed to say, but I will never forget it. "Have you thought about trying God?" he asked.

6/14/02 ~

It's been a while. Time has passed so fast yet it seemed as time stood still. I don't remember much—just darkness. Alone. Not even enough thought or energy to end it. I found some sort of safe place in the darkness. Maybe I knew it was the bottom. How could I fall further?

6/18/02 ~

It feels good to say I have been consistent with my exercises and avoiding "bad" food. I believe the groups have helped me as a person, but have not given me true light. I couldn't deal two Sundays ago, so I called Ruth, my cousin in a nearby town.

"Can I go to church with you?" I asked.

Ruth was more than happy to say "yes." She and her husband could hardly wait to introduce me to a young woman, Lena, from church. She was an ex-druggie and ex-gay. Okay, God, you have my attention. I have been inside the dark more than out. But there is an out at least.

I cried throughout the service. I can't explain it, but I felt different afterwards. It's as if I've been wrapped like a mummy. There was a time when I could hardly breathe, and it was pretty dark in there. Slowly I can again feel the brush of fresh air, and am starting to see light ahead. At least enough to want to keep going. I still can't understand what's up with my family. Rejection seems to be the theme in my life. But I don't feel it here. God cares for the beds as well as the lilies.

CHAPTER SEVEN
DIFFERENT WARD, NEW HOPE

6/26/02 ~

During the remaining days of June I got to see how it is to have the "kind hand of God on me." Lena and I went to Julie's (another person from church). The three of us prayed together. We agreed, without too much discussion, that it couldn't hurt. The hospital could only offer us pills and some coping skills. Okay, I figured, let's see what kind of relationship God and I can have.

God and I were not off to a good start, however. Workers comp wanted to close my claim with an offer of $3,000. I wasn't going to settle on that low an offer for partial permanent disability.

Bankruptcy court came next. The judge told me my five year reorganization plan (aka Chapter??) was not feasible (no doubt). I had to show proof of income within 30 days or it would be another bad chapter for me. In that chapter, they take everything I own and sell it off. No house. No convertible Mustang. I still want it, even though I can't drive it due to the cost of insurance.

Oh, I forgot to tell you about my . . . lapse in judgment shall I say? On Sunday I snorted a sixteenth of crank while working in my yard, smoking blunts (joints rolled in cigar form). I guess I was trying to have a heart attack, thinking God would have mercy and let me die in my most special place—my yard.

I told this to Lena and Julie, and they kept a 24 hour watch over me. I confessed to Helena, my counselor at crazy school. Today is Buck's (my only faithful companion) sixth birthday. I was admitted to inpatient chemical dependency, c.d. for short. I was told it was for my own safety, and I had to agree. My mental benefits were almost exhausted so they tried my drug benefits.

The best way to describe it was like, willingly, jumping back into a dark ugly pit. Only worse than the first, second, or third time. This very nice nurse helped me through the grueling two hour check-in process. She must have known exactly what I needed. A fifty milligram Valium and two Visterals to help kick-start the Valium. They told me Visteral is a drug used to ensure the other drug hits you harder and faster. Recovery people are on a completely different mind level than the mental people I was more used to.

Day has transformed into night—what will I transform to? I got off the phone with Lena. She's also been in the drug ward.

I guess everyone gets the good drugs when first going in. I think they give you more drugs in drug treatment than you're on before you come in. Like clockwork, a nurse comes in every 45 minutes to take my blood pressure. Sometimes he or she will make me walk out of my room down to the end of the hall into a little room to check my blood pressure again. I guess they want to keep my heart from going into shock with all the drugs in me.

Nothing in the drug ward was the same as when I was in mental wards. Well, actually, besides the no smoking, being locked up, jabbed, herded, and confronted, nothing was the same. The group there was totally different. It was all happy-like. "Hi, I'm Jane, I'm an alcoholic."

Or, "Hi, I'm Joe. I'm a heroin addict."

If I'm happy, I do not need this kind of facility! I remember, before I had to be carried to my room due to that great kick-start on the required Valium, my introduction to the group was, "Hi, I'm crazy and I'm tired."

The next afternoon I just stayed in bed rather than do group or group morning walk. I also stayed away from the "day room" where they had cheese, juice, cereal, crackers, bad bananas and awful apples. It was my experience that, ten out of ten times, when I'd go to get a snack, there sat a heroin addict, eating. Being around a heroin addict who's being turned into an ex-addict is not a pretty sight or smell.

Which reminds me. My roommate, an alcoholic, told me before "they" put me to bed she added a blanket under my sheets. All the mattresses are covered in plastic for protection from . . . whatever you're thinking is true.

GOD get me out of here—I will do my best to take care of what's left—PLEASE. In every way. This time I mean it.

Friday morning an older, very serious blonde-turning-gray haired woman comes in.

"Sherri, your insurance will not cover your inpatient stay after all. But I am willing to go to bat for you to keep you here," she declared.

"Oh no, don't do that," I told her.

She went on to say they would pay for day residence treatment 9-5, Monday through Friday. I declined.

Lena told me someone named Willy called about a movie job. I was discharged and met with him that afternoon. I got the "lead greens" job! It's a small production called The Dust Factory, and it's just perfect because the work days are short since there are child stars. The production staff was aware of my limitations, and I had a lot of back-up. I had to reiterate my limitations to Willy. The pain really hurts. I'd say an eight or nine on the old pain scale.

The judge at bankruptcy court gave me 30 days to prove I could pay the $900 a month for whichever chapter I was filing for as part of my five year reorganization plan. I got this job shortly before my 30th day. Hey, God, that was some week. You're unbelievable!

I read the script today and couldn't put it down until I finished it. It touched me in so many ways. I really like the song it ends with. It's Louis Armstrong's "What a Wonderful World." That was the song played at Pete's funeral. I know God gave me this script. Thank you God! For everything—from one ward to another to freedom!

7/2/02 ~

I have been "out" for only a couple of days. Mom and Aunt Harriet came to town. I got really stoned before going to eat dinner with them at Ruth's. My pot smoking was back to being abused at the ultimate level.

I didn't have any problem keeping at least one half ounce around all the time. It eased the pain and nausea. Anyway, I am trying to have improved immensely, but . . . patience.

Mom and I are on the mends. She said she was sorry she wasn't there for me. That's all I wanted to hear.

I did tell her I will never understand or forget how my brother Mick chose not to be there for me. I mean, I know they have their own lives and everything, but, call me crazy (which many people did), in the situation I was in, isn't that what family does for each other?

Family. Home. I like my new home; it's not new, but I've done a lot of work on it since Lizzie left. I'm glad I've renewed my relationship with Ruth and Daniel, her husband. And my new church. My new hope for the future.

Sherri—do you have any idea how good you should feel writing those words? Smile!!! There's hope!

7/7/02 ~

Exodus 3

As brought to you by Pastor Ron. We are talking burning bushes. As brought to Moses by God. A great revelation took place in this encounter between God and Moses.

God tests us, you see, to purify our faith. To show us he is reliable. God is a redemptive God. Redemption.

Our Sunday ritual after church has been to go to the Village Inn for breakfast. Me, Ruth, Daniel, and Lena. Sunday is a day I look forward to. Church and breakfast with family. Lena has been coming from her home near the church all the way across Portland to pick me up and take me to church. That, of course, meant she also had to take me back. She was even nice enough to stop at Walmart so I could get some dog food for Buckley.

This one time, after we got to my home, she came in with me. After satisfying a very hungry dog, we sat and talked a while. "You know, Sherri," Lena began, "I have to confess. If it weren't wrong, I would be attracted to you. I would be kissing you about now. I hope you don't mind my saying that."

Funny she should say that. I felt something between us also. "Well," I sputtered, "if it's wrong, I don't want it either."

Can a friendship stay pure after physical attraction starts stewing and is served on a platter? A very nice platter. We'll see.

Due to the incredibly hard time I had physically working on set, combined with repeated falls from vertigo attacks, I barely kept afloat.

I have not heard a thing from my attorney on what's next with my workers comp claim. So I fired him and got a new attorney, recommended by an old girlfriend who flits in and out of my life. I believe this guy will be very helpful. I've got a lot of people on my side who say they will testify that my depression is directly from my injury. With one major exception. Dr. Pilsner. And I think I know why. She wants me to believe I'm bipolar. Especially since Lizzie and my neighbor told her I was. And even more especially since she was the one who prescribed a very wrong combination of psychiatric drugs. This is what pushed me over the edge and made me crazy. The start of a horrible ordeal—one I will never forget if I ever get out of it.

7/31/02 ~

Someone called for Lizzie today. The internal injury she caused is so great I still cannot come to any closure. I know I should be over it by now. She was a shit to just up and leave like that. Okay, I will admit. I shouldn't be throwing stones. But still.

I'm not going to dwell on Lizzie any more. I have been doing some landscaping jobs as well as working on the movie, both of which are the best places for me to be. I've also been doing a lot of drawing lately. Mostly faces in pencil. I'm in the gray zone. My heart is SLOWLY starting to heal. I've dropped some weight, changed my hairstyle, and am planning on a happy future. Until then, I'LL FAKE IT TILL I MAKE IT!

10/28/02 ~

Really?

10/30/02 ~

I've been thinking about a lady that was in the mental ward with me (third time). Out of nowhere one day she started going around asking for signatures. She wanted mine.

"For what?" I asked.

"Well, if you read it you'd know that I am sane and demanding to be released," she chortled back at me.

"Yeah, okay," I replied, signing her petition knowing it meant absolutely nothing.

Like her, I think I've been trying to get signatures, but all the wrong ones.

Validation from the wrong people.

Workers comp's medical arbitrator went totally in my favor!!!!!!!!!!!!! My attorney wants to discuss an offer they've made. Thank you, thank you, thank you.

I got a shot of Toradol, an anti-inflammatory and supposedly anti-pain injection, and a prescription for Valium. I went to a free depression group as I was seeing red flags of my severe depression coming back. In other words, I feel more like dying than living.

Today is . . . or would have been Lizzie's and my first date anniversary. That special day you spend with your loved one and look back on how much your relationship has grown. How could she do what she did to me if there was any love present?

Losing my house seems more real than ever. I keep working to improve it, to beautify it, to hang on to it. I find myself telling the "collectors" (or whoever "they" are who have the horrible job of kicking people out of their homes), that I'm not buying my house back for three times what I owe on it.

"Miss," they all say, "no need to yell at me."

"Okay," I calmly say, "let me say this again in case I spoke too quickly. I'm going to shoot the first person that shows up at my door and tells me to leave. Do I need to say it slower?"

Just so you know, I did not own a gun at that time.

11/18/02 ~

Oh God—I really need some help here . . .

Thank you to the 11 people who wrote really nice letters on my behalf, stating my depression resulted from my injury. I put them away and don't want to read them.

I packed my silk flowers, including over a thousand dollars worth of silk cherry blossoms I bought for The Hunted, floral supplies, and Christmas stuff. I put the huge honeysuckle back up after I fell on it trying to fix the gutter. I actually had to chainsaw it in half due to its weight. I pruned the roses, except for my Rio Sambu which is blooming like crazy. Takes one to know one. Unfortunately, it gets the blooms and I get the thorns. I know I could just live in my yard with my plants . . .

Bottom line_____

I am broke in every way in so many ways and yet blessed in lots of ways too.

This year has been the BLACKEST, DARKEST ever.

WHAT'S GOING TO HAPPEN??????????????????????

WHEN??

Thanksgiving is fast approaching. I'm sure you can see the irony there. I've had several invites, including a nice one from my brother, Mick, who I rarely hear from. I didn't want to go anywhere. I want to pretend like the holidays aren't really coming.

CHAPTER EIGHT
TWISTED SISTERS

The name of her catering business was very apropos to her conduct: Party Princess. I have always liked (and, yes, unfortunately, been attracted to) my friend Stormy. She called and asked me to stage her home to sell it, which required some serious landscaping work. She had to sell it or lose it. I could feel her pain.

Some job. Her place is so big it has a name: Crown Vista. It's on 47 mostly forested acres in the Tualatin Hills, and has an amazing wide-angle view of the Cascade Mountains from the master bedroom. There is a pool house way bigger than my house. After putting in a few hours work at her place, Stormy tells me, "You know, you could live here when your house is gone. There's lots of work I could give you around here."

"Thanks, but I'm not giving up my house. I appreciate the offer though," I told her.

"Okay, if you say so. Just in case, you know, keep it in mind," she replied.

So, the Tuesday before Thanksgiving she comes to my house. She picks out a bottle of some rare liquor that Pete got me from one of his Baja races at least ten years earlier. We pop it open and talk as she cooks dinner. We drank, ate, and had sex in front of the burning fireplace. She and her dog Sambo spent the night with me and Buckley. Unknown to me at the time, that was the last night I spent in my home of 14 years. The next day, following my usual routine, I went to a doctor appointment. Stormy loaded her van with what she believed to be special to me, and came to pick me up. She then proceeded to kidnap me to her mansion.

On many levels, it's here at Crown Vista that the kid in me got to come out. I was surrounded by my own arboretum. That was the best part. The worst part was that Stormy lived at this amazing place, and I was thrust into our rocky relationship. I soon met a person there known as Danger. This should have been a warning sign, like the ones on the highway.

DANGER

STORMY

AHEAD

But I was too deep in my darkness to heed the warning.

12/9/02 ~

Three years ago today I married Lizzie in Hawaii. I lost . . . my home. I didn't plan on leaving. I have been living in a four million dollar mansion. I have been sleeping with Stormy in the master bedroom. It has two decks, a sauna, fireplace, and hot tub topped with a spectacular view of the snow-capped Cascades.

Stormy reminds me of a cross between Bette Midler (except her singing), Lucille Ball and Marilyn Maroe. She was unlike anyone I've ever known. She was denitely beautiful and could be both very classy and trashy. She looked like she belonged living in her 49 acre estate. With the main house being 8,000 square feet and pool house 3500 square feet with an olympic size pool. But I remembered her fitting in just as well in a dive bar singing karaoke "These boots are made for walking. She went to art school in Boston, and was truly an amazing artist.

12/17/02 ~

Sitting here in the pool house talking to Stormy all night. We have gotten close in a lot of ways. I am not yet completely moved.

I still cannot believe this has all happened and is still happening.

12/29/02 ~

I knew it would take something pretty spectacular for me to be able to leave my home. Being kidnapped and taken to this mansion fit the bill. Slightly coincidentally, it was just last year that Stormy's niece faked being kidnapped. The authorities were none to happy about this, to say the least, and threw the book at her. This also was detrimental for Stormy, because she lost the last, although small, connection she had with her family. Her sister blamed Stormy, as her missing daughter used credit cards from Stormy for her little adventure in Seattle.

Ah, Stormy. She's a multiple-volume book in and of herself. Her mom was killed in a car accident on Stormy's 21st birthday. Her dad remarried very soon afterward to a woman he had known before and probably had an affair with. She didn't like Stormy, which wasn't a big deal until a year after her mom's death, her father died. I knew Stormy had a sense of what it felt like not to have family. We identified with each other in that way.

Crown Vista and Stormy make me feel needed. Sex is good with Stormy, but I do wish she wouldn't drink so much. She really is a special friend. In fact, we promised to be family to each other, regardless of what path our sexual relationship takes us on.

Dear God,

Help send a herd of angels to keep me from straying off the road. The pain in my body is as intense as ever, especially using it so much, but I believe I am not reacting to it as much.

I need to make a list of stuff I need to do. My court date is coming up on January 15th.

Slowly I got more and more things from my house. And as crazy as living with Stormy was, it was equally as magnificent to be there. Crown Vista had a certain air about it; for me it seemed a spiritual place.

I helped Stormy with more and more things besides landscaping. I helped tie up some loose ends for her business, which she had given up. Vacuuming, laundry, it seemed endless. Keeping busy and feeling needed was really good for me, but not enough. I began outpatient therapy again. I'm okay enough to know I need help getting through this and letting go of *my home*.

CHAPTER NINE
I'M NOT BIPOLAR, MY LIFE IS

1/16/03 ~

I Am . . .5

1/19/03 ~

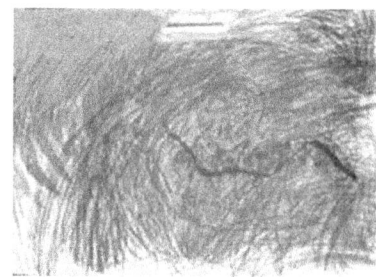

Inner Beauty

2/13/03 ~

    I'm early to group so I thought that I would write to you before morning check-in. At group we have to give our name and a number between one and ten with ten being the best, describing how we are feeling first and then how we are doing. My doing was always the same or better than the number describing how I was feeling. Today I am feeling a three and doing a five.

I KNOW I HAVE BEEN SEVERELY DAMAGED

But still waging war for my sanity while trying to prove I was sane before April 6, 2001 and am now. I feel like puking. Knowing my life is so insane.

2/18/03 ~

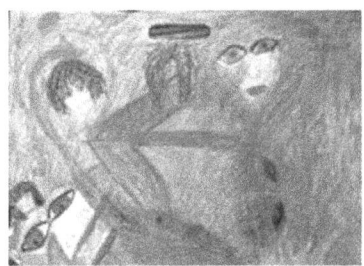

Shady Past

2/26/03 ~

Providence Partial Hospital—Journal Group

"Sherri—you have lost your house—your home. How are you going to get through this?"

"I do not know besides a lot of tears and pain and one foot in front of the next." "What will you do?"

"I do not know. Something. Always something."

I have bailed myself out of the hell of depression, I believe. Until I think about things. Then I feel alone and abandoned.

I do not believe I have bipolar disorder. If it is true, why didn't I or others such as my therapist think or see it? Why have so many of my oldest, bestest friends written letters on my behalf saying that I was never bipolar, that I've just been depressed since my accident. Why have I been having to research my life to prove I wasn't bipolar?

"Are you taking care of yourself?"

I think I am. I don't take it easy enough. If I did, maybe I would feel better.

Maybe I would feel worse. I wish I knew.

I am so entirely sick of this hell. Or the bouncing between hell and being okay and happy.

I feel:

Sick

Alone

Scared

Pain

Misunderstood

Unloved . . . for me . . . with all the ugly things inside.

3/2/03 ~

How I See Myself

3/5/03 ~

No one showed up at the auction to buy my house. I cried there all day.

Thank goodness some friends showed up to help take things away.

On my way to court for running a stop sign, I was pulled over for running the exact same sign I was going to court for. So I had two tickets for the same infraction and it made me late for court. My license is being suspended for nonpayment of a traffic ticket.

I'm sitting here in group thinking 'bout going back to my house to gather more things.

Dear God,

Yes, it's me again. I need your peace and happiness. Please.

Helena made an appointment for me to see Dr. Nina Patterson, another psych. Before I was pulled out of self-defeating behaviors group for this appointment—it hit me—I learned my best distraction was also at times my self-defeating behavior. Taking care of my hundreds of plants now meant digging them up, potting and transporting them to Crown Vista. I was sure to take my Rio Sambu and other roses I promised my home's previous owner I'd take care of. And I keep my word.

I met Dr. Patterson this morning. She changed my DIAGNOSIS from bipolar to MAJOR (the word commands capitalization) depressive episode and chronic pain syndrome. THANK YOU!!!!!!!!!!!!!!!!!!!!!!!!!!!!!

Think about this. I am thankful beyond hope that the diagnosis was changed. Maybe now workers comp will have to compensate me as this will prove I was not mentally ill before my fall. I don't know many people who would be ecstatic when told they have major depression and chronic pain, but, at this moment, I sure am!

I decided to go back to groups while I wait for a letter to be typed up to be given to my attorney. Talk to you later.

3/11/03 ~

It's been a year since I attempted to chop off my arm. I still don't think I was really trying to kill myself. Though I do have to admit, my extreme manic episode was truly crazy. My mind couldn't grasp the incredible pain. I felt . . . useless. I still don't know if it's possible to grasp or really understand—except to acknowledge—it was too much. I just had to try to make the pain go away. Somehow I put it all in my right arm. My bailing arm.

I think the hardest thing was watching everything I had worked so hard for go down the tubes.

3/17/03 ~

St. Patrick's Day

Still looking for the luck of the Irish.

If I hadn't had a breakdown, I would have to be crazy. There was no other option. To completely lose my life—my business—my home—my yard. I know I will be moving most of my plants with me here at Crown Vista.

It's an absolutely fabulous, gorgeous morning. I'm sitting here soaking up the sun as birds greet the day. It's funny, or crazy, or interesting. My life.

You have money, you have attention.

You create bad attention for yourself.

It costs lots of money to try and fix you.

St. Patrick's Day. A day for green. A green thumb. Me and greens. March was always my favorite month. I even had a "March On" party once. I get up again. I am alive!

3/20/03 ~

Stormy,

I am so glad you're getting this vacation time away. Make the most of it, relaxing, re-energizing. Reorganize your thoughts and come back ready to take on life's twists and turns—or sometimes twisted turns.

I will do my best to take care of the place and do what you asked by the time you come back. I really am so happy for you, but as well I am very hopeful—lots of good things will happen to you. Things that will give you peace of mind and freedom to allow you to run with your creative person.

Be safe and know there are two beings here that love you very much and consider you part of the family—unconditionally and always.

Love,

Sherri

3/21/03 ~

4 or .5 a.m.

Very strange. Been up and going with Stormy for three days and nights. I've been cleaning the basement, doing general hauling and moving things for Stormy. I did the basement floor on my hands and knees. I like getting things clean. I slept for a couple of hours before I took her to the airport for a two week vacation to NY, Boston, and the Dominican Republic. Buck and I are alone.

The past week we were having "problems" to the point that I told her I was moving out. She isn't aware of how she becomes sometimes, and I truly believe it's because of alcohol abuse. The legal drug.

Stormy really is such a beautiful, creative, and kind (when she wants to be) person. But there are more times than I like to admit when I feel belittled and unappreciated. Just love it when she yells at me for doing things the wrong way in front of friends. "Don't use my good towel to wipe the water spill!" she screams. Stupid things.

There are times when, between the time I leave for all day therapy and the time I get back, she's rock solid passed out. These are in between the times she has her three to six day art project binges involving all kinds of drugs.

Darren called me out of nowhere. I was happy to hear from him, and I was excited to see his girls. He asked if I was interested in dating him. What the_____????

As always, I rolled my eyes and walked away. Although I do love him, I can't see a future for us.

I don't know why I couldn't be happy marrying him. Maybe it's because I don't think he can stay sober. How could I trust him? I wish I could, mostly for his daughters.

I think I really do miss Stormy. She called a few times since she's been gone. She says she loves me and other things that make me go "um hmmm."

Some good news! I was set up with a vocational counselor with the state, who is sending me to this guy Drew, who I now have a two hour meeting with.

I feel so uncertain about my future. I am really fighting depression. Minute by minute.

3/26/03 ~

I was awakened by Stormy's call this morning. For someone who's supposed to be away on vacation she sure does call a lot. I guess I do miss her presence in different ways.

Lunch time in crazy school. I brought Buckley today. I fed him some beef jerky and let him run and show off for a little while. I met with Haley, my "cognitive therapist" (now how many people can say they have one of those??).

Drew told me today he was sure I'd qualify for vocational retraining through the state. Because of my double whammy—I am homeless and disabled. But first I go back to Haley's office for a vocational assessment to find out my cognitive skill level. My brain injury injured my memory, concentration (what was I saying?), and ability to process new information easily. It's kind of strange to be having my mind tested by filling in circles with a #2 pencil.

I've been feeling depressed, impulsive, confused, anxiety, pain, and last, but not least, loss.

Next week is my mediation with workers comp. I am anxious about the whole thing.

I know I have come a long way since this time last year when I was in my third inpatient stay.

But I'm confused about my future. What will I do?????????????????? My feelings for Stormy. For Darren. I am scared to death of that big a change. Do I really want it even?

I got a Toradol shot today. It helps so much, it's unbelievable.

Am I okay? Or am I so convincing I have all of us thinking something untrue? Am I bipolar? I said no. Finally, someone whose opinion actually counts also said no. Now I wonder . . .

Dear God,

Help me or let me die. Pretty please with sugar on top.

I apologize for not writing to you for so long. I still need you desperately.

I need your guidance and wisdom and strength.

I thank you so much for bringing me this far. I believe you will keep me on the right trail so I can know true peace and happiness.

Please keep my friends and family safe.

3/29/03 ~

Dear Stormy,

It's Saturday morning and I decided to write you another letter. Maybe you'll get this one.

Nowhere on earth could there be a woman with more potential in as many areas as you. I feel blessed just to have you in my life. Even more so to have you as family. So what a bonus to know you as a lover and a partner!

As you know, I've been thinking A LOT about my future—what's right, what I want, and what I can handle. What I can't handle is, first and foremost, watching you slowly kill yourself with alcohol. I have major issues with this, as I am sure you know. This is the one thing that will destroy any chance you and I might have for a great future together.

The other thing I absolutely cannot do is be in charge of your bills. It is giving me flashbacks of what I am just finishing going through.

I believe there is NOTHING you and I could not do if we both put our minds to it.

3/31/03 ~

Gilda just called me and told me the sheriff put an eviction notice on my house. I guess it isn't mine any longer.

I just got off the phone with Stormy. She was crying, and said she loves me. She comes home tomorrow night. I'm looking forward to her being home. I really hope it works.

4/2/03 ~

I met with Drew to go over my test results. Nothing I really didn't know. It showed I have high work values, and art and technical skills are my strong points. Now what?

Gary went with me. On the way home he said, "You always take the part you like and run with it." I guess I block out the parts I don't like.

4/14/03 ~

Friday night—best ever with Stormy. I am sure that she has many more issues than I, which is quite a statement.

BonMom. Kona, Hawaii.

With Nancy, $700 for rent. Working—swimming with the dolphins. A fresh start . . .

I need to decide what to do first and do it.

My mind feels spacey and lost much of the time. I do believe there is a higher power leading me out of this life. I have to. Peace of mind is what I've always wanted. Being happy, really and truly. Can it happen for me?

I am trying one last try to keep my home.

4/20/03 ~

Where I Am

4/26/03 ~

It's a beautiful Saturday afternoon, and I am sitting here in this amazing setting writing to you after a very long time. I have had one week now with no doctor appointments or therapy. I still haven't graduated from crazy school, but I'm getting closer.

I had my auto insurance cancelled for non-payment. I think I can clean it up if I make an overnight payment.

5/8/03 ~

I am supposed to be out of my home. Decide what to do first and do it.

Above all, keep bailing. I'm really trying.

5/9/03 ~

STORMY

HAPPY BIRTHDAY!

I know this isn't the "norm" for a birthday card . . . but it is given from the heart.

You are an amazing person that I do and will forever cherish. You are so much more than a Party Princess . . . and for your birthday I am wishing you will find this is true.

I want you to know that Buck and I consider you to be family, as well as someone who believed in us even when I didn't. You and I have many similarities in our lives: successes, hard work, determination, generous heart. As well as the feeling of being burnt out, used, in pain, and uncertain of the future.

Below is the prayer I am asking God for your birthday.

DEAR GOD,

TODAY IS STORMY'S BIRTHDAY AS I AM SURE YOU KNOW. THIS IS WHAT I AM ASKING YOU TO GIVE HER FOR HER BIRTHDAY . . .

1. **GIVE HER PEACE OF MIND**

2. **GIVE HER THE STRENGTH SHE NEEDS TO DO WHAT SHE SHOULD**

3. **GIVE HER HOPE FOR THE FUTURE**

4. **GIVE HER THE FEELING OF YOUR ARMS WRAPPED AROUND HER WITH LOVE**

5. **GIVE HER FRIENDS THAT ENHANCE HER LIFE AND NOT DRAIN IT**

6. **GIVE HER TRUE HAPPINESS**

7. **GIVE HER CONFIDENCE THAT SHE IS WORTHY OF GREAT THINGS**

8. **GIVE HER THE ABILITY TO CHANGE THINGS SHE CAN CHANGE, ENDURANCE TO HANDLE THE THINGS SHE CAN'T CHANGE . . . AND THE WISDOM TO KNOW THE DIFFERENCE**

9. **GIVE HER DETERMINATION TO MOVE FORWARD IN A HEALTHY PLACE**

10. **GIVE HER A HAPPY BIRTHDAY**

5/10/03 ~

I missed my vocational test yesterday. I've been sleeping.

BonMom called. Everything's set up if I want to go live in Hawaii! If I want to . . . Yes!

5/11/03 ~

Mother's Day

I called the women who have been substitute moms to me over the years. This took quite a while, as there are many. I missed calling my mom, but I'm not sure where she is.

Gary took me to my home and helped me get my wisteria. Cutting trees, pruning—this is how I spent the day. And many other days. It helps keep what little brain I have left sane. Well, okay, maybe not sane. Just from completely going over the edge.

This is silly. What am I thinking? What am I feeling? Drifting around.

5/12/03 ~

Yes!! Workers comp settled! I got $40,000!! My lawyer gets $6,700. I have about $14,000 in bills.

5/14/03 ~

I'm in thinking errors group right now. I should ace this one.

I could fly to Hawaii as soon as I get my workers comp money. But maybe I'll wait till August or September like BonMom suggested. Stay with her daughter and go to work for her and swim with dolphins. Big plans. Or are they drifting dreams?

6/03 ~

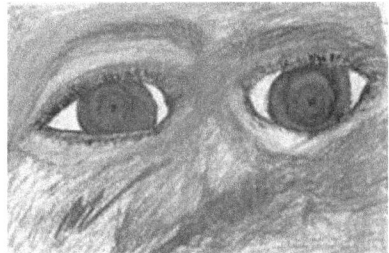

What

CHAPTER TEN
FACTS ARE STRANGER THAN FICTION

7/1/03 ~

Yipeeeeee! I got my brand spanking new John Deere mower (from the state) and other assorted tools so I can work again!! This is great! Gotta go to work—bu bye!

7/4/03 ~

Independence Day! Freedom from being led by the combination of the little girl, the victim of fear and desperation, and the controller. This one track mind, emotionless to the extreme—locking myself behind an impassable wall of logic.

Today I start my freedom! A beautiful, sunny Independence Day! I'm finally back at work after two almost unbearable years.

Stormy's supposedly renting her front lawn for an event she's catering. I'm getting the landscape in shape. I'm riding my shiny new John Deere down a steep half-mile driveway. Picking up some speed, I start to brake. Or so I thought. The bleeping brakes don't work and I'm going faster and faster down this endless hill! Emergency brake—NOT WORKING! Turn it off—NOT HAPPENING! Try reverse—NOTHING! Still faster I went. Lifting my weight off the seat was supposed to shut it off, but it didn't work! I was now going at least 20 plus mph!

"STORMY!!!!!!!!" I screamed. I'm just yards away from the front gates where Stormy's van is parked. Oh my God! I have to jump! Here goes!

I make my crash landing on a big pile of rocks. How many ways can you imagine pain? I had them all. However much the earth pummeled me, you should have seen what happened to the mower. Jumping turned out to have been the right choice. The mower continued to gain speed and met its apocalyptic demise when it smashed into Stormy's van at the gate.

This went beyond adding injury to injury. I not only re-aggravated my existing injuries, but now had intense pain in my left hip, a cast on my left ankle, and a smorgasbord of bruises and cuts.

7/6/03 ~

Artless Therapy

7/10/03 ~

Dear John,

You won't believe what happened when I was riding one of your mowers.

The response I got from John was, "Have your lawyer call our lawyers." I looked for a lawyer but couldn't find one that would take my case without a huge retainer, as this was a product liability case. John seems to have several attorneys. So, my bones slowly healed as I desperately tried to learn how to use crutches. Stormy continued her party princess ways. She disappeared for I don't know how long.

7/16/03 ~

6:41 a.m.

Ouch . . . don't know if I can do this . . .

"Don't gamble what you can't afford to lose." I broke my own rule.

My mind feels dull, then sad, then confused. God, can I get through this? The docs said the pills I took were a major contributor to my mania and bipolar symptoms.

Oh God, help me please . . . I am so sick of the pain. I really, really, am. I am so broken.

7/18/03 ~

It seems like my every day life is no more.

I sat in the woods for a while with Buck and Dad's .22. Darren had been storing some of Pete's stuff at the time of his death, and, knowing its source, gave the gun to me a couple of months ago. Timing.

Many moons ago, when EVERYTHING WAS DIFFERENT . . .

7/19/03 ~

I slept in the pool house last night. Stormy came home and was shit-faced.

I couldn't—didn't want to—deal with her.

Am I alright . . . ??? NO

Yes yes yes yes . . . And I mean it.

How can you love and hate me? This is me. You have to accept the whole package.

How can you love and hate me? This is me. You have to accept the whole package.

7/20/03 ~

Stormy says more cruel things to hurt me than anyone ever has, and that's saying a lot. The pain stabs through the pit of my stomach. Such a familiar feeling.

"Move this," she orders me.

"Move that," she growls.

"Not there, there!" she yells.

"I'm great," she struts.

"You're a shit," I think.

Those words and plenty more ugly ones I'm choosing not to print. I wish I knew what it is in me that deserves (or not) to hear all this venom. She uses it as a weapon to continually wound me. Being wounded is an every day feeling—that is a fact.

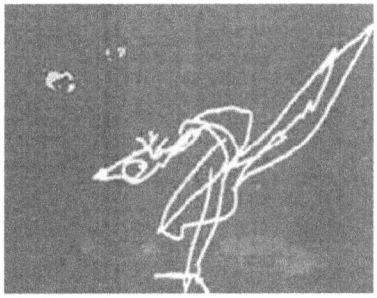

@ Crown Vista

7/26/03 ~

I figure with the lows there should also be highs in my life, pardon the pun. Watch closely, there is something good here. The guy from the lawn/ garden shop where I got the faulty mower came to pick it up a couple of days ago. I had just let him in through the front gate when a cop car pulled up. The cop asked for me, and said we had to talk. My first thought was that the drugs and alcohol finally caught up with Stormy and killed her. I asked, "Where's Stormy? Is she okay?"

All he said was, "Would you please open the gate?" About that time, another cop car arrived. I finally saw I kind of had to open the gate. As

I proceed to do so, I heard loud music and saw Stormy pull in, followed by a third cop car.

Stormy had been born with her huge blue eyes crossed, although they had been corrected. When she was wasted or overly tired, which was often simultaneous, her eyes would cross again. Let's just say at this moment, her eyes were really crossed. She had on a very blue hat which made her look like a smurf on acid. So she was alive, but definitely not okay.

During all this, the guy from the garden shop stood by silently with wide eyes and head tilted, kind of like a confused dog.

Still not knowing what the heck's going on, I watch the first two cops, along with Stormy, drive up to the main house. The third cop, a woman, offered to stay while I dealt with the garden shop guy. As he loaded the mower onto his trailer, I shared my horror story of the accident. The policewoman stood close by. Not thinking before he spoke, he said, "Obviously we did not tighten the brakes enough before you took it off the lot." He said they will not replace the item or accept any blame. Told me to take it up with Mr. John Deere himself. Knowing that he just admitted to guilt, I asked him to write that down. He refused.

The police woman, Sgt. Olman, kindly offered to testify to his statement. And then she said to me, "You have the right to remain silent. Anything you say can and will be used in a court of law. Let's go up to the house."

Sgt. Olman followed me as we both drove up the driveway. Back at the mansion, I was told to stay still by my truck. I overheard each of the five police officers try to convince Stormy to drop the domestic violence charge against me. I thought this was quite funny, considering the fact there wasn't a mark on her and picture how beat up I was from the tractor incident, cast and all. All Stormy kept saying was, "If everyone would just acknowledge the universal truth, we wouldn't have the need for law or cops."

"Miss," the cops kept telling her, "if we arrest her we will arrest you also." I have never before seen, or heard of, cops exerting so much energy to not arrest someone. The next thing I saw was Stormy being handcuffed and escorted into a cop car. Off they went. Sgt. Olman, still with me, kindly said, "We are going to arrest you. Would you like to lock up?"

"Yeah, and I gotta take care of my dog." I put Buckley in the pool house, and we drove down to the gate. I was told not to take anything with me as it would prolong my release. After locking the gate, I hid my keys. I was then handcuffed and put in the back of Sgt. Olman's car.

I've never been to jail before. Somehow that was one experience I had dodged, and even the cops tried to keep me from that experience. I was scared to death. After they frisked me like I had never been "frisked" before, even on what I could call a good date, they took my picture from every angle and stuck my hands in ink at least four times. They told me to go out into the "general population area" and wait. I've always tried to make the best of a bad situation, but this time seemed over the top, even for me. I walked to where the general population of about 20 women sat around. I tried to be cool and said, "So, this is jail, huh?" The "lady" who answered me had a tattoo around her entire neck, and a voice that sounded like Kermit the frog after a drinking/smoking binge. "It ain't jail until you bend over and cough, honey." I cried.

In the meantime, Stormy managed to land herself in solitary confinement. I was told I'd have to go in there so she could come out to make her phone call. Believe me, I tried everything to get out of it, but to no avail. Did I mention I'm claustrophobic? Well, the cell measured three by five, smelled a thousand times worse than any port-a-potty I'd ever used, and I was locked in it. My face never turned away from the teeny, tiny window that hinted of light and the outside world, where I pretended to be with all my might. I bailed like hell to reach that place. Thank goodness the officer kept his word and let me out after five minutes. Stormy spent 13 hours in there, and later said, "It wasn't so bad. I kinda liked it."

I'm out. Twenty miles from home. No money, no cigarettes, not even my cast on my foot (it and my hat were in the clear bag stamped with "JAIL" they gave me). So off I go, hobbling back to Crown Vista on this warm summer night. I just got through town when a lady cab driver pulled up beside me asking if I needed a ride. I told her I had no money, and she said I could get in anyway. She knew where I'd been. She took me all the way home and asked if she could call me some time. I was so thankful for the ride that I gave her my number, knowing I had no interest in seeing her again.

I showed up for arraignment the next day and was told I could press charges against Stormy. But when I saw her, and she asked me for a ride home, I chose to do that instead. Here we go again.

7/29/03 ~

Who are you?

Really depends on the day.

You are working too hard.

Can I make you something to eat? Feeling horny. Want to have sex.

Be polite.

Watch me doing things that in reality could be harmful to me as well as cruel for you to watch. Do you know? Do you care? Can you? Know _ _ Can you care? Can you at least be consistent?

Your eyes can be so beautiful—especially in the morning when they're clear.

Your words are clouded by untruths. Constantly.

Will you miss me?

Is anyone going to love me every day for the rest of my life?

Thanks, Buckley.

I have no home to call mine. No job. No money. No one that is "family" except Buck.

So many times I've been told, "I love you." Every time it has ended with "good-bye." I can't believe it is because I am a bad person. But why then?

My entire life I have aspired . . . I just want a family. I cannot seem to keep friends, let alone family. Many acquaintances.

I really want to write my book.

8/6/03 ~

    I have done some things lately that qualify as outrageous behavior, even for me. Stormy seems to be able to turn her feelings on and off on demand. Worse than that, she seems to believe the bullshit she says. The question is who is more fucked up? Not that it is a contest I am anxious to win, mind you.

CHAPTER ELEVEN
SICKOLOGY

8/8/03 ~

It's about 8:00 at night. I just left Crown Vista. How about that? My old friend Dotty's daughter, Brandy, came there to help move some of my stuff to her place. Stormy got back as I was leaving. She was getting ready to go to some art gallery opening and demanded my help loading up her van. Her eyes were so wild looking. She called me today. So fucking confusing.

Being with her is like being on Let's Make a Deal, as I have no idea what she's hiding behind Stormy number 1, 2, or 3. She's too much. She's not enough. It seems dreadfully awful to have a pattern of relationships similar to the last. It could be unbelievably great or fucked. It's not been such a good gamble so far.

Her loser addict friend/dealer tells me, "There's a reason you're alone." His statement still stings.

The only people she sees—the few of them—are really strange and unabashedly addicts. Will she ever see reality? Will she ever be able to deal? There really is good deep down in that soul—I hope and pray it can survive.

8/11/03 ~

I have been feeling really quiet lately. I feel too much. Feelings are not facts. Stormy bad mouths me. She wants only what she wants. She's rude, ruthless, controlling, selfish. But I know she can also be kind. I know she's scared, though she'd never in a gazillion years admit it.

Dear Friends,

To be here Or

Not to be here . . .

I did say I'd rather sleep in my truck than be with Stormy in that huge mansion.

Homeless. The only thing to do is work my way up. Have you ever slept in a Ford F150 truck cab with a standard poodle? I couldn't either.

8/15/03 ~

3 a.m.

I'm waiting for these two guys to finish getting the rest of my stuff. I'm finally moving completely out of Crown Vista.

I believe my life is bipolar. I had and lost my business. My home. I earned them. My way. I was actually respected by some, believe it or not. But I wasn't happy. No, not really. I loved all my exes. I know I can come across cold, because I could never completely let anyone know me. Or maybe what I displayed to people was, "What can I do for you?" It's like I was back to, "We can do whatever you want." Then, when I couldn't do whatever it was I'm doing for them any more, it seemed easy to discard me.

I did let Stormy know me, but she was so fucked up. Too bad she didn't know it. She was too busy creating in her head who she thought I was to use against me. Funny. Her description couldn't be further from the truth. But in her heart she is capable of knowing.

Well, I need to go. I am moving thru.

8/17/03 ~

It's Sunday. My first morning waking up and being homeless. My last moments at Crown Vista with Stormy consisted of her telling me "fuck you" because I only wanted to leave two of the last five beers I had. I got them for the guys that helped me move.

I'm officially homeless. It's a terribly strange feeling going from having to not having. I feel myself kicking into survival mode. I just hope I can find that bail bucket among the ruins.

Many of my things have a place at Public Storage. The rest of my stuff's at Brandy's Section 8 apartment. She lives there sometimes when she's not at home aggravating her mother, who keeps making excuses for her. Buck and I can't stay with Dotty because of a no dog policy. "Hope" Foursquare Church is practically next door.

If I didn't have this last load of large items in my truck and trailer sitting outside, I think I'd go to service this morning. Hmmmm. Service. Service, or maintain. Like your car, house, etc. That's exactly what I need. To be serviced. Which, it seems, my therapist thinks I need. We've agreed I'll go back to

Providence crazy school. To deal with what I should have long ago.

In my eyes, all the losses I suffered nearly destroyed me. How on earth could I have a chance to survive? By myself, there is no self-worth. Which is very much needed. I've been deserted by almost everyone I have ever loved or been close to. They are painfully not here, and history may reveal some never have been. I really want to know what it is about me that pushes away or prevents or whatever it is that keeps me from having what I have always said, since childhood, I want more than anything: A happy family and home life, which means family that is eternally, unconditionally consistently "there" for me. It is a constant. Am I really asking that much? 'Cause I don't think so.

8/18/03 ~

Here I am again. Back at crazy school. They're going to get me my own desk pretty soon. In fact, I could lead the self-defeating behavior group.

Isn't it crazy to feel most sane in a mental health facility? Since I've last been here . . .

Stormy and I had many bad fights. I've been in E.R. four or five times.

Let's not forget the John Deere tractor fiasco. Moved again.

Do I want to end my life? I am asked this more than once. I say what life?? I feel numb.

I have a headache. Ankle aches. Shoulder and neck ache. I was supposed to get my medical marijuana license today, but I didn't have the $175.

8/19/03 ~

10:00 a.m.

Crazy Providence School

I have so many unsaid things. Do I dare? Would you?

I really wonder if anyone from my past misses me. People who said they loved me. Did they? Then stopped? Or maybe never did. Just wanted something I could give them. I don't know.

Sometimes after crazy school I would go downtown to walk the Park Blocks. I'd find this old bum I met and hand him my sandwich from school for lunch. So I'm walking with Buck, who stops to pee on this really big tree. I guess the three teenage boys didn't see him behind the tree, but they saw me and my medium-sized gym bag with my meds, wallet, the sandwich and other important things. As the kid on my left grabbed for my bag, Buck grabbed a hold of him by his coat sleeve. I kicked the middle kid at the same time the one on my right stabbed me in the shin. I was shocked as I looked at the blood running down my leg to my, wouldn't you know it, CLEAN new socks. Now this was totally unacceptable. I gave the middle kid a spinning round kick that hit him pretty good. Mr. Left decided to leave with his arm and wiggled out of his coat and they ran off. Wow, we almost got mugged! At least we got a warm coat out of it. I found my friend, Mr. Bum. I gave him the sandwich and the coat. He was so thankful. And I was pleased some martial arts skills came back to me.

As I'm trying to get comfortable in the cab of my truck with Buck, it dawns on me that there's a possibility those teenage boys might see Mr. Bum wearing the coat. Worried about what could happen, I start off on my search for him. I found him passed out in the doorway at the Civic Auditorium. He wouldn't wake up, so I just took out purple and green spray paint from my truck and sprayed his coat. Yes, both sides.

I met Brandy's property manger, who was very nice. I was honest with her about my situation. Love that word: situation. That "situation" is the fact that I was homeless. She gave me legal aid names and some great info. She thought I could get a doctor to give me a prescription for Buckley to be a companion dog. Then he will have the same rights as a seeing-eye dog. He wouldn't be considered a pet on rental applications, so there wouldn't be a pet fee. And, best of all, it wouldn't be legal to deny me housing because of him. Yes!

I feel isolated—lonely—sick—in pain—confused. Yet, curiously optimistic.

Strangely hopeful. Patiently determined. I'm still bailing.

God, please help me keep my eyes open so I can find the right path.

CHAPTER TWELVE
TO THE DUNGEON

8/21/03 ~

3:17 a.m.

At crazy school, Helena told me somehow the hospital would help me get a place to live by paying first month's rent and the deposit. Cooell!

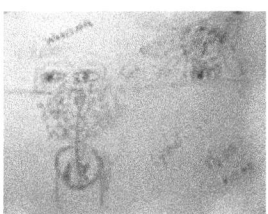

Watching Time Grow

8/22/03 ~

What to Do?

8/25/03 ~

I believe:

If it was not for Buckley, I would have already given up. I want to, most of the time. I can't kill him or leave him by killing myself. All equals—NUMB—step by step. Nothing. Hopeless.

Vision is not how things are, but how they will become.

9/5/03 ~

No matter where I wind up, these letters seem to follow me:(this one's from Farmer's Insurance)

This is a reminder that your policy was cancelled for non-payment . . ." Many of you may know how that tune goes.

9/9/03 ~

Stormy called last night. I do miss her. Especially the sex. Like she said, we did have great sex. I'm supposed to go to Crown Vista tomorrow. She wants me to haul garbage off. What an appropriate ending.

9/10/03 ~

It's really fucked up. I'm not sure if I have insurance on my truck, so if I wreck it—it might be bad. I can't imagine hurting Buckley or leaving him behind. He just gave me a nose poke, that crazy guy. My animals have always meant so much to me. They, and they alone, are my constants.

"You know it's your lifestyle that pushes people away from you," according to my mother.

Isn't that another way of saying, "We can't love you under these conditions?"

If I did push them away with one hand, with the other I was pulling them back to me with ALL my might.

I wonder if I was born defective. I know I was hyperactive and I cried every day in 3rd grade. I missed a lot of school. My teacher was a man that was mean and he yelled a lot. Finally I was moved into another room with a different teacher. I was also prescribed some pill they said for a nervous stomach. I've always felt like I was different and I believe I am. Not like I feel better or above or below anyone....just different. As well I felt like I have always had a bullseye on my back. When I was in my 20's a fortune teller told me I had the most extreme luck of anyone she had ever seen. I thought cool....until she waved her finger in my face stating luck goes both ways good and bad. My aunt used to tell me that when my head hit my pillow at night my guardian angels were pooped out. I must not deserve a family. I will leave my guardian angels here and go stop all the noise. And if nothing else, families are supposed to at least act like they care.

But there are those extra required steps *most* people do for their "family" period. And if nothing else, families are supposed to at least act like they care.

I took all the pills I could find—not even near enough. Then there's the issue of Buckley. Please put him down if he's unhappy.

I am so very tired. I'm not a quitter—just tired of the pain. The ache in my heart. I am not capable of taking care of myself right now. I've been doing a lot of self—medicating.

I am broke. My storage payment is late, my car insurance is overdue, my health insurance is due at the end of this month. And, oh yeah, one more thing. I have no place to live. And, oh yeah, another one more thing: no job. How do you get a place to live if you don't have a job? And how do you get a job if you don't have a place to live?

I need an advocate. Someone to help me deal with these things. Call my family and ask for their help. I have always done what I can for my friends and family.

I'm scared.

Helpless and hopeless in hell.

Free-loading son-of-a-bitch. That was something Dad called me when I was a kid. It became my biggest fear. So I worked for everything I had, not wanting to be a burden to anyone.

Actually, I've become exactly that. A free-loading son-of-a-bitch.

Happy now?

NO

If it wasn't for Buckley, I would admit myself to a place to live with good drugs and art therapy.

Somebody please tell me, how did I get here? No, don't.

Just got dealt too many losing hands in life to continue acquiring my interest.

Maybe I will turn my phone back on. It's so hard because it hardly ever rings, yet when it's off I imagine I'm missing calls.

9/12/03 ~

I have to get out of Brandy's place. I think the price I'm paying is too steep. I have to listen to Dot's problems all the time; problems with Brandy, problems with me and Brandy, problems with money and on and on and how badly it all affects her. Even though I paid her $200 and gave her money for utilities, it's not enough, according to her. I believe that Dot always talked more about me than to me.

I checked out a new place to live, the least expensive one I could find in the paper. It's a basement apartment in some lady's house. The best part about it is the large fenced yard for Buckley. The apartment is just two large rooms. I have to share the kitchen and bathroom upstairs. It will work.

9/13/03 ~

1:00 a.m.

Let's face it—I have no one that is saying to me, "Hey Sherri and Buckley, you have a home with us. Please come and feel loved and welcome."

I almost had to go back in the hospital today. Helena called me this morning. Said I sounded funny. "Come in to therapy," she advised, since I'd been skipping some.

I haven't been taking my Zoloft, Valium, and Toradol. It's taken a toll. I'm scared to death. Almost.

All I've been eating is popsicles. Reese's cups are good. Inside out.

9/14/03 ~

104th—my new street. The basement. My entry is in the back of the house, and resembles the stairs down to an old, cold cellar. The fireplace here is nice. I'm living in the back room and using the front room for storage. There are two tiny jail cell windows that let in slivers of light with a great view of dirt. The first time I went upstairs to use the bathroom I got bit by the crazy owner's Chihuahuas (yes, plural). I'm going to have to shower at Brandy's and pee out back. It's better than facing those dogs again. Besides, since crazy lady doesn't ever let her five dogs out, Buck and I are the only ones using it as a bathroom.

9/20/03 ~

Sorry, Helena, I just couldn't take the pain. It's sort of ironic. I was starting to learn how to deal with the pain that was not physical. But I certainly cannot deal with both the physical and the emotional pain at the same time. Please tell the rest of the staff there "thank you" from me. Everyone is so good at their job and it was both life enhancing as well as enjoyable at times. All of you did a great job. It's certainly no fault of yours my life had to end like this. It was: THE SYSTEM, THE MEDICAL DOCTORS, AND MY FAMILY.

I thought I could not do this . . . I thought I did have a chance at living. I don't know which one I was more wrong about. Was I dying to live or living to die? Dying to die.

Helena called and asked, "Why aren't you here for day therapy?"

"I know all my self-defeating behaviors and thinking errors already," I told her.

She said if I didn't come to Providence I was going to push her to do her job. "You wouldn't dare," I replied.

"I'm hanging up now," she said. I lived just across the street from Woodland Park Hospital. I decided to take a walk with Buckley. I couldn't have been more than two houses away before I heard the screaming sirens get closer as the ambulance, fire truck, and police car turned the corner and headed toward me. When they passed and spotted me I could hear the backup beep from their vehicles.

"What's with all the bells and whistles?" I asked. "There's no fire here." They looked like they were about to tackle me. "Just one call to find somebody to get my dog," I begged. "Otherwise, I'll fight to the death." I think this dungeon stuff is getting to me. They let me call a nearby friend, who came right away for Buckley.

They took me to Woodland Park. This nice nurse brought me what looked like a black licorice milkshake. "You need to drink this," she said.

I politely replied, "No, thank you."

"You will either drink it or we will shove a tube down your throat and force feed it to you." Yummy. I quickly grabbed it from her and drank it down. I later found out it was a charcoal mixture to flush out one's system in case of too many drugs.

They then sent me to Adventist inpatient. Again.

9/21/03 ~

HAPPINESS IS A STATE OF MIND.
I AM MISSING A WHOLE STATE!!!
Smart enough to know how damaged.

CHAPTER THIRTEEN
IMPATIENT PATIENT

9/22/03 ~

I just got out of Adventist on the condition that I go straight to crazy school. Donna picked me up and brought me there. I'm sort of surprised they let me out. So was Donna. I promised them I would be good, and, when I want to, I can be a really good salesman.

I feel really strange. Lost in a fog.

9/25/03 ~

I have fallen apart. Nothing is left but hurt, anger, and sadness. I'm sorry.

Okay, my plan was sabotaged. I stopped my big purple truck on I-84 eastbound. Pamela and Pete both died horribly from head-on accidents with trucks heading east. But this would be no accident. Getting out and spreading my arms like wings and ready to become one with the front of a semi-truck. The drivers always walk away without a scratch. Then there will be peace. Unfortunately, there was not a single truck heading toward me. I felt defeated and went home.

Kathy, a person in groups with me, could see I was struggling and bribed me with a Valium10 to go talk to Lynn, who was the back-up for

Helena. I'm in different groups now. They ask what traits I have from childhood.

All this stuff came pouring out. The fighting. The excuses from Mom. "Your dad loves you," she often told me. "He doesn't mean what he says to you." Her excuses didn't help. Didn't she see that no matter what she said, it couldn't stop the hurting or damage?

The sexual abuse from relatives. And she had the worst one over for dinner a few years later.

"God forgives, so we need to," Mom repeated like an annoying skip on a record. Not telling Dad about what that #%^!* did to me 'cause she thought he'd kill him. I wish she had told him.

Lynn's response was not what I expected. She said, "We're going to keep you here until we can get you a bed in a hospital." Boy, I was mad. But she kept her word. I asked if I could go outside to smoke while waiting for transportation to the hospital. They were catching on to my escape plans, 'cause they sent someone out with me.

9/26/03 ~

I hate where I am. I feel as though the therapists at Providence are really a demolition team—and very good at it. I am raw. They sent me to the Vancouver mental ward. Something about feeling overwhelmed and thoughts of self harm. Suicidal. It sucks. Here's their list of my meds:

Vioxx 25 mg AM	Benedryl 25 mg 4x/day	Morphine
Zoloft 200 mg AM	Dyazide 37.5 mg AM	Baclofen
Trazadone 100 mg bedtime	as needed	Valium
Neurontin 800 mg 3x/day	Levoxyl 50 mcg AM	Toradol

Seems like there's more, but I don't want to continue listing them.

Dotty called my family. She told them if they wanted to see me again before I was in a casket, they'd better come soon. I made bad choices. I'm out of it. Too far gone. I keep hearing excuses and reason after reason about why my family hasn't cared enough to come rescue me. They are good and I am bad. I am so confused and scared. My pains are taking all my attention.

Joe from the east coast is supposed to be here tomorrow night.

This place is making things worse, not better. It took over two and one half hours to get them to give me any meds. I now am waiting for a court evaluator to come evaluate me. Please, if ever I wanted to convince someone of something, it is now. Nothing makes sense.

They are moving one of four of us out of the room due to insanity being contagious. No, actually one woman, my roomie, was actually contagious with a virus. This was after I spent the night in the same room right next to her. And you know, I have a scratchy throat tonight. I would be safer anywhere but here. That sounds insane.

I found I had to scream, yell, and curse my request to not take any more medication. I have to convince my court appointed case-worker that I am not suicidal. This just a short time after I told my psychiatrist I was indeed suicidal. I ask you, who wouldn't be by now, walking the path I have?

I called Donna, yelling, "Get me out of here!" I thought they were going to give me the straight-jacket after the way I cried to her to save me.

Sometimes time is so unbearable. Memories of my childhood. Sit like a lady. Work like a man. Other than that I was either in trouble or ignored. Nothing I have ever done has been considered big enough to get, you know, the pat on the back or the "atta boy" or girl. Just once, I wish I heard it.

I want to thank Lynn for this journal. I almost didn't get to keep it because of the metal ring. Taken off the journal, it could possibly be a deadly weapon I'll use on myself.

9/27/03 ~

Well, the court person came to see me. We both knew that the doctors were bound morally to keep me there as they really believed I was suicidal. I put on my best face. I told myself I do have the power of persuasion. Extremely lucky for me, the court person was an old customer from Plant Pleasers and all we talked about was plants. I could be sane when it came to plants, especially when I wanted something as bad enough as I wanted out of there. I bailed my ass off and it got me out! I did a fine job, thank you, of convincing the court person to tell "them" to discharge me.

The "discharge diagnosis: Major Depressive D/O Recurrent Severe", and they added "without psychotic features" which I was pleased to see. That in and of itself is pretty sick. This diagnosis is not one a person would generally feel pleased about.

YEA!!!!

I walked away from the hospital with nothing but my hat, a few cigs, and my determination to get to Buckley as soon as I could. Walk faster. I started towards the bridge over the mighty Columbia River between Vancouver and Portland when a bus stopped to tell me it was illegal to walk on the bridge. I got a free ride on the bus and hitched three more rides to get to Dotty's. Joe was there, so the three of us went out to dinner. Joe said he'd give me $450 to find a livable place. To live. He wouldn't even set foot into the dungeon.

I made a list of people I have really loved in my life. Many do not return my love. There are a few I can say that, I think, still do. Some who did are dead. Forget the list of people I have dated.

Thanks to ALL at Providence staff. And to you crazy people. You know who you are.

9/28/03 ~

1:23 a.m.

I am extremely glad it was Joe that came. I hope he knows what that means to me. I have always loved and respected him more than anyone. I was shocked and amazed how easy it was for me to talk freely to him; about my gay relationships, Pete, Darren, Chris, Stormy, you know. And THE time (my girlfriend) Regina's mother called my mom, my brother Mick and their pastor and told them all I was a gay drug dealer. You'd never believe how swiftly both Mick and Joe came to Portland for me then. But not to take me home. I was sent to Greensboro, South Carolina.

Mick told me it would be a lovely ranch on a lake. It was trailers up on bricks surrounded by swamps. I am pretty positive the head guy's name was Jim Jones. I think it took me less than 70 hours before I figured out how to achieve my goal of exiting "the ranch" by picking the lock where they kept our possessions to get my return plane ticket.

I told Joe the thing that made me most upset at Mom. (Besides the fact she always told me she wished I could be more like Rhonda, a girl at church.) About her reasoning that she was afraid Dad would kill the ick yuk puke barf face cousin that raped me. I swore I would kill him if I ever saw him again. When Mom told me he and his new wife were there for dinner I absolutely couldn't believe it. That you-know-what was having roast beef at my home.

All these things came flooding out as Joe, Buck and I drove to the coast. I also finally told him that Mick gave me my first line of cocaine.

I'll be going back to Dotty's to clean while she and Brandy are at some get-rich-quick seminar. At least that's something I can do. And something to do helps keep my mind durable through these stormy seas. Think of positive affirmations.

Feelings are not facts. Stop my thinking errors.

And maybe put an end to my sick thought that the more I work, the more "worthy" I am.

It's now 2:40 a.m. I guess I wrote a lot. Hopefully it is not only legible but sensible.

9/29/03 ~

Dotty hurt me in a big way. Aside from feeding Joe b.s. about promising to make sure I was taken care of, she told me all my problems were due to my gay choices.

I do not feel so good right now and it's stealing all my energy. Every single nerve. Pain is always present.

It's scary to know I left Buckley in the truck a few blocks from the hospital as I sat under an overpass. Next to I-84. I don't know how long.

The color of the sky reminds me of a picture that would be found under "my favorite places." A sailor and a dog feeding off nothing more than the beauty of the pastel-colored sky and water. A red house is nestled in this beautiful garden with a huge yard with candle lights and pavers with three huge weeping willows. And finally my private dock with my boat named "Chief Get Away" waiting to take me to sea.

Shit! Huge fence, chain link with barbed wire on top. Then 2 sets of train tracks, then tall concrete barrier just to get to I-84 west. Plus, I want to go eastbound.

And now rain. This is some predicament.

This is one time where my logical and emotional and physical sides all agree.

L Loser—you look like a loser.

Well, I need to make a move somewhere. Hmmm. There's . . . hmmm.

Next mission: get back to my truck without getting caught, since I skipped crazy school again today.

9/30/03 ~

11:45 p.m.

Getting busy giving up.

10003 SE Foster. I met my potential new landlord Edward there. This was the only place I looked at. I liked it because it had awesome sunflowers.

Very strange day. I hope something of value is written. After leaving the side of Interstate 84, I made it to my truck and then to Gilda and Jeffrey's to get my mail. All without any interaction with anyone.

What is true?

Anyway, I ended up coming straight back to this hole and putting all my things together. Ready to move. Got a tremendous work-out. I haven't eaten since that shrimp cocktail with Joe.

I feel I'm getting sick. My chest hurts, and my coughing doesn't help. So, I'll sign out, draw a picture, watch TV, maybe sleep.

10/1/03 ~

Donna came and brought me coffee. We went to the place I might possibly move to on Foster. I threw up at the dungeon all afternoon. Gilda picked up Buck so Donna could take me to ER at Adventist Hospital. I promised her I would not try to get out before they said I was ready. This has to be the last time in.

Sick of being. Sick. Adventist Room 4303.

To feel the feelings to face my facts . . . To survive and move ahead while dealing with the here and now.

To balance it all with emotional and logical right choices. Seems both impossibly insane as well as emotionally draining.

Buckley—I really miss you. Hopefully this will be the last time away from you.

Me:

Quick wit

Unstoppable endurance

Painfully honest

Compassionate

Emotional wreck.

10/2/03 ~

12:30 a.m.

Dealing with all at the same time. Bailing is the only way to stay afloat, even if it's just barely.

Let's take a closer look at the losses column. Health

Home

Relationships

Business

Ability to consistently think

Additional points for:

Constant medication which constantly changes

Chronic pain

Vertigo

Living in a dungeon with non-stop (okay, they sleep once in a while) barking rat dogs

Childhood memories:

3rd grade—tranquilizers for nervous stomach

6th grade—Mom was hospitalized and I was sent to live elsewhere

BEING LONELY

In and out of love.

Very long night. Couldn't sleep. They gave me Ativan and Vistaril (2 times); the last was at 4:30 a.m. I woke up at 6:30 crying—scared, lonely—desperate.

I can't seem to deal with the past, the now, and least of all, the future. It's like my past, present, and future collide.

The past. It all started—a very long time ago. Yes, let's revisit some ghosts from my past. I should warn you, they're not the friendly kind.

I remember not making it easy for Mom to get me out of the car the first day of school. I cried a lot at school. I felt I was being left or abandoned.

During grade school into junior high I stuttered. I was very shy unless I knew someone very well. I do believe there were other things that happened to me that I have made my mind forget. I had a damaged, scared attitude as well as this strong will and character which, like it or not, comes from my dad. Although he never sexually abused me, he destroyed me with his words and emotional abuse. I have used his/my strengths and strong work ethic to overcome my little tormented mind. I became involved in things like drama, debate, choir, etc. I got my first job at the age of 15 when I picked plums, grapes, and apples. I got a job at the big McD before I moved on to Kmart and got promoted to service desk. I graduated high school six months early.

I even received awards for various school activities I was involved in. None of my family ever came to any of my school plays, debates, etc. They'd only come to the church functions I was in. My mom "found religion" when I was very young. She lost it for a little while, but then found it again. She went along as a chaperone on our church choir tours. Lots of my friends talked to Mom as a counselor or good friend. They would tell me how much they loved and felt close to her. I always believed I didn't turn out to be the daughter she wanted me to be. She wanted a girly-girl who she could dress up and who would play the piano at every church function. Rhonda comes to mind. She was the whole package. She had a beautiful voice and played and sang songs at church. Thing was, Rhonda was one of my best friends.

Two homes I lived in burned down; one of which I had to be rescued from. Our dogs had to be rescued from the second fire. I'll never forget the sight of Dad standing there crying, helpless, watching our house burn down.

Dad and his first sons by another marriage were known very well in our community. They were either very respected or very hated. Dad was heavily involved with the Teamsters.

And who could forget being in the back seat of the car in the middle of the night because Dad would get in a fight outside some bar and Mom would get a call to come bring him home. He had a strong reputation with many "friends" in town; they would call her before the call went out to the police.

I remember looking at my shoes in a bar while Mom screamed and pleaded with my dad to come home. He was dancing with a woman named Rose, whom he was having an affair with.

"Smitty, you'll take these kids, because if you don't come home with me now I'm gonna go and just kill myself and spare myself the pain," Mom threatened.

His reply: "I don't want the little bastards!"

Mom checked into Kennewick General Hospital for a while. I was sent to Aunt Dorothy and Uncle Ralph's. We often went to the Blue Mountains camping and fishing. He would get me drunk. He'd let me drive pulling a trailer. He said I was his drinking buddy. He never abused me sexually. I loved him, in spite of his continuous drinking.

Unlike my feeling towards another relative. He took me to his shed. Even while my family and relatives were there—unaware. In some sick way I needed the attention so much that I didn't care.

I craved attention so much I never told anyone.

Years later, when I was in college, I called home and Mom told me that the #$%&* (and new wife) had dinner at my house. I was furious.

"Honey," she preached, "you have to forgive him. God loves him as much as He loves me or you."

"NO WAY!" I told her. It couldn't be true. Could it?

As a kid I was in this huge youth group, or, as I see it now, brainwash the young before they wise up group. An older boy abused me in the church basement and church van. Until I was around 15. There were others.

When I was a junior in high school I got busted for drugs found in my '65 Dodge Dart station wagon. I named her Bessie Blue Beater. I paid for it myself—a whopping $200. The arrest was scary but I got through it. I knew the stuff wasn't mine.

I fell intensely in love in college. With Regina. It lasted five years.

Donna just called. What a good friend she turned out to be. She is taking care of references for me so I can get out of the dungeon. Her call also got me out of this room. It's not too bad interacting with the other patients. I like Brent. He was here last week when I was here. He is a very likable guy. It doesn't hurt that he makes me laugh either. I forgot what that was like. I guess it's both a good thing and a bad thing he's leaving today. But there's another guy who seems nice. It's a good thing to have another patient to feel comfortable around when you're in a mental ward.

This time is different for me. I'm ready, or maybe willing is a better word, to face my demons.

I just came back from motion group. That's where all the patients sit in a circle and throw pushballs while music plays. Whoever has the ball when the music stops has to answer a question.

"What are you good at?" was the question I got. "Plants," was my reply.

I still haven't seen the doctor. I feel very anxious.

I declined Ativan this morning. I only had Zoloft and thyroid pills. Oh yes, and a nicotine patch.

It's around sunset. My afternoon really sucked. For the first time I wasn't completely drugged when Dr. Flynn finally came in. I was hopeful that we could talk about my emotional being. Instead, he stated his feeling was I won't get well until my social security disability came through. Said I played the role of victim. He also thought I was a drug addict.

I cannot believe my life. Do others have to sabotage any help I will ever get?

Stormy called me. I called her back. She was mostly inquisitive as to where

I am. And the whereabouts of stuff of hers I supposedly have.

What I do have is a *raging* headache.

Dear God—

If you still love me—please help me feel better.

So close to the end and yet so far.

7:00 p.m.

Adventist Hospital

I just finished writing in the last page of my "drawing book." I also talked to my nurse about today. He is very kind and understanding.

Because of the pills, in addition to having a headache, my stomach is sick and hurting. I am trying to keep down some 7 Up, crackers, and ice cream.

Why is it just because doctors and therapists cannot help me with the real problems they have to create more?

10/3/03 ~

9:45 a.m.

Instead of saying I'm not a drug addict or handicapped or not this or that, I will focus on what I am: I am a person that wants to live a productive, full, happy, healthy life! That's all. I will focus on not what

I lost, but what I have! Tonight just might be the night I get some good sleep. Trazodone and Neurontin are on the menu.

Today I spoke very precisely and directly to Dr. Flynn. A 12 step program is not an entirely bad idea. I told him I believe drugs are a symptom of other things. And I did not sign up to collect disability due to mental illness, but rather my physical limitations. Anyway, you might be happy to know that I ate better and had a much better day.

My prayer to God for the day:

Dear God,

Thank you for all the good things you have given to me in the past, now, and in the future. I am very grateful.

Also, please help all the "idal" people out there—the suicidal, the homicidal, etc. people out there in the community and here.

Please allow me a peaceful, restful sleep tonight without the presence of any bad dreams or thoughts.

I do love you and pray you will replace the things I have lost or had to let go of with good things.

Please protect those I love.

Have your loving way with my life. Amen.

Sleep is welcome.

10/4/03 ~

8:45 a.m.

Now they're giving me Remeron too.

Guess what? Mom called me from Israel this morning. She said she is coming here to stay with me for a month. I really do love her. I hope she really comes here.

It's chapel time right now. I was going to go. I am having a lot of flashbacks to the first time I was here. I still owned my house and business, and Lizzie was my girlfriend. I called home after chapel to hear she was moving out. When I left I began a long nightmare.

Okay, I went to chapel. We ended it with my request, the song "Because He Lives." I'm starting to think I saw a pinhole of light in my darkness. Maybe I CAN face tomorrow.

I am counting on the next two to three years being WAY different than the last. No Iranian cab drivers for me today. Besides, where would I go?

2:35 p.m.

I just woke up crying. Bad dream. My life, only seen as a child. My nurse came in along with another. They took me to a group.

In group we made paper airplanes. We had to put our "things" in it, look at it and throw it away. Make another paper airplane. My imagination is very vivid with bad and good stuff. I'm sure I can use more airplanes.

10/6/03 ~

8:45 a.m.

Just had breakfast. I am pretty sure, even with my power of persuasion, there is no way to trick the cafeteria people into giving me more than one cup of coffee.

I am hopeful I get released today. The week-end doctor was way better than Dr. Flynn. I don't plan to go back to outpatient. Maybe one-on-one with Helena.

Here's some good news: I am all signed up for the Intensive Outpatient Program (IOP to those of us in the program). Here's my class schedule:

Monday:

Making Use of Therapy	10:05-11:00
Self Abandonment	11:05-12:00
Recognizing and Managing Anger	1:05-2:00
Coping with Stress & Anxiety	1:05-2:00
Healthy Relationships	2:05-3:00

Tuesday

Making Use of Therapy	10:05-11:00
Affirmations	11:05-12:00
Anger	1:05-2:00
Identity & Express Feelings	2:05-3:30

Wednesday::

Co-occurring Disorders	9:30-11:00
Thinking Errors	10:05-11:00
Anxiety	11:05-12:00
Coping with Stress & Anxiety	1:05-2:00
Journal Workshop	2:05-3:00

Thursday:

Co-occurring Disorders	10:05-11:00
Depression (a class I should be able to teach)	11:05-12:00
Life Management (why didn't I think of that one?)	1:05-2:00
Coping with Stress & Anxiety	2:05-3:00

Friday:

Co-occurring Disorders	9:30-11:00
Changing Self-Image	11:05-12:00
Self-Defeating Behaviors (who Me?)	1:05-2:00
Week-end Planning	2:05-3:00

Now you see where the "Intensive" comes from. Whew! And not just that, but there are several different group programs. There's an Activity Group, an Educational Group, a Psychotherapy Group, and Occupational Therapy. I'm willing, though not sure how able.

10/7/03 ~

I went to anger group. Erasers are put on pencils for a reason. People make mistakes.

Lose authentic self by not asserting yourself when you feel anger. Unless I act out my emotions, people will not take me seriously. Being assertive is being true to yourself.

10/8/03 ~

11:00 a.m.

Providence Outpatient Clinic (OPC)

I just walked in on the end of the 10:00 group—ooops. I thought it was the beginning of the 11:00. Where's the eraser when you need one?

I'm sitting here in the group room on this blustery fall day. I went to Ruth's last night. I got a check for $750 made out to Edward for $450 rent plus the

$300 refundable deposit. Thanks, Joe! Ruth also gave me a card from Mom. It had some explanation of why she was in Jerusalem, but I really didn't get what she was saying. I guess she really doesn't know that I'm proud of her doing what she feels she should.

I wound up taking Darren and Kathy (his other daughter) to dinner at Taco Bell last night. Darren and I walked in the park while Kathy was in the library. Darren says he wants to date me, but we really didn't talk too much about it. I am very confused about my feelings for him.

I scored a moving truck—yes! For free—THANK YOU! I have a meeting with Helena today. She said she thought I was going to kill myself last week because I was mad at her for calling emergency on me.

I will meet Edward tonight to give him the check and get the keys to my new place at Felony Flats (Foster Road with the sunflowers). Smile Face.

1:00 p.m.

Communications Group

In business I've always been assertive. Personally, I am more passive/aggressive. I've got them all covered.

My stomach feels sick. I just had my session with Helena. We talked about the "shed." (Harriet, Ruth, Mom, Joe, Pete, and Darren also.) I've made this surprising discovery. I'm really scared of dying. I'm trying harder than ever to get through. (Listen.)

Last group—

Stems: #9 The hardest choice is:

To Deal or Deny—by avoiding—

The scared little inferior girl is still in me. The one that needs to be reassured. The one that's weak. The one I hate. She'll never get Dad's approval by being weak. There is nothing good that will come of her.

What should I do with her? Forget her? Save her? Acknowledge she is part of me?

I need to deal with what I can do without anger at my limitations. If I want to be whole, I have to deal. It's a gamble. My eyes have been shut!

It sounds easier than it is. Let's look at why:

1. I am not capable of having good relationships.
2. I make wrong choices too often.
3. I'll never be close to anyone.
4. I'm never going to get through this depression.
5. I'm not smart enough to learn new things.

There has got to be enough good in me to fight to save what's left. I'm being rescued from the dungeon!! I met with Edward and we talked for over three hours. He told me with as many positive references as I had, he felt pretty confident in renting to me. Even with my bad credit and no proof of income, or a co-signer. THANK YOU!!

I only owe a very small amount for November. October and security are paid. Thanks, Joe!!

10/9/03 ~

A pretty sleepless night on Brandy's couch. This guy knocks on the door looking for Brandy. "Who are you?" I ask.

"Brian. Who are you?"

"Sherri. Well, now that we know who we are, Brandy's not here and we can say good night. Good night, Brian." He leaves and I resume my position on the couch.

Providence

Think of a pie. About one quarter of it is your biology. Another quarter is attitude. The other half is behaviors. BE AUTHENTIC.

Was practicing my shim sham shimmy at lunch. The other patients seemed to enjoy it.

10/10/03 ~

1:37 a.m.

Back at the Dungeon

I didn't stay for my last group. Coping. I couldn't. I went to Fred

Meyer's and lost my cell phone there.

I got extremely lucky. The truck lady gave me an old phone she didn't want. Major telephone issues. She also gave me the key to one of her trucks I could use to move.

RAIN! BIG RAIN!

I need to decide what I really need to take. The place is so small. I think planning ahead would be a smart move.

4:00 a.m. drawing frenzy! And then there's:

Helena,

What do you see when you look at me? Are you thinking about your kids? Husband? Me? Do I dare even think that maybe—you and I could have some laughs and be friends—that's of course if you were not my therapist? I have begun to think of you as my friend.

I have considered the thought of hiring a therapist in the future just to ensure a true conversation would happen. Have a sounding board maybe.

Am I really "sick?" Have an "illness?" After this long of a ride I have to guess I can answer that YES (with art to back me up).

It could be just because you have the most intense eyes I've ever looked into. So kind, and safe.

You winked at me the other day before you started group. Don't ya know that got my mind a wandering? Could it be possible for me to have somebody like you for a friend? I want to look more often into your eyes. But, that means you will look into mine.

I am afraid of the truth of my darkening existence. Believe me, logically speaking, it's a fucking lot of shit.

Because of you, and for many reasons, my walls have most definitely come down. It's the part of me I have always considered weak that is left. Yet somehow I am here. But dumbfounded as to what it is I should do to help myself get beyond this illness. How do doctors and therapists talk about me? How do I act? I feel completely stumped as to what I should do. Bailing just ain't cutting it for me any more.

Is it alright with you if I wanted to spend longer sessions together? I have a lot to say.

I also want to ask Lori, the art therapist, to look at some of my drawings and analyze them. Do you think I could handle it?

Last week when I came to the clinic high and couldn't look at you, you said you thought I was mad at you. Did that bother you? Can you really leave your work at work or sometimes do we follow you home? In your mind how can you care, and then turn it OFF and suddenly not care?

CHAPTER FOURTEEN
FELONY FLATS AND BEYOND

10/11/03 ~

I'm in my apartment at felony flats. It's my and Buckley's home now. I feel as though I haven't stopped moving since I lost my home last November and moved to Crown Vista, where Stormy always had me moving things around.

What a fairy tale turned nightmare. Our humble heroine goes literally from home to homeless to the mansion to homeless to the dungeon to felony flats. I am not done bringing my stuff here, and far from knowing what to do with it. This is the smallest place I have ever lived. Jim, a friend of a friend who helped me move, stayed with me. We had sex in the shower. It was pleasant, but not like the hot passion I had with Stormy. I asked Jim to leave a few minutes ago. Buck was antsy and I wanted some space. Did I mention very small space? That's all I have.

The girl upstairs said she is going to sue the landlord for sexual harassment, blah blah blah. This was within the first five minutes after my moving truck showed up.

I stayed up and worked on my apartment. I really like having my own space. I know this is where I'm supposed to be. I moved a lot of my stuff. Stuff. There's so much of it. You especially notice how much there is when you're moving from place to place to place.

I went to Bub and Scout's and had something to eat. Bub was really worried about me last week.

10/12/03 ~

10:45 a.m.

My plans today are to finish most of my move, and stop by the ward at Adventist. I'll visit and take some food or something for everyone.

Jim came by at 7:30 this morning, beer in hand. I had to turn him away. Did I tell you Jim tried to kill himself recently by jumping off the Morrison Bridge? The other night I enjoyed his company until he started talking nonsense about how "they" were looking for him. Paranoid. I almost ripped the smoke detector from the ceiling to assure him "they" weren't filming him. If the guy hadn't been "sick" and refused to take his meds, I could sort of liked him. But, as I told him, I could empathize about being "sick", but I couldn't emotionally or mentally handle him. He reminds me of a boyfriend I had when I was about 16. Beautiful eyes and smile. He made me feel beautiful when he looked at me.

Well, the saga goes on. I need to call Edward to tell him to pick a time to get all his crap out of the storage area he promised me. Endless stuff.

Last night Bobby, a friend of a friend, and I went for the last time to the dungeon for the rest of my stuff. Wouldn't you know, I had to call the police on freak lady (landlord upstairs) since she wouldn't let me in. She'd lock the top lock as I unlocked the bottom and vice-versa.

With Bobby's great help, I completed my exit from the dastardly "D" at last. I still have stuff at Brandy's, Dotty's, Jeffrey and Gilda's, who knows where else.

I took the truck back today—the lady there was so nice. I really appreciate when things go well, perhaps more than the average Josephine.

10/13/03 ~

11:15 a.m.

Sitting with Bobby. My hero for the day. I would never have been able to get it all done myself. I am out of the dungeon! The place I bottomed out. I'm so happy to be here without having to risk dog bites to use the frickin' bathroom.

7:10 p.m.

I'm alone. Done with the Dungeon. Maybe that could be the name of a chapter. Done with the Dungeon. What connotations that word has.

I'm thinking about naming my book Facing Face. I believe I am perceived at only about 15-20% of my whole being. In other words, how I'm perceived as a whole being is made with only a small amount of info. I am perceived to be outgoing, confident, fun, social. But inside, I am scared, insecure, lonely, sexual, passionate. Can I see who I am?

Who are we, really? Are we how others see us, or are we the person others don't see?

10/14/03 ~

Now I'm at OPC, sitting, just waiting for the phone. I need to call PGE since there seems to be a problem with my electricity. I also need to get another prescription for Toradol but they need a doctor's consent.

So, while I'm waiting I'll tell you a joke. What do Indians call sex stones?

Fucking rocks.

Well, the problem with PGE is an old bill for $290 that I still owe them. I got more sleep last night than I've had in a while. Sleep is very important.

Going to have to get me some more of that, since I know I feel much better with my mind and body rested.

Affirmations:

Turn negative self-talk to at least a neutralizer. Like instead of, "I am damaged physically," I can say, "There is a lot of life left in me. Not all is broken."

Pain is a constant part of my being, but not the ruler of me. I can live with my limitations.

My new affirmation is: There's always that chance things could work out in my favor.

Anger Group with Helena

Did you know there are many ways anger can be expressed indirectly? I believe my anger seeps out indirectly—in my tone of voice. I have often been misunderstood by my ex-lovers when I am simply trying to get a point across. It turns out I have been completely perceived the opposite of what I was really trying to express.

My pain level now makes me angry. It affects my writing ability. Probably causes me to drive more recklessly than I probably should, and likely drives my over/under eating. It makes me want to refuse to take my pills.

10/15/03 ~

I started dual group diagnosis (double your pleasure, double the things wrong with you) this morning with another therapist. I talked a bit with another patient, Diana, who's not been coming here as long as I have. Our conversations made me conclude that a person does not have to have any one particular thing they go to or have to have to be an addicted personality. She gave me a bunch of morphine pills and Percocet she was getting for her severe pain in the sacral area.

There is no birth of consciousness without pain.

My journal group assignment:

Five years from right now my hopes are:

To really know myself, be at peace with myself and the world around me.

To have my physical and emotional pain at a manageable level that will not affect my life in a negative way.

To be in a happy, healthy relationship, growing old and experiencing life well spent. Together.

I hope to still have Buckley. He would be 12, which is old for his breed. Benson (remember him?) lived to be 16. I held him as the vet gave him the injection and the life left his body. I want Buckley to have the same long life as Benson did.

I hope to be living part time in Hawaii and part time around here.

Maybe I will still be in therapy with Helena. I couldn't imagine having any other therapist. I can't imagine life without her now.

Four years ago I was working on Men of Honor. So many people in my life.

So little honor.

10/16/03 ~

OPC

I'm waiting for a therapist, though I don't know who since Helena isn't here today. Afterwards, Diana will come pick me up. We are supposed to "talk" for a while. I went to Jeffrey and Gilda's since it was his birthday. It's not the same with them since I've moved.

My apartment is slowly coming together. I have to get a phone.

10/17/03 ~

The first time I talked to Diana outside of group was when we sat together at lunch one day. Being the vest connoisseur that I am, I admired her vest. She told me she had to get up at 4 a.m. every morning to make her husband lunch before he left for work. She took good care of him. I joked, "I need a wife. Why don't you divorce him and marry me?" Walking back to group she said when she looked at me she was amazed at how beautiful I am. I wanted to shrink into my shoes.

10/20/03 ~

HAPPY BIRTHDAY MOM!

I went to OPC three days last week. Friday I was here, not feeling like doing much. Stormy called again. I went out to a bar and met her for a few drinks. Of course I brought her back here. We talked half the night and then had sex for a while. I took her back to her car about ten the next morning.

I got a call from Jane, my legal medical marijuana grower. Her boyfriend beat her up and was now sitting, hopefully rotting, in jail. Bobby and I spent the night at her place. He has been staying on my couch for a while, so I thought a change of scenery would do us good. And Jane appreciated the company.

Moved Jane to her friend DC's house, and moved more of my stuff. Ruth gave me a check for the phone. Thank you!!

10/21/03 ~

Yes! I got my phone installation date five days from now. I'm feeling very nervous today. Stormy continues to leave me messages on my cell phone. Yesterday she said the agency bought her place. She was very upset. I love her with my heart, but my head says NO WAY!

LIGHT does NOT exist without dark. Pleasure without pain. Good without bad. Change comes about through the synthesis of opposites. The goal is not to prove which is right or wrong, but to find and accept the truth in both.

10/25/03 ~

5:45 a.m.

Stormy called and asked me over. I brought groceries and beer. Here I am, back at Crown Vista wearing my favorite loungewear. A long, black robe with big fur around the collar. It goes well with this red beret hat. We took ecstasy at 4:20 a.m.—a hit of blue diamond. I feel everything, yet no one is feeling like taking charge.

Yesterday I had lunch with Diana at "school" again. She gave me ten more morphine pills. It seems Helena is starting to get to know the real me. I mean, at least I'm talking to her about things beside just plants.

Got my prescription for Toradol. More people than I care to count have seen my big white butt as they gave me these shots.

Knowing Diana had a connection with God, of sorts, I remembered I had this small glass vial with a mustard seed in it. It was a necklace. The Bible says in Matthew 17:20 …"If you have faith as small as a mustard seed, you can say to this mountain, 'Move from here to there,' and it will move. Nothing will be impossible for you." The mustard seed is the smallest seed in the world, which is odd as it produces one of the largest plants in the garden. I gave it to her to thank her for all the pills she was giving me.

11/4/03 ~

It's been a while—lots happened. I was with Stormy Wednesday until today. I just got to crazy school. Affirmations class and group. I stayed Sat. night at my apartment and went up to Crown Vista on Sunday. On Halloween we got dressed up and then decided not to go to some party.

I traded pot for use of Sloan's (my neighbor in the four-plex) storage unit and half the driveway. I dug up a lot of plants from Crown Vista and they need a good home also.

Do I trust Stormy not to hurt me again? NO. She is supposed to be out of Crown Vista this Friday. Sounds impossible.

I am committed to overcome my condition. I am open to new meaning in my life.

My truck broke down so I was driving my car. I'm still having bad dreams. I can't believe I missed my pain management appointment yesterday. The next opening is December 1st. Diana continues to give me morphine pills. That helps. I got a letter from BonMom, wondering where I am. I wish I had the answer. I feel very sick to my stomach, and my head really hurts. I want to lie down.

Dear God, Where am I going?

Last week Helena told me to write a letter to (one of) my abuser(s), although he is dead. I feel the small child is winning this war. It's easier to just lie down and give that bail bucket one hell of a kick, so to speak. No expectations. What is it I want? Not to feel pain all the time.

Here we go again. Anger group. There's a lot of anger in the world. And what good does it do?

At lunch Diana and I took Stormy's stuff she put in my car to her new apartment. She gave me another morphine.

Ruth said Mom is flying into Seattle the end of the week. I told her I couldn't pick Mom up. The truck's still broken, and I have no car insurance. Good enough reasons. Or bad reasons, depending on how you look at it.

11/5/03 ~

This morning Ruth called to ask me to go to Seattle with Aunt Harriet on Friday to pick up Mom. I've been having panic attacks. It's hard to breathe or think in that condition.

I talked to BonMom for a long time. It's nice to have people care.

I'm sitting at OPC waiting to talk to Helena. I need to tell her about my panic attacks. I missed the last two groups of co-occurring conditions (that dual diagnosis I hit the jackpot with). People with mental conditions plus drug problems. To take or not to take the pills. I can't help but think of the chicken and the egg and which came first—the mental conditions or the drug problems.

I am really panicked about seeing Mom. I think I am angrier than I thought. Anger comes from being hurt. How can I possibly share my hurts knowing it will hurt her?

I am proud of myself for not going to Crown Vista last night. I need to be independent. Self assured. At peace. Diana has given me three very nice poems she wrote. One says:

"Sherri, you are a woman that can change the world." Probably easier than changing my life.

How do I call Aunt Harriet and Ruth and tell them I cannot go to pick up Mom?

1. I have other plans
2. I feel uncomfortable going and I don't want to go.
3. I'm sorry, I changed my mind.
4. I don't want to go—NO! I'm afraid.

11/9/03 ~

I've been helping Stormy move out. I thought I had a lot of stuff! I've never seen anyone with more stuff than her. I moved stuff from the barn to the house. She's such a slob. I picked up the bottles, cans, trash, did a burn pile, you name it.

I saw Mom once for a few minutes and talked to her on the phone briefly. We're going to have a session with Helena this week. I love my mom. Who pushed who away?

11/11/03 ~

1:00 p.m.

I'm at crazy school. Mom is out in the waiting area right now. I had a huge panic attack last group. At 2:00 Mom and I will meet with Helena. I need to tell her she needs to go back to Ruth's. She brings up too many feelings that are very difficult to deal with. Diana was talking to Mom while she was waiting, trying to assure her that things were okay.

11/17/03 ~

4:45 p.m.

You're not going to believe this. I am here at Providence emergency room waiting to be seen. Oh, by the way, the meeting with Helena and Mom went okay. I don't know. Okay to me could be devastating for the average person, or is it the other way around? Mom's memory was not the same as mine on most things. I told her about something that happened and I asked, "Do you remember?"

"No, I don't remember that," she said. She didn't remember anything.

I told her I thought it was best for both of us if she stayed at Ruth's, and I took her there that afternoon.

DC, Jane's friend, came out with her truck and picked up the load of plants I had waiting since my truck broke down. I skipped the next two days of OPC, took my truck in, and had DC help bring over the plants which I managed to cram in the "yard" at Felony Flats.

Oh yeah, the emergency room. I was working at Stormy's, who's been having moving sales all week, not to mention attracting the strangest people to her house. A few nights ago, while working with Stormy in her huge garage turned art studio, who should walk through the door but the guy who came looking for Brandy, Brian.

Last night, for some reason, Stormy let this girl she met at some party stay in the "Safari Room." The girl was a stripper and had other habits the law scowls at. The next morning, Stormy asks me to tell the stripper and the guy she had over that they had to leave 'cause someone was picking up the bed in there. I knocked on the door, clearly relayed the message, and went to get myself a cup of coffee. All of a sudden this asshole Brian came in the kitchen and attacked me! He grabbed me from behind and starts choking me, and then threw me into the wall, causing me to fall down some stairs. Every time I tried to get up he'd kick me. I screamed over and over, "Stormy, call the police!" She finally saw me and did. Whatever martial arts skills I had were over-shadowed by fear and pain.

I managed to regain my footing and ran outside. I jumped into Stormy's van, where she always kept her keys, and took off with Buckley down to the front gate ¼ mile down the driveway and blocked the excite with the van. Buck and I got out and ran into the woods as Brian's truck came barrelling down the driveway. It wasn't long before I saw Brian grab a chain from his truck to pull Stormy's van from the gate enough to get out. I saw he cut his hand up pretty bad, and, I have to say, I was glad. He got away just before the cops and an ambulance showed up. It turned out that Brian served time in prison for beating up a cop.

11/26/03 ~

The Crown's Point

12/2/03 ~

10:00 p.m.

At Foster aka Felony Flats

Stormy and I have been together daily since she called me—all except for one night. All in spite of her working me like crazy. It's enough that my ribs are still sore from that asshole at her place. I wanted to press charges but was warned not to by people who know him. Fear rules my world, damn it.

Brian was so incredibly evil and hateful—hitting me, choking me, throwing me down, kicking me. And even though I know my "loved ones" would never in a million years want this to happen to me, there seems to be a pattern of no one standing up for me. I know I sure would for my loved ones. If anyone hurts someone I love I'm hurting them.

I spent Thanksgiving at Crown Vista. Candlelight. Fireplace glow in the master bedroom. She really tries to make me believe she's not been with anyone except me, but I know better. Did I mention she has this problem, among others, with honesty? Stormy told me Diana liked me, and I said, "No way. She's straighter than a ruler."

I've let my life here at the flats be completely non-existent, as I spent all my time helping Stormy move. And for me, I think that's worse than simply being alone.

Experimenting with hazardous behavior.

The good news is that I walked away from her without any fighting. I went to school and then to Bub and Scout's. I do have a few good friends.

12/3/03 ~

2:00 a.m.

Felony Flats

A neighbor across the street who, don't ask me why, visited me from the start, finally left. She brings her pipe with the white dope (methamphetamine) over. Her four-year-old son really makes me smile, which doesn't happen too much. Poor kid.

Good God, I need you. Big time. Help me fight this evil dark war—or help in any way you might think of. I can't bail any more. I give up. I can't seem to out-run it. Between the street drugs and the narcotic prescriptions for pain, depression, thyroid . . . I guess medically I qualify for the medical marijuana license or permit or whatever piece of paper it is that says it can help me in my condition. Do I really need a piece of paper that costs $$$ to tell me that?

So, how should my priority list read?

A program named "Starting Over" is on.

S. O. unds exactly like what should be my next adventure.

T V

A E

R R

T

I

N

G

Why do I keep going back? April 6, 2004, the day I fell and lost the life I had built will mark three years since that day working on The Hunted. Now it feels as though I am the hunted.

Congratulations. I have finally jumped through all the hoops and met all qualifications to now get disability and will receive $600 per month starting this month. I guess making it into mental hospitals six times in three years helped. Severe depression and anxiety. Who wouldn't be if they lost their home, business, relationships . . . I lost my identity. I was only what I did.

As difficult as it has been, and as weird as this may sound, I feel very fortunate that, through much therapy, I have gained a new awareness. I am learning who I am. I have been given this luxury. I plan to make the most of it. Since this whole life-changing ordeal started, I have been drawing, writing, journaling . . . I would very much like to put it all together in a book. Life is truly unbelievably amazing!

I am in my starting over house.

Be come mindful.

Addictive behavior comes from avoidance.

I've been in the same groups for six months, at least, with Diana. She didn't talk much, but when she did she spoke quietly and everyone was quite attentive. One thing she said, repeatedly, was that she planned on leaving her husband when her daughter graduated from high school.

All of a sudden, Diana stopped coming to group, so I called and left her messages. Finally, she called back. I said, "Hey, if you want to be friends, don't make your friends worry. You stay in contact, especially considering we met at crazy school because we're suicidal." She apologized.

Diana took me to pain management at St. Vincent's hospital, as Stormy had my truck. I got 30 ml of long acting morphine. Twice a day. And something they call a tens unit, which sounds like shock treatment through an electric vest for pain. Starting up physical therapy soon.

One afternoon I was trying to organize my things, and Diana came by to help. Before she left, when we were in the kitchen, I remember feeling so nervous, as the energy between us was so thick. I stammered to her, as I stared out the kitchen window, "Diana, uh, are we just friends?" I turned around to look at her. She was so beautiful with the sunlight on her hair. She said, "I love you like I never loved, and, yes, you are my friend." She gave me a really long hug and said she'd be back that night. True to her word, she came back and spent the night. There was no sex involved, which was fine, but it was important to her that I tell Stormy about us. While Stormy pretended not to care, I think she did. I still fought with the feeling that I would be accused of breaking up Diana's family, something I couldn't do. Diana insisted it was already broken.

We went to Washington Park one night with champagne and had a picnic dinner on top of the morphine pills and whatever else I was on that day. When we got back to the car cops were there and a tow truck was pulling in. The park had closed. We wondered why it got so quiet. I told the officer that I had a brain injury, which I thought might cover up how high I was. He said we could leave, but then I couldn't find the car key. Who knew where my keys were? I reached into the cop's car and took his flashlight, asking if I could borrow it, and retraced my steps to find them. When I got back, Diana was telling him we were in love and how happy that made her. I think he couldn't wait for us to go.

In my past I had a reputation of wining and dining my girlfriends, and now, I wanted to do that more than ever for Diana, but I wasn't able to, physically and financially. This relationship was unlike any I'd had before. Previously, sex, never initiated by me, happened at the beginning of a relationship, and then we got to really know each other. With Diana, we grew very close without sex. I didn't initiate it, and she didn't know how to begin the sexual aspect of her first gay relationship. So Diana and I became intimate in a way I didn't know existed.

12/4/03 ~

6:30 p.m.

Crown Vista

I have done nothing but dig up more and more plants. Stormy already started her impossible behavior. She is so completely blinded by her selfish attitude and controlling obsession. And whatever her drug du jour is.

I am in so much pain now. Stop the cycle, Sherri. Be smart. Not much will change with anyone in my life with these bad behaviors until we are all completely honest to ourselves and each other.

12/16/03 ~

9:50 a.m.

Diana helped me move my bed into the living room last night. Darren came by for a minute. I then proceeded to fall into a much needed sleep. Diana even cleaned before she left. What a very nice person.

I stayed at Stormy's Sunday night. Went to pain management yesterday. I asked for a lower dose of morphine.

Mom is supposed to be here today. I plan on talking about all the things she said she didn't remember during our appointment with Helena. Sometimes I think my words come too fast and my memory leaves too early.

12/18/03 ~

11:50 a.m.

Crazy school

I spaced out, checked out, and just quit thinking during my morning groups. It's easy to do with so many more people in attendance. I see this pattern: more people attend crazy school during the winter holiday season.

Affirmations Group

I am open to finding new meaning in my life.

Diana called and asked if she could stay at my apartment tonight. I'm pretty sure she is leaving her husband. But I will not be the reason, although I do want to help and support her.

These are the only affirmations I can find right now:

1. I am not capable of having a good relationship.
2. I make wrong choices too often.
3. I'll never be close to anyone.

One night Diana stayed over without telling her husband, Richard (previous times she let him know). I convinced her to write a letter to him out of common courtesy. This is what she wrote:

"Richard,

I felt fine this morning and thought about driving myself over, however I thought it would be best if I didn't drive first thing this morning considering the residual effects of the medication. I am being more responsible with my medications. Last night/evening I was in a lot of pain, and without my meds. Sherri's doctor had prescribed her Valium, and it helps with her pain as well as her vertigo. She asked me if I wanted to try it and I said yes. It did take the edge off my pain as well as make me drowsy. It was responsible of me to stay at Sherri's and not drive home. I am sorry to have caused you any unnecessary concern.

Earlier this week, last night, and on several other occasions you have threatened to leave or divorce. If that's what you want, I respect that and understand you have to do what's necessary for your peace of mind. Just know that I don't take your words lightly, and don't want or deserve any more idle threats. I hope we can sit down and talk without yelling or harsh words. I only want to talk if it is a calm conversation without disrespecting each other."

I told Diana she needed to deal with Richard as best as she could so she could look back with no regrets. I also gave her a key to my apartment so she would have a safe place to come to.

12/31/03 ~

(aka my 44th birthday)

I received this notebook from Sabrina (a former girlfriend of seven years) last night at her house. She made my favorite meal, fried chicken with mashed potatoes and corn. Stormy went with me. I dropped her off at her place on the way home.

I saw Candy this afternoon. I've known her over twenty years, but haven't seen her in a long time. I went to DC's, then Bub and Scout's. Bub made me a cheeseburger pie—yum—just her and I. Then I went back to Stormy's. She put together some snacks, accompanied by good wine and pot. We watched the very exciting Home and Garden channel, and fell asleep by ten.

1/1/04 ~

When we woke up it was snowing like crazy. Diana called. Unknown to me, she spent the night at my apartment, and asked when I was coming home. "Right away," I answered. I told Stormy I was leaving, who then decided she wanted to come, since she heard Diana was there.

At home we made a great dinner and watched movies. I really didn't feel like taking Stormy back home. I have to say, I had a very hard time sleeping, as Diana was on one side and Stormy the other. And Stormy was being her bad self and I had to keep moving her hand off me.

1/5/04 ~

Stormy got locked out of Crown Vista. She now lives in her friend's apartment complex. Our talks turn into fights over the insensitivity that we both feel we are given by the other.

Diana and I have new rules now. As Stormy was, and will always be, invited to Thanksgiving and Christmas dinners (I had promised to always be her family), she will have to spend the night at DC's if she doesn't want to drive home.

People come and go in and out of my life. DC's in, Gilda and Jeffrey not so much, Bub and Scout on and off, then there's . . . Diana. So wonderfully different from anyone I have ever known.

1/12/04 ~

1:00 p.m.

Crazy school

While eating the indescribable hospital lunch, I talked with this elderly fellow patient. I told him I liked his black beaded necklace. He took it off and gave it to me! He said he had studied several religions, but believes in THE Bible and in his past lives. As I looked at him, into his small, sparkling blue eyes, he said he believed I had been a great artist and am one now. He wanted to buy some of my artwork. Something about his words gave me goose bumps. I told him I'd love to give him a couple of my masterpieces.

I called Aunt Harriet and told her I really wanted to spend time with her. I'm angry about this endless pattern of what turns out to be poor choices of self-defeating relationships. Things to bring up at my 2:00 with Helena.

Pain med. Ask to see my doctor for prescriptions. Valium.

Dad saying hurtful things I know aren't true. Like Stormy does. True or not, they pierce my heart.

When Dad was yelling at me calling me a free-loading son-of-a-bitch, Mom's reaction was, "Honey, you know he doesn't mean it. Ignore it. You know he loves you."

I've done this with my relationships. Ignore Stormy's harsh words to me. If it's too much, then I go to Plan B: AVOID.

Helena.

Self-abandonment.

Capacity of the real self.

Is it possible, really, to support oneself when under attack? Not with Stormy.

Here's another one of "those letters" that seem to follow me:

*** FINAL NOTICE ***

This is your final notice.

Total Account Balance   10,126.77

Wow. It's hard to get good mental treatment for much under that. It adds up fast.

1/13/04 ~

Felony Flats

2/4/04 ~

Affirmations

Today's subject: "Attitude." Today's worksheet:

"Describe a situation where your positive attitude has made a difference in your life:"

I had to say where I live, compared to where I was and what I had. I am blessed to have a place for me, Buck, and stuff.

"Describe a situation where your negative attitude has prevented you from finding a positive solution to a problem:"

My relationship with Stormy. I mean, I'm constantly wondering why she does what she does when I should be thinking more about how I respond. My pattern has been not stopping the involvement with Stormy until it becomes detrimental.

I have to learn the ABC's of relationships again. I want to go through the whole alphabet with someone. I need to experience a good relationship.

Last, but certainly not least:

"Think about one regularly occurring situation where your attitude could make a difference:"

One just couldn't cut it for me. I had two. Stormy. Physical pain. The worst is when they go together, which is way too often.

2/18/04 ~

ABSOLUTELY NOT

I am not going to find a way to manage my depression and anxiety because I believe its stem is my physical pain, which reminds me of my initial injury, then my losses due to the injury, then my life as it "isn't" now, and, finally, I believe my future is not worth going to.

No negative thinking. Just statements of reality. Mastering reality is only being able to get to the point of practicing living it.

3/3/04 ~

Reporting to you live from Felony Flats. 3:30 a.m. Pacific Time

It's a very rainy, cold, dreary day. I have a splitting headache with a dose of nausea. I'm having a tooth pulled tomorrow, then a bridge built. The fun never stops.

DC, her grandson, and I have gotten very close. Like family.

I just came across the contract I made when I gave away my business, and copies of the letters I wrote to tell my loyal clients. Ouch.

Crazy upstairs neighbors. Tall man (I swear he's over seven feet) and crazy lady. I've seen them use their food stamps to buy pop at the 7-11 and then go outside, pour out the pop and return the empty cans to get money for cigarettes. Could write chapters and chapters on them. But I'll spare all of us.

Diana is still very much in the picture. I asked Helena, "Should I go out with her?"

"Not hardly," she said, exasperated.

Our relationship has continued to get more physical, bringing us both pleasure. We spend as much time together as possible. She often takes me to the dentist. She used to be a dental assistant. She told me she asked Helena if she should go for it with me, and Helena said, "Yes." I'm confused.

I believe Diana loves me and I believe she really wants to keep from sinning against God, as do I.

Stormy now has bright pink hair, lost her van and had to walk home. She didn't have insurance, so it was impounded. That same day I got pulled over. I have no insurance. Lucky for me the cop got another call, and I got to leave with my truck and no ticket.

I wrote a letter to the editor of the Oregonian about John Deere and company. I still feel the need to tell my story. Somehow it makes me feel better, I guess. Little else does.

CHAPTER FIFTEEN
PRIDE KEEPS ME FROM BEING PROUD

4/4/04 ~

I rented a tiny house today on Salmon Street, just down the street from DC. I rented it from Sam and Shelly. The house and landscaping are in serious need of a lot of work to make it livable. There's no heat in the house. But I love the huge shop area and an even bigger yard with lots of room for my hundreds of plants. They will be very happy here.

I believe things are looking up. I think there's a possibility things could work out. Diana stays with me more than not. She takes really good care of me. No one has ever come close to caring for me in the warm, cheerful, loving way she does.

4/6/04 ~

Why it happens, I don't know. But I got scared and went inside my head and wouldn't let Diana in. I just ignored her. I hate how much help I need.

4/8/04 ~

Salmon Street
Home

It happened. She left after making this house a home.

I was lost, and wanted to run. So I planted plants instead. I set up lights outside, as I planned a long night of plant therapy. To see the things she had done in the house was unbearable. The fruit in the bowl on the table. The green rug covering the cold tile in the tiny bathroom.

4/10/04 ~

Knock knock. Who's there? Diana came in, and with a big smile proclaimed, "I'm home!" J

Okay. This is where I completely numb-out. Or try but can't, due to the overwhelming emotions that scream inside me.

I don't quite know how these new emotions will work in my life. But, thus far, I am completely convinced. I love her and I like her and it feels right, warm, and safe with her. I trust her. I can't seem to see life without her. I'm glad she came back to stay. Even with Boomer (her cat). I am NOT a cat person, but I was getting attached to Boomer.

This relationship exploded and now 4-10-04 will forever be a holiday!

4/28/04 ~

AFFIRMATIONS:

I Sherri: Am working hard

Am making improvements Know my reality

Can make my own decisions Can get better, stronger

Am worthy of love and compassion

Am learning so much about myself

Know it's okay to feel sad and disappointed

4/29/04 ~

Salmon

5/4/04 ~

My time with Diana has grown along with my feelings for her. She is so good to me. I really do love her and I love the fact that she loves me too. I helped move her things from Richard's to her parents' home. We call it "Boomer's Cottage" since it's way up in the woods and Boomer's been staying there.

5/9/04 ~

Diana wrote and framed this for me:

A Story of Love

Once upon a time . . .

In the darkest of dungeons and a very lonely place . . .

There came to be a glimmer of light that shone forth much illuminating insight into a depth of despair, which surrounded a heart lost, but evidently not forgotten.

As days and weeks turned into months, the glimmer became a radiant source or emerging energy that would continue to engulf the forgotten soul, and bathe it with a renewed spirit of belonging.

The brilliance of this light source never fades, it only grows into a more magnifying attraction as the months turn into years and the years will lead off into an infinite unison of spirit.

Sherri, I love you more as each day passes and desire to spend all my days enraptured in the beauty and everlasting spark that has ignited a burning fire in every cell of my being.

I exist to love you and I will love you the rest of my existence. Forever does not begin to describe the time in which I will be devoted to you.

As I am blessed with the opportunity to show you how much I love you, I pray that you will recognize my sincerity and not close off the pouring out of your spirit into mine. I want to be one with you. My heart beats to the sound of your name and therefore, cannot go on without your presence in my life.

As each day passes, I look forward to the approaching time when we will unite by means of a marriage between our two souls, and when we will then become one spirit for all eternity.

Please do not doubt the purity of my words as they are spoken directly from my heart to yours.

Hugs and Kisses Forever Diana

Okay. This letter hit me hard. I don't think I can be all she needs from me. Is suffocation from good stuff possible? I feel it is. I'm too broken to be what is needed for me to heal, let alone be everything she needs and deserves to live happily.

I distract myself by doing things. I think I need to build a carport or two for here and for DC. The yard needs work. I have to get out.

5/10/04 ~

4:30 a.m.

I feel very torn. I said she could not use me as the excuse to divorce the rat.

I'm an alibi now. I hate to be even a part of any family breaking apart.

Diana,

I see love in your eyes. I feel love when you touch me. I hear love when you speak. These feelings over-power me. Could it be—this time— that feelings are facts?

It really doesn't matter what anyone says as long as our love can continue to be a good thing in each other's lives.

Oh, by the way. Do you know I honestly love you and plan on marrying you and having a very full life with you?

Will you marry me?

5/27/04 ~

My head hurts. I just swallowed a handful of pills. Ahhhh shti.

5/28/04 ~

Sherri—

Why are you snapping at me so much?

Are you deliberately trying to sabotage the love I have for you? I'm a bit hurt that you could treat me, or talk to me, in that manner.

I can understand an occasional snap as we all have bad moments. However, it appears to be happening on a frequent basis today and yesterday.

I try to comprehend the reason behind your anger, and I try to convince myself that you are not really angry at me, only hurting physically and perhaps emotionally as well. Probably in part to being triggered by me so often.

What do you want? Do you wish that I go away? I'm sorry for getting on your nerves. I realize I have been here a lot and that you must be tired of me. It's okay to tell me that you need some space or time alone. Maybe it is best if you go back to asking me to stay over, if that is what you want me to do. I didn't mean to impose myself on you. I tried to respect that you needed time to do your own thing and I thought I was showing this by allowing you time to be your creative self, outside with your plants and organizing your tools, etc. I even was respectful enough to not stay on your heels all the time and give you privacy while you visited with Sam outside on the porch the other day as well as with Shelly in your bedroom, etc.

It has been my intention on trying to be an asset for you, but I feel like I've failed you. I like doing things for you, such as trying to stay a step ahead of you by remembering to put your keys in your bag, picking up cigarettes before you run out, trying to keep the inside orderly so you won't become too overwhelmed, putting clothes and towels away after I launder them except for that one load yesterday that I left on the bed.

I don't ask you for money or to be paid back when I use my own.

I give 100% of myself to you freely. I talk with my therapist for one hour, out of an entire month, about problems I'm having between my mother and soon-to-be ex-husband, and suddenly I'm "letting Richard control me?"

I have done rather well at not allowing Richard to control me. I pick and choose when to answer his calls and I try to make arrangements to not be left alone with him. I don't buy into his bullshit and I certainly don't waste my time and energy allowing him to occupy my thoughts.

I have learned to expect a certain amount of respect from other people if they want to have me around. And if they don't want me around, then I hope they would have enough respect for themselves to ask me to leave.

I ended a relationship of 19 years about 18½ years too late. The next 19+ years will be spent in a respectful environment, even if that means I must live all alone.

I want to spend my life with you; however, if I do not make you happy then I would not respect myself for staying and causing you to be miserable.

Communication is the key to any successful relationship, but the communication needs to be mindful of the feelings of one another.

I am trying desperately to communicate my feelings to you because I *REALLY* love you and I don't want to see "US" end.

If you want me to stay, then let me know, and if you desire me to go away then respect me enough to tell me so. I will love you always.

6/7/04 ~

My days are spent with Shelly's daily visits, working on DC's yard or something or other, and my carport. There are about five or six teenage boys that come by a lot to work on whatever I'm doing. We like working in my huge shop doing some kind of artwork.

6/15/04 ~

Sitting here alone in the crowd.

D.H.S. Department of Human Services. It's time for my "face to face" interview for food stamps. It was a very depressing time for me the first time I applied.

Diana,

Do you know how I feel? Can you feel what I know? Babe, I love you. You have given me a reason to live.

As you and I know, the feeling of pain and despair may be replaced with feelings of love and belonging.

I miss you when you're away from me. I have become an addict of your love and touch.

When we met, my life was full of chaos and Stormy. You helped me through without any conditions.

You left the life you had to start a new one with me. Thank you—

6/22/04 ~

9:00 a.m.

Me and Diana.

I am sitting on her bed in her parent's home. Her mom is very kind. Her dad looks younger than her soon-to-be ex-husband.

Boomer has stolen my heart. He is all the great cats I've known morphed into one.

6/27/04 ~

Diana took me with her to her church. They told her that I was not welcome there, and if she continued to see me, she wasn't welcome either.

6/30/04 ~

I had a hard day yesterday. I have this knot on my head and a black and blue eye from a battle I had with a tree branch. My teenage boys heard about what happened. They came over after they all died their hair black and put on their baseball caps backward like I wear mine. It cracked me up, and though it hurt to laugh, it hurt good. It seemed like only a few minutes had passed when Diana would come out and tell us I needed to come inside to rest. If I didn't go in she would come back out and just look at the guys and they would tell me bye and leave. I wasn't sure how she did that because there wasn't a mean bone or look in the girl.

There were many days when Diana would fix up something for me to barbeque to feed us along with DC and our neighbor George. Diana noticed George had no visitors and soon found out he had no family either. So from that point on he was added to the list of people invited to all our family functions. I love this about Diana. She is so open and caring to all.

Sam, Shelly, and I tried to have a discussion. The one and only thing Sam promised me he would finish before I moved in was a fence for Buckley. It takes time. It hasn't happened yet, but I kept up my part of the deal—of course.

Depr

E

SS I ON

RAGE

TURNED

INWARD

Looking away from the pinhole?

It's as if I built a machine, taking careful steps to acquire the outcome I so desperately wanted. Had I only known. These steps would eventually take me even further away from my biggest want—a family.

7/4/04 ~

We went on the roof of the house to watch all the fireworks. It was great.

Diana,

Happy 4th of July! This has been a day that will become a most excellent memory. I love you now and forever.

Always yours,

Sherri

I

    Love

        You!

Things to do to keep my sanity:

To write or draw is the ?

7/11/04 ~

I feel VERY fortunate today. Mostly because Buckley is here with me.

I watched helplessly, completely horrified while a truck hit Buck. It happened right in front of my house. The impact threw him about 20 feet. I got to him before he could try to stand up. The guy in the truck stopped. Then Diana got her car and the truck driver and I got Buck into her back seat.

We got him to emergency care in about 20 minutes. He was in shock. The outcome looked dark. But thanks to the good God up above, to everyone's amazement, that night we brought him home. He was very bruised and was pretty cut up (sounds familiar) but no broken bones!

7/24/04 ~

12:24 a.m.

Diana came to bed before me. She's sleeping. Today we made the first major improvement on the house. I arranged my living room, and brought a LOT of stuff to store at DC's. This was a good day!

7:30 p.m.

Sweet Tomatoes

Present: Diana, DC, and yours truly.

My first visit here has been a pleasant one. I used some of the money Mom sent me—the second $100 check I received from her—along with the postcards with absolutely no writing or signature.

7/28/04 ~

3 p.m.

Diana and I are at Wendy's drive-in having lunch. We went shopping and I had a wonderful time spending the money I received from Edward for "Wilbur the Wire Man," my art sculpture.

I bought some shelves for my bathroom and beads for both the bathroom and bedroom doorways. Now it's time to head home and play with my new toys.

Hey Diana—

I was just thinking about you. I really love loving you! My teeth are showing big time! I really do love you today and forever and ever and ever—

S

7/29/04 ~

11:55 a.m.

This is my "I've learned" list so far:

No matter how much I care, some people just don't or can't care back. I've learned it takes years to build up trust, and only seconds to destroy it.

I learned that it's not what you have in your life, but who you have in your life that counts.

I've learned you can get by on charm for about fifteen minutes, and by then you had better know something.

I've learned that you shouldn't compare yourself to the best others can do or be.

I've learned you should always leave loved ones with loving words 'cause it could be the last time you see them.

8/1/04 ~

3:09 a.m.

I have been putting down new tile in my bathroom.

8/6/04 ~

Yesterday morning Stormy called, crying, saying the owner of her apartment, had a huge dumpster out in front of her apartment and told her whatever was left in her apartment after that day would be thrown in the dumpster. She had more than worn out her welcome.

So here we go trying to help Stormy get and move as much of her stuff as possible with my truck and trailer, DC's truck and Diana's car. When we got there indeed stood the biggest dumpster I ever saw. We could have taken her stuff to one of the storage units she had, but there was no room.

There was another storage unit close to this apartment that she and I also stored things in, and, in the beginning, I paid for. But we couldn't go there, as prior to this, the owner called telling me he caught Stormy and what seemed like a gang of homeless young people there decorating the place with things from our storage unit. He said if I wanted any of what was left in the storage unit I would have to pay the overdue bill and come get it. He just sold the business and the new guy was selling all the stuff.

8/12/04 ~

The kind man from the storage place called later with the place and time where this stuff was being auctioned off. Diana, her mom, DC,

Sabrina and I went to the auction. I lasted about two minutes there as I saw some of my things, as well as Stormy's, being rummaged through by all these strangers. So Sabrina and I went for a drive to waste some time while everyone else stayed.

Later Diana gave me a couple of boxes of stuff she purchased there, hoping it would make me happy. It sure did.

8/15/04 ~

I could not help but wonder where and how Stormy was doing. I heard someone called the cops on her when she went dumpster diving. How could someone fall from a three million dollar estate to being picked up as a transient going through garbage?

I knew I could not understand, even if I knew exactly how and why . . . I know where I was and how far I had fallen and how and why. But her how and why was completely different from mine.

8/20/04 ~

9 a.m.

Salmon—(Home)

I gave Diana money to pay my health insurance bill. It was the first time I ever had to pay, as the production companies I'd worked for had been putting money in my flex plan and there was enough to cover all my previous medical bills since the accident. Since I wasn't quite all there, it was a while afterwards when I finally asked her, "Did you pay my medical insurance?"

"Oh no! I forgot," Diana answered, feeling awful about it. She forgot to pay the bill and I lost my insurance. I tried to get it back, but with all my medical "issues" they would not re-insure me.

As I headed out of crazy school for the last time, I sang as loud as I could, the song from the movie The Sound of Music, "So Long, Farewell"—GOODBYE! Although I was happy I didn't have to go there anymore, as it has been the better part of hmm . . . two or three years, I knew it wasn't because they fixed me but 'cause my insurance had ended.

8/23/04 ~

It's odd, what I call getting a lot done now compared with the old me. I am broken but I am finding myself trying harder, and I know this has everything to do with all the positive input I get from Diana. She can make me actually believe there is something in me that is still salvageable. Of course, she didn't know me before . . . when I was someone who set goals and then not only achieved those goals but went beyond them. And then set new goals.

Bub gives me a lot of good input. She calls or stops by often, telling me she cares. Knowing she will tell me the truth, every time I see her I ask, "How much better am I?" She would say, "You have a ways to go, but if anyone can make it back on top, it's you, Sherri."

I hope I can be the person Diana sees. When she comes back over I'm going to tell her I love her and am so sorry I cannot give her all she needs and deserves. And also, that my rage is turned inward at myself, not at her. That it's my fault I have trust issues . . . not hers. But I want so desperately to give her my trust and respect. It's just so hard to believe she can respect me as I can't respect myself knowing all the help I need that she gives so easily without hesitation. Seeing me at my absolute worst. But showing me such love and care with her eyes and actions. This relationship is so foreign to me. There is such a war going on inside me. When I see her, knowing she is concerned about me, ready to help, I get angry that I need help. This same blasted cycle of rage, pain and even denial starts inside me. My grandma used to tell me relationships are not 50-50 but 100-100. I am so far from 100%. From what Bub, Scout, and a few others tell me, I am only about 40% of what I used to be. That's on a good day. And I know they're trying to be nice.

8/24/04 ~

I no longer have health insurance and am out of Zoloft and, of course, my mind.

I feel overwhelmingly sad and helpless. I can't take care of myself. The copay for my prescriptions with insurance was often more than I could pay; without insurance, the price is way higher. Like from $5 to

$200 each. I continue to have not only tremors in my face and arms but full blown earthquakes all over.

If it were not for Diana, DC, Donna, and Buck, I really would love to end my life. It just doesn't feel like much of a life. I feel like I am on the verge of throwing up most of the time. It has been three years and four months since my fall. I have hit bottom, bailed out of it, only to find myself at the bottom again and again. I feel I am stuck, just hanging on, bobbing around in this storm going nowhere, and never completely free of pain. Because my body is shutting down on me, my heart hurts in an almost unbearable way.

Dear God,

I hope you are having a good day. Please, God, help me overcome the pain and confusion that is warring against me and please allow me peace and happiness.

8/25/04 ~

Trying to get through my day by keeping busy. Still working along on getting settled here. I do believe things have started coming together. But, damn, my arms are sure tired from all that bailing.

I haven't had my meds. I think I might need them. Not allowing the feeling of withdrawal from all the drugs I was on before get the best of me. I stay completely stoned most of the time and sometimes give in and indulge in other drugs that seem to be everywhere. Shelly comes over a lot. She or Sam or both bring over some kind of white powder.

But what was on my mind the most was Diana. Not understanding her. Or for that matter, not understanding myself. I knew I didn't or maybe couldn't trust her. Yet I knew I trusted her more than anyone. I guess I just wasn't used to anyone loving me the way she does. One minute I was all for it and ready to believe this might actually work out. Maybe there can be a happily ever after then the rage or suspicion and lack of trust would come flooding out of me. Sometimes it would be just inside my head. And other times I would either ask or answer in tones that would be so much louder than my intent. One arm pulling and the other pushing.

I see DC all the time. She told me last night she wants to adopt me.

8/26/04 ~

9:30 p.m.

A Song About You
I'd like to take the time
To let my mind unwind
Forget about my sorrows
No use calling them to mind.

You see, this song, it's about you
Your heart is so kind
Your words are like a song so sweet
I could eat them all the time.
You gave me yellow when I was feeling blue
Your love like colors shine so bright
You are my beaming smiling light.

Because of you I look forward to night
When our bodies together feel so right

But, honestly, my love is true. Never before have I felt so sure of something I have no history or experience with. I love experiencing it together!

CHAPTER SIXTEEN
WALLS COME TUMBLING DOWN

8/31/04 ~

I acknowledge I definitely have tons of "trigger" issues. Today, with Diana helping her dad, and "enjoying each others company." It was like there was a target on my back with lots of soldiers shooting at me. Even the tool shed became an issue with me because of my own monstrous shed memories.

Diana says she loves me completely. And ya know, I think she just might. I am on Skyler Road. I am choosing that for my name. Minus the "road" part.

9/1/04 ~

S & M
p e
e d
c i
i c
a i
l n
   e
for special people.

Objective: To enhance the life you have now with the passion you had before or with creative new passions.

Set up a structure and be accountable. Kind of like a personal lifestyle plan.

9/2/04 ~

Looking back with the face I have now—and after facing many unrecognizable faces over these past three years or so—I have to say I finally accept or acknowledge this face in this place. Yes, I had a good life in lots of areas, but I wasn't really happy. What made me happy was working in the profession I gave 100% of myself to. Other than that, I can say I do not want that life back.

9/3/04 ~

"INFERNO" still smoldering!

I just talked to someone at Providence and she's calling my former insurance company.

9/9/04 ~

My mind. It keeps things interesting.

My stomach. It feels sick most of the time.

My head. Has continuously been at the very least a dull ache.

The things that enrage me are so small. The things that hurt me are so many. The things that scare me, at this point, are so few, as I dodge taking chances.

I think my meds cost about $5,000 a month. Being off them has opened up a chasm of darkness within my mind. Unfortunately for those around me, my mouth unleashes words that are sharp and full of suspicion and doubt.

9/12/04 ~

Diana,

It's 8:00 a.m. and I'm sitting here on my couch trying to "face" facing face.

You're on my mind as you are so much of the time. I'm looking forward to seeing you today. As well as taking you and your mom to "Miss Saigon" tonight—I know you'll love it.

With the words you read on these pages I hope you find the meaning behind my actions.

I feel as though, while trying to establish a relationship with you, I lost sight of our pre-existing friendship. There are so many emotions that come up in me with the mere thought of you. We truly have been through many experiences together.

I believe it was not your intention to place me in a detrimental situation. As I believe no one is capable of making anyone do anything. It's that "free will" thing.

You see, I truly know I am not a whole person.

Also, I feel so many people were affected in a harsh way just for us to be together. I saw and felt the pain of you leaving your life, husband and daughter. But I believed it was what you wanted. I saw the confusion in you when you felt you sinned against your religious beliefs. I believed you were still doing what you wanted.

But now, as I have so fucking many times, I feel I have unintentionally caused chaos in people's lives to the point where I question if I am a good thing in your life. In fact, your life is just much easier without my presence.

I understand I do not get to avoid all the feelings inside as I try to file my newest information away regarding my personal life.

I am so tired, Diana. It's hard to say who will win the tug-of-war inside my head: physical pain, emotional scars, depression, or what's left of the true optimist in me. My days and nights drag on and I can't seem to sleep longer than an hour.

The confusion and darkness seems to almost engulf me. My thoughts are not happy ones.

If there is a positive reason why I'm in your life, I hope it is that I helped you realize how capable you are.

This letter is not to end or start anything. It's just a letter to explain what's going on inside my busy little head.

9/14/04 ~

While building the carport, I taught Diana how to use the compressor. She loved using it and the staple gun. We used six mil plastic so we could see through it to the sky and moon. She was stapling some of the plastic down. As I was walking around, I saw my sailboat was collecting a bit of water on top. As I stood on a hill, facing downhill, I reached down to get the trailer's tow bar to move it so the boat would be on an incline, where the water would drain

better. Before I knew it, I slid and found myself under the boat with the tow bar across my arm and chest. There I lay. The compressor was loud, so I knew Diana couldn't hear me shout. I pulled my glove off my free arm with my teeth and reached into my pocket for the three joints I stashed there. I proceeded to smoke them all. It could have been a minute or an hour, who knows. The compressor went silent, and I heard Diana call for me. Although I couldn't yell loud, because of the weight on my chest, she finally did hear me. You know how they say people do amazing things in time of crisis—well, it's true. When she found me, she took her coat off, threw it over my head, and said, "Stay there." Needless to say, I didn't move. She lifted that 28 foot catamaran off me, which was amazing considering how slender she is.

The ambulance came and paramedics cut off my boots and vest, which really pissed me off. This was my favorite vest. I mean this was my VERY FAVORITE vest. Diana came with me in the ambulance and I was taken into triage at OHSU. They ran CT scans and all kinds of tests, but I was fine. They sent me home with a load of major drugs and something they injected into my vein. I whined about where my vest was. I wanted it back, even if it had to be duct taped together.

9/22/04 ~

My Dearest Sherri,

This is the hardest letter I have ever had to write, however I do hope that it precedes an amount of growth for both you and I.

My love for you is so deep, and magnetizing, that I find myself letting go of my common sense at times. It is not healthy for a relationship, our relationship, to involve such suspicion all the time. What chance is there for you coming to trust me? Where there lies no trust, there exists no future.

I have tried to place myself in your situation, having had so many relationships gone badly, with such misery and strife, and being lied to so often. I have been more than patient with your lack of trust in me because I can recognize, and understand, why you would display such unhealthy, paranoid, and relationship sabotaging behavior.

From the time that you drove to Boomer's cottage because you couldn't believe I was not with Richard, to the time you waited at the end of my driveway, stalking me, and not to forget all the time in between where there were hurtful comments made such as I am "just leading you on," or I'm "not really getting a divorce," and I've been "heartless" to name a few. And the sarcasm I hear in your comments when I give you an honest answer to a question and you do not believe me. Your comment last night about not being able to move in together until you knew you could trust me and the hypothetical question about private investigators opened my eyes to the reality that this was going to be an ongoing issue. My patience and understanding ends here.

Maybe you should have someone watching my every move. You will ultimately see that **I DO** get my divorce, that **I DON'T** have an intimate relationship, or even a friendship, with Richard anymore, and that your lack of trust in me has pushed away someone that *completely and truly loves you.*

Do you realize that I chose you over everything else in my life, especially my religion? I made the conscious choice, because it was my deepest desire to be with you! If that was unacceptable to my friends or family members, then that became their problem for *I was with you* and **chose** to keep you in my life even if it meant losing touch with other people.

The thought of not having you in my life, intimately, is enough to cause me to cry uncontrollably for hours at a time. I know this because it has happened to me on more than one occasion.

I am having a difficult time with our "trust" issue. To be honest with you, I cannot deal with it any longer. I trust you completely and will continue to do so until I have reason not to. I only wish you could believe in me. I am not giving you an ultimatum, just sharing with you my feelings. My own state of mind is not 100% and my anxiety level has come to its limit. I am not implying that you give me the anxiety, just that I am not dealing with my feelings well at this time. I do not know what else I can do to help you see that you can believe in me. I am tired and cannot keep trying to jump over the same obstacle.

I am not leaving you, however I am requesting that we put all intimate relations aside until there is a balance of trust between us. I love you as much or more than ever. This is a hard thing for me to do as it causes me a lot of grief and places my heart in great turmoil, yet I believe it has to be. I cannot start a new beginning with suspicion and a lack of trust being two of the cornerstones of our foundation!

Please try to understand that I am not rejecting you. I understand that you need the peace of mind that I am being truthful and while you come to that conclusion I will continue to be your friend.

I will not have peace of mind until your suspicions go away. I feel we may continue to be friends, but only friends. When our friendship reaches a point where there is a balance of trust then it will, for me, be a time to rejoice because I desire to be much more than just your friend.

This can be a time of growth for both of us. Please do not give up on me or on yourself. There lies ahead a beautiful future for the two of us when we can overcome our present obstacles.

With all of this being said, I do not feel it would not be a good idea for you to come camping with me. It would be very hard to sleep with you and not be intimate. The time apart may prove useful for us in looking at, and grasping, the wonderful friendship we had and hopefully will continue to have.

I love you,

With every cell of my being!

Diana

Reply:

Diana,

Honestly, I feel the more I know you the fact becomes clearer—I don't know you at all. As I reread your letter to me I will respond to your words . . .

Why is it the hardest letter you have ever written? Because your love for me is so deep you lose your common sense? You ask what are the chances I will ever trust you—well, not too good judging from your reaction of such defensiveness. How long have you been more than patient? Unhealthy? Paranoid? Sabotaging behavior? What?

As far as you say I am suspicious. I find nothing wrong with my questions to you as to where you have been and what you've been doing. I find nothing wrong with it! As far as a private investigator, I find nothing wrong with it. It will answer questions you won't answer without being HUGELY defensive. As well, Diana, you know I know for a fact I do have sufficient provocation for my questions!

As far as your patience ending—mine already ended.

As far as what you gave up for me—I never asked you to, nor am I the one who pursued you, but rather you me.

Your actions speak loudly. You want to enjoy your life with your dad and mom and whoever else, and a life with me, but not mix the two. I wasn't invited to your family reunion, and you continually kept me away from your life in Washington unless you wanted me to "work" doing stuff for your dad.

When you know I wanted to go spend time with you at your place you always seemed to keep me from ever going. Or if I did come up, it was never for more than a day. Now you are telling me you don't want me to come camping?

Have you ever been completely honest to anyone?

This letter has taken several attempts. It's now 24 hours later, and I will continue.

I could only come up with two reasons anyone could check-up, or whatever that means including a detective, on someone else.

1. Fear: to make sure this person will never be able to hurt them, and

2. Peace of mind: to know as completely as possible there is someone trustworthy.

I have to say, I would like to have someone care about me enough to check up on me. My response would be, please, go ahead. I have nothing to hide.

I believe I got the chance to meet a part of you as far as you threatening suicide again. Were you lying when you PROMISED me we would never contemplate suicide again?

It's our choice what we allow our minds to dwell on.

I will not allow your words of blame and guilt thrown at me for the mental state you're in or the demise of our relationship.

Yes, it's been my experience that if a person is so quick to be that defensive then there is usually something to be guilty about.

I told you I would always be your friend and wanted you in my life. But the rule I have is that, without exception, I want to be around people that are positive.

I really don't think you calling me a stalker, untrusting and paranoid is in any way supportive or encouraging.

I have friends that really want me to be happy. What if they hired the P.I.'s to make sure I wasn't getting into another black relationship? So, maybe I didn't come up with the idea on my own, but I feel it is an acceptable thing to do and was done with the right motives.

I wanted you to be honest with me. Let's face it, I know there are and have been occasions when you were not. I believe you could be so much more alive and present in your life by being real.

Enjoy camping with your dad. I really hope you get your shit together.

9/24/04 ~

Where do I start?

What is my goal?

10/9/04 ~

2:37 a.m.

Salmon Street

It's been all about free clinics and places that offer free groceries.

My doctor (knowing I lost my health insurance) wants cash up front for my Toradol injections.

I find it so absurd that I have to go to these places and need their help. While Diana is camping with her mom and dad my days went on as usual.

The most consistent thing in my life is the constant inconsistency.

I received a call from a friend of Stormy's, telling me he had her phone number. Not only was I glad to know she was alright, but it would be great to get rid of all of her stuff I was storing. I called and got her address and loaded up my truck and headed to Sauvie Island following the directions Stormy had given me. It's odd. While driving there I looked up to where beautiful, massive Crown Vista stands, and remembered looking down on Sauvie Island from there a million times. Now I pull into the trailer park Stormy calls home.

There's a huge field on one side of this dirt driveway, and on the other about eight old run down trailers. As I looked out to the field again I noticed the little silver tiny trailer that used to sit up at Crown Vista. Around the trailer were all kinds of things, from the best silver to weird hanging art.

Stormy seemed happy to see me. She was staying in one of the trailers, although nothing in it was hers. I told her I had more stuff of hers to bring. She asked me to go on a beer run, so I did. When I got back there was a LARGE woman staring at me as I walked in. Before Stormy or I had a chance to talk she introduced herself to me and asked who I was. I told her I was a friend who had stored some of Stormy's stuff. She said her name was Sybil, and asked Stormy if she told me who she had introduced her to. Without waiting for Stormy to speak, she said it was Jesus.

"Great!" I said with a big smile. "I like him. I hear he's a good guy!"

That was the end of that conversation. Stormy then told this LARGE woman all about my landscaping skills. Sybil told me she had just gotten a bid for over $10,000 to top the huge 60' black walnut trees that lined the driveway. She asked if it was something I could do. I had already saved Stormy's friend thousands by arranging a couple of union buddies to do the same thing for him. So Stormy answered for me, "Oh yes, darling, it would not be a piece of cake for her to do but a crumb of cake." Sybil said she would pay me $1,000 and the cost of the 40' lift required to do the job.

After she left I asked Stormy who the LARGE lady was. She said she met Sybil about 20 years ago, and the two of them plus Sybil's husband shared a lot of coke and sex.

I said I sure hoped she was less of a person then than she is now. Stormy recently ran into Sybil at a supermarket. When she heard about Stormy's situation, she brought her to this trailer park she and her husband own. The owner of the trailer Stormy was staying in is on an extended vacation.

Sybil and her husband live in California but she comes up alone to check on things. She has a new husband now since the first one killed himself. This one does not like Stormy.

Anyway, I hired Sam to help me trim the walnut trees, and we finished some extra work Sybil added. Diana and I went out to Sauvie Island and saw Sybil, who talked to Diana about us renting the soon-to-be available trailer there. We declined to rent there as it was too close to Stormy.

Diana and I never figured out why I didn't get paid by Sybil, no matter how many emails and calls we made to her. But soon our attention centered on our home, our own daily troubles. And looking forward to the day she would be divorced.

After Diana won her disability hearing, and received a chunk of cash, she bought herself a new car. We then traded my truck in for an Izuzu Amigo, paying them the $3,500 difference. No one has ever given me such an expensive gift.

I was in bed or, at best, just lying around most of the week. It felt like my head just wanted to tip forward to the right and lead me into a nose dive to the floor. I finally got almost all my meds back, so I'm actually feeling slightly better.

Mom sent me a poem along with a check. The poem was actually a few sentences, which was more than she wrote on most postcards I received from her. She didn't even sign it. I am sure they were from her because I know no one else in Jerusalem.

Anyway, her words made me feel really sad. She said she knew I didn't want to spend any time with her, and I didn't want to talk to her. I finally called Ruth, and through the knot in my throat and tears in my eyes, asked her to get a message to Mom that this was just not true! I also told Aunt Harriet I thought Mom and Mick would be very shocked to see me in heaven.

People often judge others' Christianity on whether or not they go to church. I do not go. I believe church is a place of worship, not just a requirement to get into heaven.

I couldn't finish my letter to Mom. Too many words to say; too overwhelming to get on paper.

My wonder-friend and co-author took me to Clackamas Social Services to pick up a voucher for another one of my prescriptions, and she paid the money I owed so I could get a new phone here at home. It's supposed to be turned on the 12th.

Diana called me at DC's and asked if I wanted to see her when she came home from camping. I said yes, and then asked if the fact that I was uninvited to the camping trip was my punishment for her thinking I am too suspicious. It takes time to build trust. Just because I ask questions doesn't mean I don't trust. Trust has to be earned.

I am so tired. Good night—morning. Good grief!

10/10/04 ~

Dear Mom,

I realize that I haven't written to you or called since the last time I saw you.

But nothing has changed about how I feel about you.

Mom, I love you, and respect your ambition and your strong will to do what you feel is right. Where did you ever get the idea I don't want you in my life?

My life. What is left of it.

I've lost my insurance, both health and auto.

My days are difficult to get through. I've been off my prescriptions for quite some time.

10/12/04 ~

6:00 a.m.

I finally got most of my meds through different free clinics.

Stormy was here, but nothing happened between us. I mean, there will always be something between us, but no longer in an intimate way. We're just friends.

She had her van FULL, and my truck was full, and together we took the loads out to her trailer. I told her I'd help her build some kind of shed to keep the things she has outside dry. Imagine moving from a mansion to a mobile home.

Stormy said she was going somewhere and would be right back. Well, I unloaded and organized her things that had already been sitting in the field, as well as the wood and the things I brought. After three hours flew by I figured she wasn't coming "right back," so I left.

Saturday night I visited Bub and Scout for a while.

PACS Health Clinic, another free clinic Diana found, got two meds for me: Neurontin, (which, without insurance, would cost me over $12,000 per year!) and Zoloft. I haven't started taking it yet, as I've been off it for over a month. I wanted to go in really bad for a Toradol shot, but the doctor said not without insurance. This system is so wrong!

After Bub and I took a couple of loads to the dump, she helped me work on the awning I'm/we're putting up over DC's patio. And, wonder of wonders, Stormy showed up in time to make us all dinner.

I get a phone today—Yea!

Diana, whom I only briefly spoke to on the phone last week, is coming over tonight. We talked mostly through letters to each other for a week or two.

My pain. It, or should I say they, seem to get much worse the colder it gets. My emotional pain still makes me acknowledge its existence. Which obviously hasn't helped emotionally—I think it causes me to say things to Diana I don't really mean. My good feelings are stored in the same place my bad feelings are stored, and they get all mixed up.

Dear God,

First, thank you for loving me even though I am much like whoever wrote the scriptures in Romans Chapter 8. I do what I don't want to do; my spirit is willing but my flesh is weak.

Thank you for keeping your ever loving hand on those I love.

I ask you to continue to give me the desires of my heart. And that those desires are good ones.

Just in case you want some hints, I ask for:

Peace of mind

A purposeful life A fulfilled life

And, while I'm asking, a happy, joyful life is welcome. It would also be good to have only people come into my life that you plan to be here. And last but not least, it would be nice to have some sort of income. And, please, give me the ability and strength to spend it wisely.

I love you Lord.

Sherri

10/16/04 ~

Dear Sherri,

I love you with all of my heart! Sometimes it feels like I can't live life without you there beside me. Sometimes I think you would be happier if I were not in the picture.

I found a stash of Lorazepam that I had set aside to take all at once. It is the easiest way I am aware of to go to sleep and not wake up.

I am so incomplete when I am not with you, yet when I am with you I fail to do what's important to you. The last thing I'd ever want to do is to cause you grief, however I seem to manage just that and it is certainly not my intention to do so. My efforts seem to be in vain as I continue to mess things up and be misunderstood. I feel like a fucking failure when it comes to our relationship. I wish we could "get outta Dodge" and start someplace new with just the four of us: you, me, Buckley and Boomer. Always and forever my love for you is there. Should I pass before you, my dearest one, my love for you will remain and overlook you with care.

Each blessed moment that I have left in this world my lips will long to kiss you. I declare your lips the only ones I will ever press upon mine.

The spark you have ignited within me burns hot and will never extinguish. Should your love for me cease, as I have seen in my darkest fears and nightmares, I vow to never love another or have the desire for love again. I say this not to manipulate your feelings or place concern in your thoughts, but to express my eternal devotion to your spirit. I can never love another from the depth that my heart loves you.

I'm scared as I listen to my anxious heart beat for the thought of not having you leaves me trembling in fear. I would rather see to my own demise than to live without your presence in my life.

Can you imagine the despair of losing the one thing that drives your spirit to see the light of day?

Can you comprehend the devastation I feel as I view in my nightmares that your love for me has extinguished?

How great it is to be loved by the one your soul desires most. How tormenting it can be to love and not be loved in return, or to believe and yet not to be believed. The desperation can certainly suck the air out of one's lungs and leave the spirit drowning in a sorrow so deep it cannot bear another breath.

How long can a heart continue to beat to a rhythm so out of tune? Does the song exist that can bring comfort and melody to complete the empty verse that echoes in my mind?

I love you I love you I cannot live without you. I am here and you are here, yet where are we? Do you love me or have I destroyed the love you once felt? My heart aches as I fear the loss of my soul mate. There is no blame to be placed but on myself. With ignorance I have treaded water when I should have had faith to swim ahead, but now I have consented to allow myself to drown while no longer looking for a lifeline.

I can see no justice for my soul, but there does remain a pit of darkness in which to submit.

Forgive me for the hurt I have bestowed upon you.

Forgive me for appearing to control our relationship; it was never my intention to come across that way.

Forgive me for becoming defensive when I am scared as I am not understood or believed.

Forgive my quiet nature and my reluctance to answer promptly. After years of being misunderstood, I am slow to speak as I fear my words will fall on deaf ears or will be heard differently than what I intended.

Forgive me, too, for retreating inward as I fear I've nowhere else to go.

It's sad that all I hear is my own demise calling out to me. You deserve so much better than I have offered you. I will love you to time indefinite. Even beyond my last breath of life will my love for you remain.

I am sorry for my shortcomings. My desire has only been to please you, not to cause you pain, but there again I fall short. You are beautiful and special and deserve better than me. I love you!

Love, Diana

10/17/04 ~

Dear Diana,

I love you when I'm breathing

Sleeping

Alive or dead

NOTES FROM OUR PAD:

| Post it notes | Tape |
| Colored stickers | Pockets |

Highlighter   tabs

Paperclips

The only constant thing in my life is—change Printout sheets

Starting over TV.com

If we compare

We live in FEAR!

Check into: Fearless living.ORG

D—

Jealousy is a distraction

Emotional willingness to face it?

Startingover.com—*Audition*

Go over fearless living book

If you don't fill your own self first

You will be too empty

To be able to fill anyone else.

Food stamps re: Phone

Drs. Office

Walmart

Post office

Cigs

Movies

        Shovel

        Dog food

        Pills

        Clothes

        Rain gear

State changes that have already occurred—changes occurring now.

11/18/04~

11:59 p.m. Face to face with me

Readiness to face the difficult challenges ahead of you in daily living. The need for a crutch to help direct your energy so you can achieve goals because the traumatic brain injury has damaged your cognitive thinking.

You are willing to face changes in your life. However, you need direction as your brain injury resulted in your mind becoming overwhelmed by not knowing the order in which events need to take place to accomplish your goals. It's like you need someone to make you an outline of how to go about daily living, help in setting new routines in motion and help in creating a way to establish new healthy habits and routines and chart your accomplishments.

You lost much monetarily, physically, emotionally. You still have the courage to face reality as it is and make the best of where you are at in your life. You know the answers lie within you; however you need help in identifying a system of approach to your abruptly changed life. You need to not only bail, but set a course. A navigator would be useful.

11/19/04 ~

12:00 a.m.

REACT or ACT

11/27/04 ~

Sam called frantically. Shelly is missing.

My mind is not even toying with the possibility of losing another friend—great friend. Where could she be?

I know lots of people would come to the same conclusion about Shelly. She is very good looking—due mostly to a gift from her maker plus many trips to the cosmetics counter. She is really shy—but comes across curt, short, even rudely stuck-up. She can be a really good friend. We've spent a lot of time together since I moved here and she became one of my landlords and a friend and, dare I say, family.

Sam and I have been talking on the phone. I even went to see if she was at her dad's. She is "missing." She lost her job today. Sam was told she was fired for drug abuse. God please keep her safe.

11/28/04 ~

Diana left today after being here for the last few weeks. I am sure causing her a bit of unrest. I told her I plan to confront her father the next time I see him. At first I was led to believe I was uninvited to the camping trip because I was too untrusting and suspicious. Then Diana said that it was her dad that did the uninviting because he lost all respect for me after learning I had come out to their house checking on Diana without acknowledging them. She also said she caught her dad spying on her during the camping trip.

I have told Diana that one, if not both, of us needs to confront her dad.

Stormy showed up for Thanksgiving, the third year in a row we celebrated this holiday. George, a widower, would have spent it alone had we not invited him over.

Thinking of new names for myself.

Sky

Siouxhapi

Siouxsea-Q

Slim Fast

Misty Sara Greens (MSG)

My next dog will be named D.O.G. pronounced Deogie

NOTES FOR DC:

Carry meter

Blood sugar test before dinner

Make eye doctor appointment

Do U.A. for protein in urine

D—Things to do:

Wash rugs

Wind chimes

S—4 George & David's yard:

1ˢᵗ clean mower

Hair dye removal

Shoestrings

12/15/04 ~

I

LOVE

YOU!

Sherri . . .

You are the love of my life; my one and only Soul Mate. How blessed I have been by your presence, wisdom, and love.

Thank you for the time, attention, and presents you showered me with on my birthday.

My day was made special by you and your thoughtfulness. I will never forget December 14, 2004; the horse and buggy ride for my birthday was wonderful. However, the first gift you ever gave me will always remain my favorite . . . the mustard seed necklace.

What means the most to me is your unconditional love. Through you I have grown and will continue to grow. Thank you for your patience and acceptance and your willingness to put forth effort in maintaining our friendship and nurturing our relationship to the point of my rebirth. You have given me life and you continue to sustain me.

I am honored to be by your side, and more honored that you want to be by mine!

12/31/04 ~

Diana gave me a birthday party!

Diana's mom was sitting next to me at DC's and gave me a present. You can't imagine the joy that I felt when I opened it and saw my FAVORITE vest duct-taped together! Even though Diana cautioned me to be careful, and I was, as I started to put it on some of the duct tape came off. But, the vest didn't fall apart! Knowing her mother, I can only imagine how hard it must have been to take this dirty, raggedy vest and sew all the pieces back together. That was one of the best presents EVER!

This beautiful woman, Diana, gave me this journal with a beautiful woman facing me on the cover as a birthday present from Boomer. That cat has good taste! I'm happy. Looking forward to the New Year!

1/1/05 ~

Letter from DC to me:

Tears well up in my eyes and I want to cry and can't because the laughter make the tears of happiness show up. When gravity keeps them in the middle. It's the oddest feeling. Can you believe God wanted us to meet? You knew! Facing Face!! I love you and admire all that you can do and will do. Not for money OR gain or whatever! You are supposed to have a Mom and I'm supposed to have you as my daughter.

Love of self and each other; as one looking into yourself and admiring what the other has to give. What I give of myself, you give me back what I need in me. Standing face to face.

When you were giving me the thread from the towel, I was giving the thread to you. That's when I really knew we love each other like ourselves. Does this make sense?

I don't think so either.

2/1/05 ~

We spent the month of January, it seems, looking for a bigger place to rent. Of course we knew the bigger the place the bigger the rent, but things were settling for Diana. And I. Didn't realize how much BIG $$ is needed for decent housing. How do young families and old families and the in-between families make it?

???

2/13/05 ~

I have been sooo sick—couldn't even make it to the bathroom in time. Diana, as always, with love beaming from her eyes, would clean up after me. She gives me better care than I deserve. I don't have any self respect right now—how can she love me? I just don't get it. But I really wish I would quit playing tug-of-war—pushing her away and pulling—needing her at the same time.

2/14/05 ~

Valentine's Day

Dearest Sherri,

How quickly the tides have turned and taken you away from me. We have ridden many waves together thus far, and have held our heads above water. The difference now is that the waves have separated us from one another. I cannot stop loving you at the sudden onset of a storm. I pray that when the after effects of the storm have had time to settle that there will be a chance to ride the waves together again.

God only knows the depth to which I love you and I have to trust in Him to keep us both afloat in these rough waters. Remember we are made in His image and we have the capability of forgiveness. I hope that you can forgive me for the hurts I have flooded you with. I have to accept the fact that my actions may have forever altered my future, however I hope that at some point you can allow me to be your friend for I always will love you and you will forever be in my heart. I truly want what is best for you and if I am not your sacred soul mate then I pray that you find that person soon for you deserve to be happy.

Just remember that it is impossible for me to go a day without thinking of the love I carry in my heart for you and that you will remain in my prayers till time indefinite. If we continue to drift apart I hope that we can keep a lifeline between us for communication. I never want to lose sight of you even if we are in separate vessels.

Namaste (The divine in me honors and respects the divine in you)
Diana

2/19/05 ~

A lady called me from . . . somewhere . . . the county? She told me I qualified for additional care and full medical benefits. I asked her, "Is this a joke? Who is this really?" She said it was no joke and she would come for a home visit the next day.

The next day . . . she drove up while I was in my front yard with all my beautiful plants. She seemed very nice, so I excitedly offered her a plant. Only after she agreed to take one did I agree to sit down and talk with her. She told me I could have someone get paid to help me by being my caregiver. So I went inside to tell Diana, thinking WOW, this will make our relationship easier. Finally she will get something in return for all she does for me. Get paid for what she already was doing! Sounded great! How lucky!!

2/28/05 ~

10:03 a.m.

It's all about choices. Individual choices. Playing fair is all I want. Maybe it's time the "system" will even "work" for me.

I've been coming to a lot of conclusions lately. I see myself standing in front of a group of people—people at the bottom. I know their torment. I say, "Anyone have someone in mind that you blame for your hurts or why you're here? What have they done to you? List them." I believe this list will somehow lead back to drugs and/or alcohol and/or people who have chosen "the dark side." Now, was it a good choice to do those drugs? Drink that alcohol? Hang out with that person? Maybe, backing up and taking another route, or, just maybe, a life full of other things than the usual menu.

I'm thinking of changing my legal name to Sky Siouxhapi. The Sky's the Limit. It's better than my status quo: the sky is falling.

I'm in the "system" now—unwillingly thrown on the big, dirty, greasy chain. Another linkage is all I am. I feel I've only got the dirt and none of the grease to help me glide more smoothly. But maybe it's my time to be greased. It certainly seems logical. I'm trying to make the right choices and "doing" optimistic while "feeling" like dying. It could lead to I'm "feeling" a two but "doing" a five. I always seemed to be doing better than I was feeling.

I went to Tri-Cities last week to see my brother Joe and his wife, Mitzy. Diana took me. Rented us a car and made reservations at the Hanford House. I knew I needed to go to see Joe, if only for a short time. I asked Mom who she wanted to bring me, Diana or DC. I respected her wishes, and she said Diana, Buck, and me. I was so happy. We visited Dad's grave, my first time since he died seven years ago.

Joe told me he heard some woman say that what is really important about the dash between the year of birth and the year of death on a tombstone is what we do with and during that dash.

I saw the inconvenience, at a minimum, I caused Joe, Mitzy, and Mom to accommodate my not wanting to see Mick. The one big hurt that I've held so tightly to. I mean, Joe came across the country for me. Only me. No other reason.

He saved my life! He and Diana talked me into seeing Mick. It would be the first time we'll have talked since I called him from double lock-down in 2002. As Joe and I walked into the coffee shop, I saw Nancy, Mick's wife, first.

I love her. She has been my "sister" since I was about 12 when she and Mick got together. He was a coke dealer in those days. I lived with them after I ran away from home.

Then I saw Mick. We hugged. This was a start. I told him, "Mick, I'm sorry you were mean to me, but I forgive myself." The visit was kept short and the conversation light.

3/12/05 ~

Diana,

Do you have any idea how much I love you?

Your love broke thru the blackness that surrounded my heart and life. You made what was just a small pinhole of light turn into a bright, warm, loving light. As I was lost in a dark, stormy, scary, lonely night in my boat that was sinking rapidly out at sea, YOU shined through as a lighthouse that guided me safely into your arms.

I love you!!

Forever & always,

S

4/25/05 ~

There is this person that loves me more than I thought was possible. One minute I love it and take it in and the next minute my anger spouts out from my intense pain, physical and emotional. Diana and I spend a lot of the time we're together doing stuff I hate doing. Like going to the doctor, no, make that free clinics. Or looking for a place to move to that we can't afford, and going to places that give away free food.

The times that were good really were amazing. The picnic at the rose garden, hot tubing, the 4th of July on top of the house, the horse and buggy ride on her birthday in December . . . she showered me . . . .

My body and mind wage war against me. Going through withdrawal from all the drugs I was on before I lost my medical coverage. I know my anger came out in a lot of ways other than yelling. It wasn't even aimed at any one certain person or thing but it engulfed me and would seep out in many ways, sometimes quietly, or with extreme frustration, or just my defeated spirit hovering thick in the air. More than anything I think it came out in my tone of voice.

4/26/05 ~

6/1/05 ~

Bankruptcy

There are more chapters to pick from in bankruptcy court. I get a whole new chapter today.

So many chapters ago I was sitting in the exact same place picking a chapter.

6/15/05 ~

You know how, when you love someone, I mean really love and connect with someone, words can be so feeble? I guess that's what keeps the greeting card business alive and well. So, here is a greeting card I got for Diana. Thanks to American Greetings for the words in quotes.

Cover:

"I'm so *thankful,*
that if I were a dog,
I'd be wagging
my tail."

Picture: cute dachshund wagging tail
Open . . .
"I'd also be sniffing your crotch,
Humping your leg,
and leaving 'presents'
in your shoes.

Just be glad I'm human."
    or sort of.
"Thanks!"
  for just
    existing!
Love you with all my heart,
Sherri

CHAPTER SEVENTEEN
FACING THE WHITE COATS

Now, some of you may be thinking, "Did she go to that ward again?" I know I think of the guys that come to take you away to the funny farm. For those of us that have been on that ride, I can tell you . . . funny it is not. Neither were these white coats.

6/23/05 ~

It finally came through—Diana's divorce! Yipee! At last she was free! It was a day to celebrate, a beautiful summer day. We met with my bankruptcy lawyer, had lunch downtown, and had a big BBQ to celebrate with friends. We picked out a house to rent from Edward that we even put money down on.

At about nine p.m. we went to the local tavern where George hangs out to plan a surprise birthday party for him. Diana and Buck stayed in the car while I went in. The bartender was busy so I waited. After a while Diana came in. Her eyes met mine. She smiled, and said she decided to walk home. I figured she needed the time to herself. No problem. I hung out, waiting to talk to the bartender. People come and go, as do screaming sirens. Finally the bartender came over long enough to tell me to come back the next day. I left.

As I pulled up to my house there were cop cars and a couple of cops standing behind them. At that moment I was propelled into the twilight zone.

Buck and I jumped out of my car as one cop approached and said to me, "There has been an accident. Why don't you put your dog in your house and we'll give you a ride up to the hospital."

Thing was, I couldn't do that as I only had my car key. With my habit of losing keys, Diana was in charge of them and had only given me my car key.

I raced to the end of the street to DC's. I banged on her door to ask if she'd keep Buckley while the cops took me to the hospital, only to hear her say, "No," she couldn't.

As I pulled back up to my house, one of the cops was talking to George, who said he would take Buck. So I jumped into the female cop's car, still asking, "What happened? Is Diana okay? How bad is she hurt?"

The cop told me she just knew Diana was hurt bad, and then asked me if I wanted lights and sirens to get me there quick. Of course I shouted, "Yes!" as we drove by the place Diana had been hit by a car while crossing the street. I saw one of her sandals in the middle of the street.

The cop got me there quick. I had to wait before I got to see or talk to anyone. I was so scared. She suffered serious head injuries. Was she undergoing surgery?

I couldn't sit still. Pacing. Tapping my right foot. Left. Both. Hold my head in my hands because I couldn't stand the pain piercing my heart. Oh, God, don't let her die! Please, please, please, you can't, she can't . . . she's too nice, damn it! Oh, Jesus, she just got her divorce! I should have driven her home, I knew it. Why did I let her walk? Fuck! She's gotta make it!

All this time the cop stayed with me. The hospital assigned a social worker to me. About 1:30 a.m. I had the police officer call Donna. She was on her way. The social worker wanted me to go to the ER to see a doctor who could give me something to calm me down, but I refused. I wanted to have my wits about me (what was left) when she woke up.

A few minutes later I was told I could see Diana.

I was about to enter yet another type of emergency room. Have you noticed that emergency rooms are usually laid out in a circular pattern? That is the common ER. Then there is the emergency room with green reclining chairs and cops outside rooms. As the elevator door opened I saw this ER in the basement of the hospital. It was a hall with a dead end. I remembered how I felt as I walked down this hall . . . pretty hopeless.

When I saw a patient roll by me I thought I would get sick as his head was broken all the way open. I remember wondering why there were not any doctors working on this guy. Why they were not acting as though this was an emergency. I am sure he was not dead, since, first of all, there was no sheet over his face which gazed back at me, and, second, well, I saw his heart beating on the little box he was hooked up to.

Then I was there. With a cop on one side and a social worker on the other, they helped me get down that hall as my knees became weak at times.

"Are you alright?" they asked. "Do you want us to go in with you?" I said, "No," as the white curtain was parted for me to go in.

I could not see Diana at first, as there were at least four or more white-coated doctors just standing by her bed. I pushed my way through them. In the back of my mind I wondered why there were so many doctors there, yet none were working on her. No tubes, monitors or anything else.

Here lay motionless the person that took care of me . . . the one that had shown me so much love.

Diana loved me at the time of my life I was most unlovable. I lay my head on her and asked her not to leave me, and cried I was sorry for all the times I could have been more understanding and that I didn't know what to do without her.

I noticed one of the doctors kept wiping her head by her ear, although I didn't see any blood. And her eyes were moving rapidly, although they were closed. A tear would roll down her face. Without turning around I asked those doctors, "Can she hear me?" I heard all of them quietly answer, "Yes, she can hear you."

A few moments later a short, blonde lady doctor walked in. As I turned to her, I cried, "Is she dead?" With a tear rolling down her cheek she answered, "No, she is not dead, but she is dying."

Oh my God. NO NO NO NOOOO—what do I do . . .

I heard someone say, "Tell her what you think she would want you to say." I leaned down and struggled to find the words. "I promise to try my best to take care of myself and fight to become whole again," so that all the effort she put into me wouldn't be in vain. "And I promise I will try not to kill myself for two years." I thought two years was a good amount of time. Diana would know this is all I could do. She always told me she believed in me, and no matter what the obstacles were I could overcome them and have a fulfilled life. I told her how very much I loved her.

I went back with the cop and social worker who waited for me in the hall. Donna showed up, and so did DC. I wanted to go home and wake up. I couldn't. We sat in the basement waiting area. I didn't know what to do with myself. My body was tired, yet I kept tapping, pacing, crying. Then it happened. A nurse came up to us. "I'm sorry," she began. I didn't want to hear any more, but she continued, "Diana passed away." I crumpled to the floor.

NOOOOOOOOOOOOOOOOOOOOOOOOOOOOOOOOOOO! !!!!!!!! !!! !!!!!!!!!!!

I asked Donna to come with me to see her. Her head was covered with a towel. Her body was covered with a clean, ghostly white sheet. Not a spec of blood. Other than being pale, she could have been sleeping. I prayed she was sleeping. She would sleep eternally. I told her I loved her more than anyone, and I was so sorry. She knew.

Diana's family came to the hospital. I was so crushed, I didn't know what to say to them. Her parents talked to me, but her daughter and sisters, and certainly her ex, wouldn't. DC, Donna and I stayed there for a while. I had to wait to get her belongings, which included our house key. Our.

6/24/05 ~

DC gave me a ride home from the hospital. It must have been about 6 a.m. She was upset 'cause I didn't want to go to breakfast with her. Outside my house, before I could get out of her truck, George came outside to ask about Diana's condition. DC yelled out the window, "She died!" The sound of her words burned my innermost being to the core of my heart and soul.

I was carrying a clear bag with Diana's bloodstained clothes. Buckley ran up to me and smelled death on her clothes. He tried to take the bag from me, which he never does. I thought I had to hide the clothes, somehow get rid of them. I went into the shop and climbed the highest ladder to put them on the highest shelf I could find.

It's you and me again, Buck. He was what comforted me the most.

The phone rang, must have been three or four hours after I got home. I was just sitting, staring out the window, trying to wake up from this horrible dream. The house was quiet, which was unusual, as there was usually music or TV on. When it rang I jumped. It was Stormy's mobile home park landlady, Sybil. Her voice sounded shaky as she told me, "Oh my God, I just heard on the radio about Diana. I'm so sorry."

I choked out quietly, "Okay."

She asked, "Would it be alright if Stormy or I came over later today?" I just answered, "I don't care," and hung up.

Whether I was sitting looking out the window or standing and staring into space, it seemed I died too. Everything in me died with the exception of the ability to breathe.

The hospital social worker called to check on me. I don't know what made me think of it, but I asked her why all those doctors in there were just standing by her bed?? She paused, and said, "There was no one but you in there with Diana." She said there were other people who asked the same thing. "They must have been angels," she concluded.

I heard somebody walking through the shop. It was three teenage boys that loved to come over and build things with me. I taught them how to use some of my tools. They had heard. Their young faces seemed so distraught and concerned. We spent so much time in the shop together. They were my friends. They all seemed unwanted by their families, or, at the very least, didn't get the love and nurturing kids should get from their parents. They asked me what they could do. I said, "Could you help me build a cross?" The process was too great for me, and they agreed to do it.

DC came over. She said, "I said something to upset Diana yesterday, and I wonder if that's why she killed herself."

"I don't think so," I yelled back to her. "She didn't kill herself!" I said I wanted to be alone, and walked her to her truck.

I went back into the house sick over what DC said. Stormy showed up. She gave me some kind of pill or something, and asked if I wanted to smoke with her. I said sure, thinking it was pot. It turned out to be a meth pipe. I really didn't care. She got me up and took me into the shop where I made a silk flower arrangement for the cross. I used all the boxes I had of silk cherry blossoms that were leftover from the day I got hurt working on the set of The Hunted. Sabrina came over, and the three of us started drinking and smoking pot. I remembered to take my meds that day, at least the morphine. I was so drugged up that I finally drifted into a deep sleep while we were talking in my bedroom.

6/25/05 ~

I woke up to noise coming from the kitchen. While it was not uncommon for me to wake up in a confused state, not knowing the day of the week or date, my first reaction was to yell out, "Diana?" With a pause, and a cracked voice, I heard, "No, it's Stormy." It was then I turned my bed into a waterbed. I cried until I could cry no more. Though the flow of tears would eventually dry up, the pain stabbing my heart hurt more than everything and anything. Ever.

Raw

6/26/05 ~

I'm in the shop. It's 4 a.m. I'm afraid to go to sleep because I don't want to wake up again. I want to sleep. No way can I sleep in our bedroom. I'm listening to the group Train's song "Calling All Angels," which was both my and Diana's favorite song, before and after we met. Okay, I am willing. Good. So much, so much. She's in me. All around.

I walked out of the shop and watched the boys paint the cross. It was about six-feet tall and three-feet wide. They painted it white and put it on a stand.

Sabrina finished putting together copies of a picture of Diana along with a poem of hers to put in envelopes with confetti for the memorial. It felt good to have people around and keep my mind busy, as horrid as this was.

Something caught my eye. Three females were walking up my driveway. It was Diana's two sisters and her daughter. I was a bit taken back, but greeted them with open arms. They were there to pick up some of Diana's things. I took them inside and said, "Take whatever you want."

They were only there about 15 minutes, but in that time they took some pictures off the walls, some of her clothes and her purse. One sister kept whispering to Diana's daughter, and then her daughter would point to something and ask, "Was this my Mom's?" I would tell her if it was or wasn't, but either way I'd say, "If you want it, it's yours."

When they were gathering everything together, one of the sisters told me that Richard's lawyer said the divorce wasn't finalized. Even though both of them signed the agreement, it seems that it hadn't been filed in court yet. "And Richard has taken full charge and is making all the arrangements and paying for the memorial service and funeral, and you are not allowed to come."

It was as though somebody had hit me right in the stomach. Again. How is it that somebody so beautiful, so full of love, could be so quickly discarded and forgotten? It's now all about her stuff and control. I invited them to the memorial service I planned for Diana the next day.

After they left, I called Sally, Diana's mother, and told her what happened. It was only this morning when she called and asked me to hide Diana's car. She asked if I hid the car, which I did. She also told me to hide my car, as both our cars were in both our names. This brought out a different reaction in me. This made me angry, and I wasn't going to hide my car. I yelled at her, "Doesn't anybody care that she died?"

6/30/05 ~

Salmon

Memorial Service in Loving Memory of Diana

A poem by Diana:

Rejoice...In The Hope!

It is hard to understand the pain felt in our heart When a person truly loved from this life had to part.

Remember our Lord God above on whose strength we can borrow When our eyes grow weary from tears cried in sorrow.

Sleepless nights we will have as our soul feels lonely For the one alive in our heart who is gone in flesh only.

We have been given a promise of a grand resurrection Where our loved ones will return to us in perfection.

Until that time arrives let us put faith in our maker For He who's keeping our love

One's spirit has the power to rescue her!

Bub and Scout, DC, Edward, Sabrina, and some others were present. I got up and said the biggest thing I learned from Diana was forgiveness. She had forgiven much in her life.

Diana's father, a usually quiet, conservative, dare I say redneck, got up to speak. He said, "I loved my daughter very much. I was not a fan of her life change, but if she was unhappy with Richard she couldn't stay with him. I came to see the drastic change in her. I have never known her to be this happy. I've grown to love and accept you, Sherri, and I thank you for making her last year of life on this earth so joyful and full of love. There is no disputing that."

Diana's spirit is now among the angels.

CHAPTER EIGHTEEN
FACING MY DISINTEGRATION

Diana gave me love—no bars held. And I was even starting to accept her love—something new for me.

We met in crazy school. When I first saw her, I could certainly tell we shared one thing: CHRONIC PAIN—inside and out.

She talked mostly about being in a marriage that was more like a job she had to do, and wanted to do, for her daughter, the apple of her eye. The only bright spot she had was her love for her daughter. And for Boomer.

This was early fall 2003. I remember the first time we went to lunch. She said, "I look at you and see how beautiful you are, inside and out." This embarrassed me greatly. Mostly because I was in shock. She talked to me, taking me in with her eyes. I knew she was someone special.

We went to lunch and talked on the phone quite often. Her words were so quiet; it was hard to hear her. When my mom came to town to go to a session with Helena and me, it was Diana who went into the waiting room to explain that this place wasn't a bad place.

Diana had stated many times that she planned on leaving and divorcing her husband when her daughter graduated high school. She didn't hate this man—she was just not in love with him. And true to her word, that's what she did. What neither of us anticipated was the deep, pure love that blossomed between us.

She came up to Crown Vista the last week-end Stormy was there before moving. I remember seeing her and Stormy play dress-up in all the beautiful dresses and costumes available there. This was the first time I really saw her smile—in fact she was glowing. Her face beamed when she laughed.

After that she spent her time helping me with the task of moving Stormy out of Crown Vista. She didn't have to be asked to help—she was just always there.

Winding up at Felony Flats, and having people in our lives unlike any either of us had had before, she somehow made it not only bearable but fun to be there. She helped me arrange the place. It was then I realized the unseen pull we had toward each other.

When I moved to an actual house on Salmon, it seemed huge and unreal that I could be so fortunate and have a big yard! I think it was April when she knocked on my door, announcing, "Hi, I'm home. I told Richard about my feelings for you and asked him for a divorce."

Whoa—was I scared! At that time I still had huge issues with having anything to do with the breakup of her marriage. As you've learned, I also managed to get myself into quite a lot of unfortunate situations over the last year and a half. Was that pattern going to stop or continue? And, besides, the Salmon house is so tiny (it's the yard and the shop that's huge). So she moved into her parents' home for a while.

It was extremely hard for her, and I believe her parents were very helpful.

They were willing to do what was necessary for their beautiful daughter.

She was there for me. Whether it was to pick up and throw my boat and trailer off me, or to take me to Tri-Cities to face my brother and my family and myself, or in the kitchen cooking up some healthy food (which, for the longest time, I thought I was allergic to), she was there.

7/4/05 ~

Mustard seed necklace. Small miracles.

Diana's name changed when her divorce came through. I think it was India Jaiden Nevaeh Neiashea

I wish I knew...what to do with unbearable pain.

I miss you so very much—my heart is broken

7/5/05 ~

Yesterday was very hard. I reminisced about last year when Diana and I got up on the roof to watch the fireworks. We then went out to "Boomer's cottage" and sat on the bench. A dog named "Happy" circled us two or three times.

I feel so *nauseous and dizzy*.

My prayer to God:

Please forgive me for my shortcomings and sins. Remember I am human. This is A LOT God—I don't like it one bit! But I am asking you to let me *know* if Diana is with you! Please, I really need to know. Please have her in your arms.

7/6/05 ~

I can't stand to look at the stove. Diana always had something cooking on the stove. It has to go. I can't look at it any more! Luckily, my teenage boys came over. They moved it out on the side of the house. I put a table and chairs in its place.

I forgot that the stove/oven was the only source of heat in the house. I didn't care; my heart was so cold anyway.

The phone rings. I thought it was probably Sally, Diana's mom, since it was almost always her. Night and day. Instead I hear a voice I didn't recognize. "Hello, my name is Kacie. I'm from Aging and Disability Services, and I'm your new case-worker. Is your caregiver Diana Anderson there?"

I remember just saying, without emotion, "She's dead." Now this was probably something Kacie didn't hear every day.

"Oh my gosh! Are you okay?"

"No," I answered. She then hit me with a barrage of questions, the first of which was, "Is someone with you?" I said I had friends coming in and out, which was true, although my friends were just the teenage boys and my cantankerous neighbor, George.

Kacie called me several times and set up an appointment for me that afternoon to see a social worker at Kaiser. DC took me. The social worker was very kind, and gave me a stack of papers with places and numbers to call in situations like this. I wonder if I am the only one who never even looked at the papers.

7/7/05 ~

The social worker called to see if I had made any calls for help. I said no. She probably figured I wasn't going to do anything. She suggested I see a particular therapist with Lutheran Family Services. I told her okay, and thanked her. But before I hung up, she said she enrolled me in a day treatment at Kaiser for depression, doctor's orders. Or else I could lose my benefits.

No sooner had I hung the phone up when it rang again. It was Janna, the therapist with Lutheran Family Services. She had a British accent, which I loved. If nothing else, I would go to hear her accent and get my mind on something else.

Kacie called again. She told me if I didn't have a new caregiver by the end of July, I would lose my benefits. Losing my benefits would have been nothing compared to what I just lost. She gave me a list of available caregivers. I didn't care. How could I replace Diana??

7/8/05 ~

Kacie called again. Stormy talked to her and said she would take care of me. I heard this before when she kidnapped me to Crown Vista. And we know what happened there. The one big difference now is that if I didn't get another caregiver, I would lose my health benefits I thankfully got a few months ago. After she hung up the phone, Stormy left.

It's unbearable. Not even a bear could bear what I'm going through.

Time to visit Kaiser. The Kaiser intake form asks a lot of questions that are supposed to help them select effective therapies for me. Good luck. On a scale of 1—10:

"Please circle the numbers which describe how much, during the past week, pain HAS INTERFERED WITH your ability to do these:"

General Activity—I circled 10 "Can't do" Sleep—I circled 10 "Can't sleep" Mood—I circled 10 "Very poor"

Enjoyment of life—I circled 10 "Don't enjoy"

"How many minutes can you walk before pain becomes severe?" 5-15

"How many times are you awakened by pain each night?" *Too many to count*

I checked eight out of nine boxes worth of symptoms, from feeling sad to difficulty concentrating to everything is an effort.

"With whom do you live?" *Alone I lost my girlfriend/caregiver 2 weeks ago she died in an accident*

"How do you let your family/friends know you are experiencing pain?"

They do not hear from me—I hide

"Please circle the number which describes the intensity of your pain at its WORST in the past week"

10—Unbearable pain

I circled all of the following which described my pain: "Aching

Burning

Constant

Dull

Sharp

Shooting

Stabbing

Throbbing

Other: *unbearable*"

Medications

Diazepam 10 mg oral tab

Promethazine 25 mg oral tab

Zoloft 100 mg oral tab

Morphine 15 mg oral tab

Levothroid 75 mcg oral tab

Maxalt-MLT 10 mg oral ta

7/9/05 ~

Noon

Me and Buckley

As I keep telling Buckley, I'm not bipolar. My life is . . . .

It's been more than two weeks and still somehow I still do not believe it. Aunt Harriet called this morning and we had our normal great conversation. She is so very special.

Sabrina took me to my new primary care doctor yesterday, Dr. Sax. I like him. He kept me on the same meds I've been on. Everyone agrees I should have mental health therapy. There's no doubt in my mind I do need help. This is on the list of many things I need.

7/12/05 ~

It seems so unreal. My best friend, partner, lover, caregiver, is gone. My life became entangled, willingly, with Diana that she was my life. My grief is too much to bear.

What keeps me going is nothing more than the respect, and honor I have for her and all she did to help me adjust to life with a disability. Her love showed so very much—in her eyes and words and actions.

I am unable to ever comprehend.

7/15/05 ~

The first time I met Diana's sisters was when I went to Richard's to help move some of her stuff. I thought it was strange they were at her home with their sister's soon-to-be ex-husband. The only time they interacted with Diana was once or twice on the phone when one of them wanted information.

I remember the first time her daughter was here at our home. She came to yell at Diana and told her she hated her. She said it wasn't so much "the Sherri thing" she was most mad about, but rather it was now she was left alone to take care of Richard. This deeply hurt Diana. We talked about how kids as a norm hate their parents one time or another. We both agreed her daughter would come around one day. I am happy to say we saw changes in her that made us believe she was doing just that.

I really cannot understand Richard's actions since her death; although there were many times before she died that I didn't understand or like his actions. Such as when he called here 17 times in a row and just hung up.

Now the hardest thing for me to deal with is my grief. It's the biggest, most agonizing, most dreadful thing that has or will ever happen in my life.

When I found out that because of a very small technicality Diana and Richard were not yet divorced when she died, it wasn't a big deal to me. The only thing I could think about was that she was really gone. I know she believed she was divorced, as I have her message to me on the answering machine. She was extremely happy about it before she was tragically, accidentally killed. When it became a big deal was when I was told I couldn't come to the funeral, as Richard was calling all the shots.

Well, I went to her funeral. She was my partner and lived with me for well over a year. The minister spoke of her as a rose, so I found it odd there were no roses there. Every picture of Diana was years old, and in none of them was she smiling. At the memorial I had here, I realized every one of the many pictures of I took of Diana shows her smiling big time!

Richard, nor her sisters, could care less about the life she led this past almost couple of years. Now, after her death, they do not even respect or allow the people who were close to her to grieve. Now they come to our home, storm in like vultures, cold as sharks, carelessly rifling through her and my stuff. Do these people know or understand the extreme pain and agony her parents and I are going through?

My God, please help me keep bailing myself out of such a massive loss. It's surreal. She was so very amazing.

I will not let anyone interfere with what we had, and how she was, is, and always will be sacred in my life. How dare they look me in the eyes and not see the love we had together and try to make me focus on "stuff " or paperwork or anything. I will not. I will treasure this pain and loss because what these feelings mean is—I finally had it.

Love is great.

To be loved is greater.

But to be loved by the one you love is greatest!

I am very confused when it comes to religion, but I have no doubt God is love. I want love. That will always be my only true intention and goal.

Mom got here Wednesday, five minutes before my landlord, who's talking about selling the place, and three other people showed up to look at it. One of them asked if I was interested in continuing to rent after the house sold. I started crying and went to my shop. Then I went to do my dishes, which hadn't been done in three weeks. I think I only had two showers in that time period.

I really had the best time with my mom. I feel close to her. And I believe she felt closer to me than ever before. But she only stayed the same amount of time she always does: one night.

7/17/05 ~

India Neiashea. I truly loved you with all my heart. Thank you for all the proof of your happiness with me as I have to deal with those who were not involved in our life at all. At least not in a positive way.

7/20/05 ~

George—Big Yellow Truck

Last week was George's birthday. Without Diana. Tomorrow he is taking me to Sally and David's, Diana's parents, to mow the lawn. First time I'll be there since she . . . Lindsay is my new caregiver. I do not recognize her, but she's friends with Sabrina. I remember ripping up the list of potential replacements for Diana.

NO one could ever take her place, or look me in the eyes—deep into my soul—with such love. All the time she was like that. Okay, a couple of times love is not what I saw in her eyes. But that was, say, three percent of the time. I need to find out what happened. I thought, repeatedly that day, she's leaving. I did think but didn't really expect it. Was I the biggest pain that night? I don't think so, but what if? Or was it the feeling and emotion of finally exiting 19 years of unhappiness? God, I want to know. Do you want me to know? Please, God, why? My Diana. Why? Why did Sally tell me she was seen crying and distraught by the witnesses? Who told her that? I don't even know. Oh my God, did I have something to do with this? Oh my God. If there was something going on, why didn't I notice? I've thought about this so many times. I knew she was going somewhere. She's doing all the things she does when she is going away somewhere. To Boomer's cottage or her Grandma's at the beach. She went to Costco and got me a case of mango juice. Sally told me Diana said to her, "I don't want to forget to get Sherri's mango juice. She loves it, and it's better than her pop." She cleaned the house. She got the laundry done. Carefully, she would put outfits together in my closet. I didn't, or maybe couldn't, wear some of them because I know she arranged and touched them.

7/22/05 ~

I spend nights on my couch, as I can't bring myself to sleep in my bed without Diana. I guess I was more tired than hungry, as I fell asleep before I could get the handful of gummy bears in my mouth. Instead they found their way to my hair, as I apparently slept on them. It was a pretty sticky situation. My hair was so matted, it was horrible.

Lindsay came to pick me up so we could do the necessary paperwork to have her officially appointed as my caregiver. We left for our appointment with Kacie, and got to Aging and Disability Services while they were having a fire drill. Kacie and about forty other people were standing around in front of the building. Kacie had brought the paperwork with her. We found her, and so while Lindsay was signing papers with her, I sat on the curb trying to get gummy bears out of my hair. Turns out scissors were required.

8/2/05 ~

3:00 a.m.

Buckley & me

I received a notice to pick up a certified letter from "The Estate of Diana Anderson." Sally wants me to wait to pick it up until she contacts me. I don't know what to do.

Going over bankruptcy papers I received in the mail.

Sabrina and I argued. She told me I was yelling at her. I was not. She let someone take my piano. This did not make me happy. I called her an "insensitive bitch." I didn't yell it.

8/9/05 ~

My mental health is now in the hands of Lutheran Community Services. Janna is my new counselor. But they made me sign a "No Self-Harm Contract." It reads as follows:

"I, Sherri Smith, recognize that keeping myself alive is my responsibility. If I am feeling suicidal, I will take the following steps.
Call or speak to:

Janna cell #1234567890
Lindsayphone#1234567890 and cell #0987654321

To make for a safer environment, I will:

Remove knives and guns I will not take pills
Will not stand on or go on the road or freeways
Will not go outside in the dark

I will use these skills:

Draw or write
Plants—(will water, prune, love)

If I feel I cannot control my suicidal urges, I will immediately go to a hospital emergency room for evaluation. If for some reason I cannot go, I will call Janna at 1234567, or (after hours), 1234567890.

This agreement will remain in effect permanently, unless I'm notified by my therapist."

They not only made me sign it, but they also had a witness sign it. OK. I'm in.

8/22/05 ~

10:38 a.m.

Buckley & me

I spoke to an old friend, and former coke customer, Joy, a little while ago. She and I go back many, many moons! Ironic—one of Diana's new names means the moon or "light of the moon" I think. Diana always reminded me of Joy. In fact, Diana and I spent time with Rachel (Rachel is Joy's twin sister). We joked about Diana looking more like Joy than Rachel did. Jasmine was someone I met when I was 21. We were instant friends. I thought we were lifelong friends, but that shows my ignorance. I have so many memories with Jasmine. Her and I had a booth at one of Portand's oldest events, Saturday Market, in 1985 and 1986. We sold dog leashes and collars made from the beautiful colored hiking straps. At that time, the only dog leashes were either made from chain or leather. We also sold christmas ornaments that Jasmine would write on the spot whatever they wanted. She was a pretty talented artist. I loved being around artists, seeing that they got a lot of attention in my life.

My heart is broken; my head is unable to stop the millions of thoughts. I can't make any sense or any order of them. My mind is like a rolodex spinning and I have zero control of where it stops. Sort of like a slot machine. Where it stops is not up to me.

I've often said I don't gamble with more than I can afford to lose. Maybe because I didn't follow my own rule is the reason my grief is bigger than I can handle.

Tomorrow I go to bankruptcy court. My name will be changed. I know my last name will be Raye, because that's Dad's middle name. George wanted my first name to be Skylark. I thought Sky Raye sounded funny. Lindsay suggested Skyler. Even on my way to court I wasn't sure who I would be.

Hopefully a new life, maybe new hope!

I feel so bad too much.

I need help. I am very aware of my inabilities.

8/24/05 ~

Dear Sherri,

I just looked at the photos on the CD you gave us. Thank you!! Now I'm listening to a music CD that belonged to Diana that we'd like to copy before we give it back to Richard. I need help. Maybe sometime in the very near future you could come over and give me a CD burning lesson and then while I practice you could give our flower beds some attention?

Etc., etc., etc.

Love you,

David Dad

9/5/05 ~

No one wants me around them, but it's okay if I do things for them. Just barely alive.

9/7/05 ~

I can't breathe if I think about my reality now. It's more than I am able to wrap my mind around.

Shelly, my landlords girlfriend, met someone who gives her drugs. I did some with her. Then she and I went to see this guy MR for more drugs. Shelly was always good at sharing, and her drugs were no exception. I kinda wish she wouldn't have. Snorting this stuff is like snorting battery acid. Besides, I don't want to be awake now. Actually, ever again.

Tammy is a person I met who was born a male, but is going through steps to become a girl. Really long blonde hair. Oh, and also sells drugs. He/she has been coming over and trying to show me how to smoke meth with flavored water. I'm not that great at smoking it. It really stinks.

I remember seeing Stormy smoke it. I would find blackened foil everywhere. She would have black all over her face at times. That, with her wild cross eyes, was a pretty alarming sight, quite opposite of how she normally looks.

9/14/05 ~

> Kaiser Visit Summary
>
> "New Internal Referral
>
> ALT IR PAIN MGMT MULTIDISPL GROUP VISITS
>
> New medications:
>
> Seroquel 25 mg tab
>
> Methadone 5 mg tab
>
> Discontinue the Relafen
>
> Mark your calendar for the group visits . . . Tuesdays . . . for eight consecutive weeks"

9/18/05 ~

They're upping the methadone and lowering the morphine.

9/20/05 ~

My psychiatrist said I need stronger Zoloft, so now it's 200 mg.

9/23/05 ~

Diana, I miss you BIG. Three months of intense pain. It's time to heal.

9/24/05 ~

6:15 p.m.

What a beautiful day!!

For the first time in a while, my to-do list includes just laying here in my yard with the warmth of the sun shining on my face. I get these waves of so many thoughts and emotions that my mind gets flooded. It's just like when a motor gets too much gas—it gets flooded and will not start.

9/26/05 ~

4:30 a.m.

Facts are facts, right? Why—Why do I why so much?

Slept on Stormy's couch watching a movie (more sleeping than watching), and then we went to sleep in her bed. When sleeping with her I made sure not to sleep close.

Is it because I don't really have any other place to go?

10/2/05 ~

4:50 p.m.

Fourth day of rain; only the beginning of much more to come. My teenage boys came today. It's the first day I can sit up.

The joy she brought to my life. Way bigger than the feelings of the loss of her. Right?

10/22/05 ~

I'm learning—

It's not the things that happen in my life that is important. It is how I react to them. This is what I know to be true.

I am sure I never felt more confused or alone. I sit here, day after day, alone.

Letter to DC:

There are things I need to get off my chest, so whether I give this to you or you respond is unimportant.

The night Diana got hit by that car and I could not get into my house as she had the keys I came to your house hysterical, told you what had happened, and asked if Buckley could stay there. You said no. I was already in shock over something bigger than the shock of your reply. So I justified it in my mind that you were half asleep and didn't mean to react to me with your, "What are you doing here now?" response and the fact you wouldn't let Buck stay there.

At Diana's memorial here at our house, when we were sitting together in a circle, you out and out lied when you said she had come to you early in our relationship and asked if you thought it was bad or sinfully wrong for her to be in a relationship with me. Your answer to her was to go for it. You lied so far from the truth. Why did you do that?

The truth is you were dead against her from the start, telling her to leave me alone, etc.

She then came to my house and broke out my bedroom window.

When she didn't pay my bill on time and I lost my insurance, you really were not even a little bit nice to her at all.

At her service I was not able to deal with anything due to the traumatic shock and intense grief I felt. This is when I told you, "No input please." I wasn't really sure I was going to even continue to live, so I chose not to deal with the lying.

When I called you, I remember you telling me I should keep busy because it would be good for me. So I did, as you requested, and put things together for you that you ordered. I remember you started laughing, saying, "I don't even know what's in most of those packages" piled up. I cleaned your gutters. Built another shed. Potted plants and weeded your yard. When I didn't get your lawn mowed exactly the way you wanted, you went and paid someone else $40 to do it.

The more work I did at your place, the more abusive you were toward me.

Why?

You told me how you stuck up for Diana when I was being mean to her.

Why would you want to needlessly say things like that?

You told me your family wanted you to pick them or me. Why would you ever repeat such stupid lies to me?

Then you said you were tired of all the promises. What the hell does that mean?

I asked you to please not say anything else to me. I wanted no input from you unless you thought about it first. I said if you care about me at all, you would not say anything else to me until you thought about all you have said.

It seems every time from then on I felt horrible after talking to or seeing you. And I don't need any help in that department, thank you very much.

Then you blow up at me for saying I was tired of you and Sabrina continuing to bitch about your money situation to me—especially since both of you just had returned from vacations. I cannot believe there was any concern for me at all from you. Meanwhile, I wonder every day if I will be able to live until the next day. How could you be so cruel?

I looked back in my journal the day Diana and you made the deal concerning the computer. At that point I was out of any obligation regarding this deal. But I still told you after her death I would make sure you got paid.

It didn't matter. Nothing I said got through to you. You were so self-indulgent. It was all about you. Even my friends didn't want to be around you, as you'd immediately start talking about your personal problems. Things no one needed or should have to hear except maybe a priest or therapist. Like your mother's abuse, what your brother said to you, all the Joe stories, etc., etc.

I did not want our friendship to cease, but I am no longer capable of the abuse I feel continually coming my way. I really hope you do what is necessary to get back to the DC I met because I miss her friendship.

Please do not send any more letters like the one I'm sending back along with this. First of all, I have never begged for anything. I helped you from losing thousands of dollars on scams I told you not to fall for. I have never ripped you off or taken advantage of you in any way. In fact, I have given you many things, including, most of all, my time.

Hopefully you understand now. No one forces me to do anything. Same as you.

10/26/05 ~

> Kaiser Visit Summary
> Medications:
> Increase the Methadone to 20 mg every 8 hours
> Discontinue the Valium

11/4/05 ~

I found out recently that November is National Caregivers Month.

Well, I would like very much to honor my caregiver—she was actually more than a caregiver—she was the love of my life. I know you understand all the feelings of hurt, of anger and detachment.

This brings me to what I am asking of you. To honor the best caregiver, Diana.

I've been wondering lately—why do I keep existing? I really do not want to, as, well, logically, the case for my existence in the world is weak—very weak.

As I look around my world, there are more reasons to not want to, as life continues to get more overwhelming. Things so small in reality, for example, like those stinking dirty dishes in the dirty, gross kitchen. This is the easiest and most doable thing I face in here. Yet, I sit paralyzed. In a state of indecisiveness. Which pain is it I need to deal with?

11/15/05 ~

Tammy came by today and brought a friend named Cari. I'm pretty sure she's a real girl. She seems nice. They brought their homemade bong, which tasted like strawberry. The blue smoke filled the room. I could still taste that awful yuck in my mouth. I've got a really bad headache, so I've decided not to allow anybody else to talk me into smoking this shit again.

11/17/05 ~

I unplugged my phone and locked my door. I'm locking the world out.
11/20/05 ~

I hear George outside my house again. I hear him say, "Skyler, is that you crying again?" I seldom let him in, but he frequently checks on me. It soon became painfully obvious to me that I don't have to lock the door because nobody wants to get in. Except for George and my teenage boys.

1/1/06 ~

Dear BonMom,

Happy New Year!

I am convinced that my life has purpose. That there are reasons for all that happens, even if the reason is for no reason at all. To be still and listen is something I've failed at in my life, until now.

Since Diana died, so much has happened. Mostly inside me. I have taken a six month period to be alone and work on the things I needed so I could grow and allow my inner child to grow and mature.

I believe my personal/emotional self is about between the ages of 10-14. So part of me is still quite young. But I'm very happy I got back to that part of myself. I am sure in time the onset of maturity will do its thing.

I'm still working on my book. And during the process I have been so blessed to have been able to grow and learn so much.

My goal is to have an art opening in March. It would be the first showing of my art. This is something I have never done. I have allowed some people/ artists I trust and respect look at some of my art projects and have gotten only positive feedback. The theme of my art show will be "Celebrate Your Scars."

Way back, when I worked creating designs in people's back yards, etc., there would be a stump or concrete lump or something that was a huge eyesore. I would, almost always, transform that to something beautiful. With this in mind, I started going through things that have been boxed up more or less the last four years. I started "fixing" some of my favorite things that got broken. I soon learned I could not "fix" them to their original state, so I added things to make the broken part the focal point.

Anyway, there is way too much to tell you in one letter, so I will end this for now.

Most importantly, I want you to know I am doing well and look forward to seeing you at some point. I love and miss you and there is not a day that goes by that I don't think of you.

Love,

Sherri

P.S. My name has changed legally to Skyler Raye.

1/15/06 ~

My life is as sad as it is ironic.

All my life I've tried to push the sadness aside. I can't even acknowledge it, as it hurts so bad. I feel like I am dying. I'm five months in to my new therapist, who tells me this is as bad as it's gonna get. If it can't get any worse than this, and I don't know how it possibly could, then I can get through it. Just knowing I've undergone the worst helps, in a sick sort of way. To get through it I had to go through intense sadness. Cry a lot. Scream a lot. It's important to feel it. I don't have to keep the "No Trespassing" sign on me any more. If I can help someone else, that helps me heal.

2/22/06 ~

I fell again.

Kaiser Permanente Summary of Visit Clinical Laboratory
CULTURE WOUND
Procedures
I & D, SKIN ABSCESS, SIMPLE
Medications
CEPHALEXIN 500 MG CAP

CHAPTER NINETEEN
FLASHBACKS OF THE WORST KIND

3/5/06 ~

Stormy called from the beach, where she was "working" for Joy on her condo development, and invited me over. "Oh, and bring your trailer, I've collected some great things here," were the last words she spoke before hanging up.

I was scared to go, as I hadn't traveled by myself for so long. But I thought it would be great to see Joy, as it had been I don't know how long. I guess it should have been longer, because I was way wrong to think she was my friend. Although there were many times I had been hers. She had me "do a few things" which were endless for her "project" that already had one lawsuit against it. Joy wasn't just stand-offish, but boldly cold to me. She said I should be over Dianna's death; after all it's been eight months. The truth was over her head like a huge neon sign. I was way out of the "in" crowd and there was no place in her life for me. I was broken. I really was so caught off guard by her actions and words. It cut me deeply. I cried all the way home.

3/28/06 ~

Loneliness is bad for your health. It leads to crying.

4/3/06 ~

They put my house up for sale.

6/1/06 ~

I just heard this Michael Jackson song, "Man in the Mirror"—wow. If I start with the person I face in the mirror, I'm not sure who it is that I see, but I often suspect it can't be me. My faces changes. Maybe it's the different pieces of me.

"Plant Whisperer"

I am old—I feel a sense of great pride. Because, I feel—oh, I know, feelings are not facts. But most of my life I've made it through the facts via my feelings. So, hey, feelings can also be facts.

Feelings are not facts.

I never would have believed anyone who told me this was how my life would turn out. From here, it doesn't look so good. BUT, appearances aren't everything, and in some important ways I am better than I could have been. Through it all, I can say I'm proud to have had the luxury to get to know myself. If I work at it, maybe I will discover who the real "me" is.

I probably learned the most when I was attending the mental health outpatient clinic. It took me six times in the inpatient mental ward, plus outpatient time. You have no idea (I hope) what it's like to wake up in double lock-down, in the hospital. Only to go into two-and-a-half years of intense, all day mental health clinics. But this is where I received the "tools" to accept myself, even when everything seemed like, looked like, felt like, undeniably, the worst time in my life. Ever. But, really, in my vulnerability I was stronger than I've ever been or will be in my life. I always say a person is strongest at their lowest, absolute worst times. Otherwise, I don't know how I would have kept bailing.

6/14/06 ~

Shit. The house sold. I have a little more than a month to move.

6/20/06 ~

Although she was slightly better than nobody, it was obvious to everyone who came around that Lindsay the caregiver was not doing her job, to say the least. Lindsay was getting paid for something like 79 hours a month, but only worked approximately 12 hours a month. Her jobs were supposed to be managing my meds, doctor appointments, transportation, paying my bills, cleaning, etc. I wasn't happy to find out she neglected to pay my electric bill for the last six months. I wasn't aware of this, so imagine my thrill when I was called by a collection agency. After losing everything, and filing bankruptcy in attempt to rebuild my credit, it was quite disappointing to have collection agencies calling me.

A friend, so I thought, came to save the day. What the hell was I thinking?

Stormy stayed at my place practically all the time as we got me ready to move. She was "managing" the trailer park for Sybil, who's in California. They talk at least three times a day. Sybil does manage to come to the island a lot and visit Stormy. They probably spend all their time drinking, being the total alcoholics they both are. They've come over a couple of times and looked around at my stuff like it was a garage sale.

I was beyond sad. I didn't want to move. I didn't want to leave the home where I had so many memories of my life with Diana. I was grieving the loss all over again. And let me tell you, once was one time too many.

Although my house was small, my yard was huge, and I had hundreds of plants. I also had a ton of stuff in the huge shop, like my tools, art supplies, etc. It was stuff I moved six times over the past five and a half years. Even when I was homeless, I rented storage space for this stuff. I know it wasn't much to some people, but, to me, it was the remnant of who I was once upon a time.

Stormy told me she wanted to be my caregiver. She just couldn't stand by anymore and see me taken advantage of. It would, I thought, be impossible for Stormy to convince my case worker that she could be my caregiver. My case worker, I thought, would remember when Stormy came to "help" after Diana died and wound up stealing my meds before disappearing. Stormy really talked a good talk. She won over my case worker and therapist.

My plan at first was to just move everything to George's house. Stormy would ask questions about what I had and would dig through my things. She and Sybil kept telling me how great it would be for me to have my things at the trailer park. There was a huge field. It wasn't too hard to convince me. They told me my heart and soul were in the yard and art world. After all, it was my best therapy. So, Stormy decided what was going to my new apartment and what would go to her place. I could bring all my plants and art supplies out there and keep them there rent-free. Then I could set up a plant stand and sell some plants and give them a commission from my sales. She proceeded to load up her van with my stuff, including special stuff of mine and Diana's. Many loads. For "safe-keeping." But she didn't completely take everything. I did leave some of my good tools and other things at George's.

Thanks to the extra $1,000 incentive to vacate on time from Steve the realtor, and with help from remaining friends, the move was completed by August 3rd. I made several trips to the dump on Steve's dime. I also gave Stormy A LOT of the money for gas, time, good will. After all, she practically conducted the entire move. Sometime in the end of July, I heard Stormy outside firing Lindsay, saying she was taking over. I was pretty sure I would, or could, not ever be happy again. But at least when I was working with my plants, well, it was the closest I came to any kind of peace of mind or happiness. The plants' stories were intertwined with mine. Some of them we worked on at Diana's parents' home, and I dug them up to keep before they moved. All of the plants were very special to me. I also had a large plant shrine I built in Diana's memory.

8/1/06 ~

My caseworker Kacie decided I needed to live in a building designated for disabled people only, so she got me a place at Pine Point. It's right next to a funeral home/crematorium. It stinks and I hate it. I didn't have any choice. I believed I'd be welcome to spend time on Sauvie Island and be with my plants and things, so that made it a little better.

8/5/06 ~

Sybil flew in from California. She came to pick up Stormy for a two week vacation in Napa Valley, full of spa treatments and wine, according to Stormy. I paid Sybil $50, the rental fee to have my things there, and then she added $25 per month for my boat and shed storage. She also wanted commission from my plant stand.

8/7/06 ~

Before Stormy and Sybil left, Rosie (Stormy's room-mate who paid rent, unlike Stormy) and I were given a sketch and instructions to build a wall around the area where Stormy's stuff and now mine sat.

Rosie and I did everything she asked and more. I also cleaned Stormy's refrigerator, toilet, pictures, mirrors, and floors. I maintained her garden and potted plants. We were excited for Stormy and Sybil to come back and see all the extra work we did.

8/20/06 ~

Rosie calls, crying as she explains that Sybil and Stormy came back and yelled at her, telling her she didn't do a good enough job on what they told her to do.

I called Stormy to find out what was going on. She warned, "Do you want to get in the middle of this? You are not in trouble, so stay out of my and Rosie's business." She hung up.

8/22/06 ~

Sybil and Stormy came to my apartment with some contract for me to sign. When they got here, both in dark glasses, they were very intimidating. Did I tell you Sybil is an Amazon woman? Her presence alone can be intimidating. Sybil tells me I have 72 hours to get what was special to me out of there. "Are you kidding me?" I asked in shock.

"No," was Sybil's reply as they walked out. All I could do was sit and cry.

8/24/06 ~

Tammy and I went out to the island to pick up some of my things. I rented a U-Haul for the occasion. Sybil and Stormy came out and told me, "Just take the plants and go."

I was thrilled by this reception. Tammy asked, "Why are you kicking her out of here?"

"She dumped trash in my field," Sybil snarled back.

"We'll take away anything you consider trash," Tammy replied.

"Just take what's most important to her, and get off my property," Sybil ordered.

So Tammy and I gathered about 60 of my gallon plants, and none of the bigger ones, when she got a call that required us to leave. So we took off with the U-Haul only a quarter full. When I first brought stuff over it took three trips in a 28' truck, plus lots of trips in Stormy's van and my truck and trailer.

8/25/06 ~

I went by myself to the island to finish packing up my plants and things. On my way I stopped at a 7-11 to get something to drink. I saw three strapping young men there, and I offered to pay them if they could come and help me. They agreed and followed me to Sybil's. My idea was to have them load the big stuff, but they just loaded some small stuff. The truck was half loaded when Amazon woman, who seemed fully loaded, came out and snarled about calling the police if we didn't leave immediately. When the boys heard the word "cops", they took off lickety-split. I was horribly upset, crying, snot and tears flowing, begging her to allow me to get my things. She laughed.

Three cops showed up. One seemed like a friend of hers. I was in the field trying to hook my trailer onto my truck. As I was about to leave, one of the cops came up and told me to unhook the trailer. I said it was mine. He said that's a civil matter and I had to clear out. He said someone else will have to come pick up my things. I was sobbing, trying to explain that she had given me 72 hours. I thought to myself, if Sybil knows Christ and introduced Stormy to him, I'm sure glad I didn't get introduced. I cried all the way home.

8/28/06 ~

Sam went to pick up my trailer. When he got there he was told not to come back or send anyone else because they were keeping the rest of my things. When he brought the trailer back it was full of garbage—food, trash, used Kotex, fish heads . . . it must have taken some doing to degrade me this way. What few things of mine that were there were mostly broken or damaged. My good tools, furniture, and art supplies were all AWOL.

I couldn't believe this. It was beyond mean. This was lower than low. Among other things, I wanted to take them to small claims court and get my things. No, I didn't really want to take them to small claims court. I wanted to kill them. This was over the top. I couldn't respond in any way because I was, frankly, in shock. I believe mean Sybil was scheming to do this the whole time, and Stormy went along with it because she needed a place to live. It makes me want to switch sides, from suicide to homicide. Either way, it's all too much. Too, too much!

CHAPTER TWENTY
LIVING IN PINE NEEDLES

9/3/06 ~

I'm at Pine Point. It's a facility for the disabled. Those who lived on the first floor were the most disabled and had 24 hour care, as two aides lived there. The second floor people had someone come in every day. Those on the third floor had someone come in multiple times a week, depending on their needs. I'm on the third floor.

When I learned the term the government refers to us by, I understood why it was next to a funeral home. The government calls us throw-aways. The one thing I didn't mind so much about being there was that I was the tallest, as everyone I met to that point was in a wheelchair. I always wanted to be tall.

I had a nice, clean one bedroom apartment, about 400 square feet. It had a small balcony. Living there shouted out how broken I must be.

It was obvious that I was disliked, since people were pretty rude to me. When I locked myself out, and people could see that I wanted to come in, nobody would open the door. Fortunately, one resident there started a conversation with me, and kindly said if I couldn't get in I could go through her first floor apartment.

I met my neighbor today. Her name is Marie, and she seems nice. We met when she saw me fall down the stairs. She was nice enough to offer to take Buckley out for me. Sadly, I had to live with the smell of burning people. My bed was right under the window, and I could always smell the crematorium. I would just lay there.

While walking Buckley, Tammy's friend Cari pulled up. She asked if she could sleep on my couch that night, lying to me about having to work or something. I said yes, as company was welcome.

When we were upstairs she offered me some meth. I said no, I can't handle smoking it. She said she didn't smoke it, but rather preferred the use of a needle. I excused myself as she whipped out her paraphernalia.

10/7/06 ~

My neighbor Marie was moved to the first floor. A week later a new person moved in. My other neighbor told me the new neighbor was bedridden.

On this particular day I wanted to end my life, even though the two years I promised Diana weren't up yet. So, instead I chose to throw the ball for Buck in my long third floor hallway. I heard a man's voice yelling, "You fucking bitch!" and other assorted profanities. This enraged me. I banged on the door, and when this young man answered I asked, "Is that your mother in there?" It was. I said, "How dare you treat your mother that way? If I ever hear you yelling at her like that again, you will be in worse health than she is." I continued on, taking out all my anger on him

I peeked in through the narrowly open door and saw this woman lying in bed with a big smile, looking at me with amazement. I asked her, "Are you okay?"

She simply said, "Yes."

I asked, "Would you like me to come back and check on you?"
"Please do, yes," she replied.

Later that day I went back to talk to this lady. She told me nobody had ever stuck up for her before, and thanked me profusely. Her name was Kerry Grant. Approximately 25 years earlier her car was going 90 mph and she crashed, paralyzing her below her breasts. She told me she thought it was God's way of telling her to sit down. The more I hear about this God of Kerry's and Sybil's makes me think this could be the God I'm writing my prayers to: mighty, mean, and uncaring.

Kerry invited me over to watch The Dog Whisperer with her. She thought I was shushing her when it was actually the TV guy communicating with the dogs. She thought I was so rude!

Kerry has a four-by-two sized bedsore that went all the way to her bone. I could never look at it.

10/24/06 ~

Cari started coming over more and more. It seemed like I was always in bed except for the times she or someone would stop by. She always offered me some meth. In an "I don't care" mind-set, I started to say yes, and would snort it. I guess it was just a different kind of awful.

The attitude of the residents continued to make me feel unwelcome. I found big scratches on my car. One of them called animal control on me and said Buckley bit her. He wasn't even close to her. The only time he bit anyone was when he was defending me that time in the Park Blocks downtown.

The few plants I had in the outside patio area were abused continually. I had to move them to Bub and Scout's, along with the very few plants I retrieved from Sauvie Island. It made me so sick to think about it. Mostly because I know they'll probably die. I cared for them so well; they were like a part of me.

No Words

11/24/06 ~

Day after Thanksgiving

Holidazed. Alone. One day is no different from the next. Not even holidays.

I have spent so much time in bed. Minutes turn into hours, hours turn into days, and days into months, months into years. I'm not feeling very thankful. In fact, I don't want to think at all.

Cari came over. I was thinking I was ready to try meth her way. I asked if she had a clean syringe for me to use. She said yes, and fixed it up for me. I had to look away as she stuck the needle into my arm. I felt a warm sensation, and my heart started pounding really fast. I could still taste it a little bit, but it was better than the horrible taste I got from smoking or snorting it. Plus, I actually felt like staying out of bed and actually doing something. Even something as simple as laundry was doable after she left.

After I walked back in my apartment with the last of my laundry, the phone rang. It was Mom. I didn't even know she was back in the country. She called from my brother Joe's in Maryland and asked if I would like to come to Joe's for Christmas. I said sure. I knew Buckley would be fine with my two good friends in the building. Still, I worried about and hated to leave him.

12/17/06 ~

Cari came over frequently. It wasn't because she was invited or anything, but anyone was always welcome.

12/19/06 ~

I'm on a Southwest airplane, headed to Phoenix and a two hour layover before going on to Baltimore to Joe's. I asked Mom to pray for Buck's peace of mind as I left home this morning and hoped God would answer.

12/27/06 ~

3:21 a.m.

I'm back. It was wonderfully, sadly the same. The happiest thing about being home was seeing Buckley.

They paid my airfare and for all the sightseeing in the D.C. area. I came home the day after Christmas, a little earlier than planned.

Strangely, my mother has the capacity to talk to me in two ways. Both her ways made me guilty. I slept almost the whole day when I first got there. Then I needed to nap several times that week. She would say to me, "Sherri, are you going to get up or sleep the day away?" as I lay there thinking about how much my head and knee hurt. I'd been to the emergency room twice due to falls, in December alone, hurting my injured knee. This was two days before flying there, I reminded her. "I still don't feel very good. Besides, there's also the time change."

Her words were almost boastful. "Well, it can't be the time change. I fly all the time and I don't need so much sleep."

I started crying. I am such a great big cry baby. "Mom, I really don't feel good. I'm not trying to sleep away my time here. I wish I could just be with Buck in my apartment in my own bed."

"I'd let you go if I had another six-hundred dollars to change your ticket. I know you don't want to be around me. You slept the first day away. Then we went to D.C. Then you slept until 2:00 the day after that. Now, honey, all I'm saying is that it's 'cause you're sick, not the time change. That's all."

And then that line she repeated to me so often, "Honey, you've always been so strong!"

I could hear myself scream inside my head. I am not who I used to be. She couldn't accept any of it. She was, in fact, less likely to accept the person I am now than I am.

When we go shopping she buys me things. It's not like I pick out something and ask or expect her to buy it for me. She buys me what she wants. But it seems we never talk about what I want, or anything of significance. Just shit chat.

My brothers never ever talked to me except to acknowledge I was there. No "How are you?" or anything like that. Which I've come to accept is okay, especially since I do not know how I am. I am so not me. Not anymore. It was especially evident the me they knew was gone.

They all drink wine before dinner. Mom was so against that for so many years. I guess she got a note from God that says it's okay. They also act like being gay is so forbidden, the sin so unforgiveable. I wonder what would happen if I ask to talk more with my brothers. I wonder what they would say. Are they so used to having me out of their lives that they prefer it?

Both my brothers had changed their names. Both their new names were on the name tags placed in front of their seat at the Christmas dinner table. I asked Mom why my name change hadn't been honored, although I guess it wasn't that big a deal. I was a little taken aback when she replied, "Because I don't like that name."

"Oh," I replied. I can't believe I actually wanted to come home, back to a living dead place. But Buckley is here, and he is the only one that hasn't left me. The only one I know loves me.

1/11/07 ~

I continue to stay in bed, unless medical transportation comes to take me to a doctor or therapy appointment. I met a couple of people through Cari, and when they would come over on rare occasions it would be either drug-related or they'd steal something from me, probably to buy more drugs. That's it.

1/23/07 ~

I went to Kerry's next door once in a while, checking in on her. This one night she found something on TV for us to watch besides The Dog Whisperer. It's called Dead Like Me. Perfect.

3/22/07 ~

I get this call from Janna. "Skyler," she says, "I've just been made aware of a grant I think you'd be perfect for. Unfortunately the cut-off is in one hour. Can you come by?"

"Well," I told her, "I'll try to fit you into my busy schedule. I'm on my way."

At her office, one of the questions for this study was why I would be a good participant. I said because I was making a map on my way out of hell.

It was an Empowerment Initiative grant to study and help those who got their previous life knocked out from under them get back on their feet. The study part was to understand "the system" better by talking with those who had been in it. They were also studying what was needed when or if a person wants to regain employment after major incidences. The help part was a $5,000 grant to help me accomplish some of the things I wanted to do. Wow!

I wanted to get a decent laptop and art supplies to do art therapy with others.

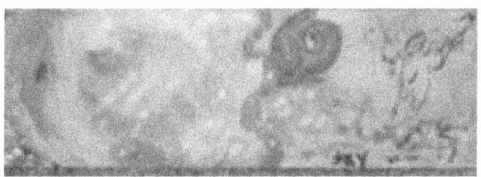

My World Straightened

4/7/07 ~

Someone told me I created Skyler Raye because Sherri Smith could not handle what has gone down and was happening in her life. She said I had told her that, though not exactly in those words. Could she be right? Yes.

4/23/07 ~

My mind spins around so fast I cannot make any sense of it. My pain is the thing that has my attention. My physical and mental and emotional pain is so intertwined that I don't know what hurts most anymore. It could be my bailing arm.

4/30/07 ~

Don't wish for it! Work for it!

Small steps. Do what you are physically capable of. Plan it out. Wise words from a Kaiser nurse after Diana died.

Today is Goals Day with Empowerment Initiative; one of their classes connected with the grant. I can make goals for all this week. Goal 1: I am going to start shutting down earlier in the evening. I'm going to start to pick up good habits. Start with sleeping, and then, with small steps, move on to better eating and exercise. These Empowerment classes are definitely intense. They ask questions like, "What's your primary concern right now?" I answered, "My self care." One thing leads to another. I'm going to start to plan meals at a reasonable time, get some exercise to get back in shape, and get to bed at a decent hour. My goals have to be reasonable, attainable, specific, measurable, and time-dated. A goal without a deadline is nothing more than a dream.

I have a long-term goal of moving to a bigger place with a yard. A couple of short-term goals can be getting all my things together and start doing my artwork again. I will compartmentalize. I will finish one room at a time so there is a place to retreat. I will set boundaries for what is helpful and what is not. Buckley is helpful.

Is it but a dream to achieve my desire to be loved again? How we view the world affects our mind and our mood.

Neiashea—I miss you

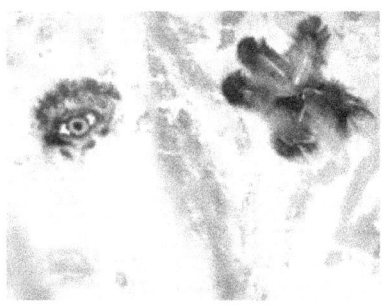

Neiashea

Neiashea . . . Why did you die?

Why is a word I say so much. About so many things. Why did I end up in the place I was (hell) when I met you? I still remember the first time I talked to you. I felt something big inside when our eyes met. I complimented you on the vest you were wearing. And how you dressed in general. Then why did you fall so deeply in love with me? But you died. Why did you die?

5/3/07 ~

Self-soothing. Thoughts, feelings, and actions. If I think I don't deserve something, I need to give myself self-affirmations. If I think I should think of others first, I'll remember the words of advice from flight attendants. Put the mask on yourself first, right? I should get soothing from others—why should I do this for myself? I should be stronger. I shouldn't need this. I have no time for self-soothing. Invalidation vs. self-soothing.

Power for self-soothing comes from within. It comes through vision. Look at flowers. Clean your house. Go to art museums. Look at magazines with good pictures (no, not those kind). Your environment really counts. Sounds. Music is soothing. Humming can be soothing. Smells. Flowers, perfume, candles, fresh air. Taste. Tea. There's always candy or popsicles. Touch is also important. Nice skin creams. Clean sheets. Petting pets. Close your eyes and have a three minute vacation.

I need to be in a better place so I can tell these people here there is hope. I hope for more than just hope. I hope to start a support group. It will be held in the conference room here at Pine Point.

I feel the air go in and out my body, but other than that there is noting alive in me. I feel more dead than alive. I am all but buried.

I have mourned Diana every second of every day since the day I came home from the hospital after she died . . .

9/12/07 ~

Haven't written for a while. Seems like doing meth is the only time I've done anything. I've been expressing my feelings doing all kinds of artwork. I know the holidays are coming. I just want to pretend I'm a bear and hibernate. But I've been hibernating for two and a half years now.

10/1/07 ~

My eyes are searching through so much bad, through so many lost people, wanting to be close to someone. I should give it up. But then I think of the possibility of a happy ending. There is always a chance things could work out.

10/5/07 ~

This is as close to death I could be and still be alive.

Bed of Needles

11/13/07 ~

Buckley and I are the whole famdamily.

I have always wanted one thing more than anything else. As far back as I can remember, the one thing I always asked from God was to have a happy family. I do not know what that feels like. The thing that makes this more painful is I do have a family that is obviously happy. They just don't include me. They don't call, email, or probably even think about me. How can my mother really believe that her reasons for not wanting to be with me are justifiable and I should not have hurt feelings? Well, I do have hurt feelings. Why do my brothers cut me out of their lives?

WINTER 07/08

HIBERNATED

I've been awoken by the different caregivers I've had these last few months. All I ask them to do is take care of my weekly meds and they do my dishes. They come and go. I don't know who they are. Luckily Bub and Scout somehow took over.

3/4/08 ~

It's time to go visit Dr. Saks to check in on me and my meds. I complained that I'd wake up out of a deep sleep and sit up because I couldn't catch my breath. He listened, and my lungs were clear. He sent me home, no major changes.

3/5/08 ~

Dr. Saks called. "I didn't realize your psychiatrist prescribed Lorazepam. You need to come in again so we can change this. You shouldn't be taking both that and methadone. People have died because of this," he warned. At first I was shocked to hear I was on methadone. Was I a heroin addict before? No matter, right now I have to stop taking it.

I would not wish the experience of kicking methadone to my very utmost worst enemy. Not even mean Sybil. Well . . . maybe . . . hmmm. Methadone is a great pain reliever. It's man-made heroin to control and get junkies off the real heroin. Parts of your body actually absorb the drug. So when you withdraw, your joints are affected, and it's like you're having epileptic seizures, on top of feeling like you have the flu, are burning up like on menopause, and can't sleep or eat 'cause you feel like you're on speed. I saw spiders on the walls everywhere. Somebody was twisting my muscles. I was aching, freezing, and then sweating, sometimes all at the same time.

3/24/08 ~

On my 17th day of withdrawal I went to turn on Dead Like Me, but since it was Easter there was some special Easter service programmed from this Living Hope Church in Vancouver, Washington. It got my attention because the pastor looked like my cousin, who had died. At the end they listed a phone number in case you wanted to have someone say a prayer for you. I called it. In between feelings of nausea and writhing and fragmented speech, I said, "I am kicking Methadone and I haven't eaten or slept for seventeen days. Can you please say a prayer for me?" I think even before the nice woman's prayer for me was over I was out. That night I slept like a baby. And all the next day and night.

Maybe this God isn't the same God as mean Sybil's, but it seems like He's pretty good so far. I got a letter congratulating me for being eligible for Section 8 housing. I'm now rich enough to be poor and get assistance with my rent. I am so out of here.

I grabbed the end of the lighted robe, asking for help with doctors, drugs, pain, hopelessness.

3/25/08 ~

I went next door to Kerry's and told her about my calling the church on TV, the prayer, and sleeping. I also told her I was moving. But first, I was headed to the church to get baptized. I asked her if she wanted to go, and she said yes.

After the ordeal of getting Kerry into her wheelchair and then into my car, we were just about on our way when Cari rolled up. After telling her where we were going she said she also wanted to go.

My new birth: I was baptized. After I changed out of my wet clothes I walked out to see Cari getting baptized, and then she and I baptized Kerry. "ONLY GOD!" was on the t-shirts they gave us, and we sang "Jesus Loves Me" all the way home.

4/08 ~

Marie and I looked at tons of possible places for me to move to. It was really discouraging. All of the places were gross. Hideous. Filthy. I've never seen so many disgusting places in my life. Made Pine Point look like a five star joint. But I still wanted out of there. I'd rather live in my truck.

Kerry was also helping. She asked what I was looking for in a home. I said I wanted a yard for Buckley, two bedrooms for stuff, a place for my Mustang, and a fireplace for me. It was also important that it be in Multnomah County so I could keep Kacie my caseworker. She checked the papers for me daily.

6/08 ~

They found it. A place that met my qualifications and I could afford. Marie went in and told the slumlord I would take it before I ever went in. After all, it met my short list of qualifications. Okay then.

Come to find out that I am now two blocks outside the Multnomah County line. I lose Kacie. I also have to find a new caregiver, as it's too far for Bub and Scout. I'm so alone. Even I don't want to be with me.

CHAPTER TWENTY-ONE

IN THE GHETTO

7/4/08 ~

Independence Day!!!

Wow, I am really moving out of here. There is a 28' truck with a hydraulic lift helping me. I can't believe this is happening . . . and I can't believe gas is the highest it's ever been, like almost five dollars a gallon.

I can't believe I am so scared.

I can't believe I still can ACCOMPLISH TASKS . . . no matter what. I am convinced that when I die, like a chicken whose head's chopped off, I will still be able to run around taking care of business. That's kind of how it feels now.

I can't believe there are so many well wishers here. Especially after being so hated when I first moved in. Maybe seven or eight neighbors came to say good-bye. When I first got here I always locked myself out. Then was ignored when waiting at the front door for somebody to let me in. Only one lady, who was nice to me from the beginning, would allow me to go through her first floor apartment to get into the building.

I was the only one here not in a wheelchair. The only time in my life when my dream of being taller than everyone came true.

The Fourth of July. Fireworks, or gun shots, are going off. I know this Independence Day, for me, means moving into the middle of the ghetto.

7/5/08 ~

I'm not in Kansas anymore. Not like any place even I've ever been. The part of society that society doesn't like and wishes didn't exist.

7/24/08 ~

I now live on 183rd, in a low income housing slum. AKA not Pine Point. I brought the Mustang and put it in the garage. I still sleep at Pine Point on Kerry's couch, 'cause I'm scared to stay in the ghetto at night. It sounds like July 4th all the time there.

Joe, his wife, her mom and my mom visited me for a couple of hours.

7/25/08 ~

How many me can you see? The shape of change. Facing faces. My only hope is new growth from my rotten roots.

7/27/08 ~

I'm an island. I believe that islands are created by volcanoes.

I always wanted to be a butterfly because butterflies are free. I know butterflies come from caterpillars. Hmmmmm.

Right now I think this is how I've felt since childhood. Except when I camouflaged myself with this personality bigger than me. I know I am walking not down the road less traveled, but down and through places where there are no paths at all.

So many hurts. God has brought me and kept me through so much. I praise you, Lord, and have to believe that you are there, no matter whether I live or die.

Having to say good-bye to someone I loved and needed. Not getting to enjoy every dance on the kitchen floor. I wasn't going to give up and you promised not to give up. Diana, you left.

Don't give up. I am about to come alive.

8/1/08 ~

Kerry's aid is going on vacation for ten days and she didn't want a substitute caregiver because you don't know who you get. I said I'd do it, though the emptying of the milk jugs of pee she collected from her bags took a lot of gumption. Her bed sore was bad—it was the size of a man's fist from her skin to her hip bone. I saw she was getting sicker by the minute.

My car broke down across the street from Pine Point. I went to the closest service place, looked around, and said, "Hey, I think I used to work here like twenty years ago!" The manager heard my voice, came out and recognized me. He remembered the good job I did when I was there and he gave me a 50% discount!

I walked back to Kerry's and she was semi-conscious. I called 911 and felt awful that I didn't call sooner. The lady who moved next door into my old apartment, Sheila, and Esther, from the second floor, came off the elevator and saw me crying in the hallway. They asked if I wanted to pray, and I said, yes I'll pray to any and all Gods to help save my friend. As they began to pray, Kerry was wheeled out and winked—she was still alive!

Sheila and Esther asked if I wanted to come to church with them. This meant picking them up and taking them there. I said sure, and I'd be happy to pick them up.

8/3/08 ~

Whoops, I slept in till 11:30. I missed church. Damn. Do I call and tell them I won't be taking them to church? They already know that.

8/5/08 ~

When I went to Kerry's I was trying to duck Sheila and Esther and wouldn't you know it, I ran right into them. I apologized for missing church last Sunday, and Esther said, "That's okay, we'll wait for you next Sunday, and if you don't come then, we'll wait for you the next Sunday, and the next and the next." I knew I had to go—I wanted to go.

8/7/08 ~

I sit on the floor of my own apartment. No one thought I would move. Except my best friends at Pine Point, who, without them, I wouldn't be here. Okay, it's the ghetto. But it's my oasis in the ghetto.

I've been unpacking the mishmash of stuff I've picked up along the way, and there's stuff that actually made it from my home on Cora. Funny, I don't know what happened to some major furniture/antiques I once had. But my special rocks, sticks, and plants are mostly all accounted for. Opening boxes I feel an assortment of feelings, like, "Wow, you made it too!" Or, "Whatever happened to ?"

On the floor with my artwork from the past six years. One thing that was definitely a common theme for me are eyes and faces. Now I get it. I need to face all my faces. Like Michael Jackson's song, it starts with "The Man in the Mirror." Who am I? Will, or can, the best me stand up and face me?

Sitting here, with my artwork around me, I see the eyes staring at me. It's oddly crowded all of a sudden. Look how I felt. Oh my God. You had to have carried me because even now I still can't believe all that's happened. I can see the prevalence of anger competing with fear in my 2002 artwork. Scary.

Here I sit.

I finally see—

I need to file—

Dealing with all the things from my life I couldn't handle in turn created another me that escaped from feelings instead of having to feel.

I've gone from my home, to Crown Vista, to homeless, to Brandy's, to the dungeon, to Felony Flats, to the Salmon house, to Pine Point, to the ghetto. Whoa. So many places. So many faces. They're all in my artwork, staring back at me. Eyes at the very least. All probably some part of me. No words can describe the feelings—just my art.

You know, I was once a ward clerk in a mental health facility during college. I wanted to be a psychiatric nurse. Up until I found out I would have to cover all aspects of nursing. I couldn't handle the blood. I'd never have thought that I would one day be a patient instead of an employee.

8/10/08 ~

I picked up Sheila and Esther and we went to their church. I was so fidgety that I only lasted there 15 minutes before I had to leave. It was a small group of 30 or so people meeting in a high school cafeteria.

8/11/08 ~

Marie and I are at the ghetto and I hear her unpacking my wind chimes. I'm outside in the back, about to hose off the green moss from my very off-white fence. I hear this little voice say, "Hey, you got me wet!" Of course I apologized.

"Hey, look at this!" he called to me. I peeked over the fence and saw this scrawny little kid with a crew cut. He squirted me with his hose.

"I'm appalled!" I shouted to him. "I don't even know you!" He laughed.

This scrawny little kid was my neighbor Roxy's son, Jessie. He's seven.

8/20/08 ~

I finally took off the ring Diana gave me. Like the one she made for herself. Now I have both hers and mine. What do I do with them? File away—How? I feel like she gave up. But then I tell myself I really do not know what happened. It could have been an accident. Maybe it was the time God planned to take her.

I've always been told that it was a sin to kill yourself, so if you did you would go to hell. So I asked Pastor Noah at my new church if suicide was a sure ticket to hell. He said God will not send sick people to hell. And they have to be very mentally ill to do that.

So here I sit in my yard, watching low-flying planes come in for landing. For some reason this helps me file things away. Flying filing meditation, I guess.

9/6/08 ~

I got another letter threatening me that I'd lose my benefits if I didn't get another caregiver.

9/8/08 ~

Roxy came over and had to borrow my bathroom. I was re-reading the benefits letter, when she came out. I told her about the problem, and she said she knew a caregiver, Kimberly, and would call her right away. With my phone, she did. About an hour later, as I was lying on my couch, a regular habit, there was a knock on the door. It was Roxy and Kimberly, who was approximately 5'10 with long hair and fingernails longer than I'd ever seen. I wondered what she could possibly do to help without breaking a nail. At this time in my life I didn't care about much, and I was afraid not to agree with Roxy, so I hired her there and then.

The first time she came over as my caregiver I remember saying she didn't have to work much, just change the sheets on my bed weekly. I noticed that Roxy was always interested when she saw Kimberly leave. It finally dawned on me why Roxy was so interested—she was getting her drugs from Kimberly as a "finder's fee" for me. I finally asked if Kimberly could get me some drugs also. So, my new caregiver became my meth-giver. Every week Kimberly would leave me a nice chard and I became a regular user. Now remember, I was also becoming a regular church-goer, with Sheila and Esther, so the two nicely intertwined. I'd save some of the methamphetamines to get me up Sunday morning to make it to church. Once there, I'd keep my head to the ground so I could pretty much duck everybody.

Kerry has been put in an old folks home temporarily. I visit as much as possible.

9/11/08 ~

5:00 a.m.

Bright spot in the ghetto. I found out that Jessie isn't really Roxy's son. He's her sister's son. The state took Jessie away from her. I think it's a really sad situation, because Roxy's lifestyle isn't what I'd call a good example for Jessie.

The world, the torture.

I don't deserve and am unworthy of God. Oh. I can't believe I said such an awful thing.

I was talking to a different neighbor Jessie, a grown up who'd come by now and then. He compared time with me to a mind expanding experience on LSD or something. Without the hallucinations.

9/23/08 ~

I am so aware of the stinking awfulness that happens every second of every day.

9/27/08 ~

I was sleeping on my couch. Yes, again. All of a sudden I woke up to find big Jessie kissing and smelling and rubbing my feet. He's lucky I didn't kill him right then. "What the fuck are you doing?" I shouted. "Get out of here!"

He tried to apologize. "I know I have a little foot fetish," he lamely explained. I was done with him.

10/1/08 ~

You are a child raised by concrete walls. That means you spend a lot of time in your head. I guess if that is all you know I cannot blame you for your thoughts.

10/2/08 ~

So much has happened. My house is looking so much better. It's been pleasant to spend time alone working and creating. Me, this place I'm in, emotions and whatever. All this combined.

10/6/08 ~

The faintest light along the dark road to recovery came from art therapy. The suggestion was that I show with art how I am. I can only color what I'm feeling. The first thing I would do when I heard the task was color small circles within circles black. It made sense. I even switched from smoking Marlboro lights to cloves called "Black" when I was in crazy school. Hmmm . . . did I graduate?

I would feel myself fall into the darkness of this color as my despair grew bigger and bigger. I noticed it without hesitation: the invitation of death. Never did I move away from the depth of that blackness, but rather I became death's neighbor. I guess I kept from being completely submerged because I would not give up bailing.

Soon I felt I used the black crayon long enough and set my eye on the dark purple. Then came orange and yellow. I remodeled my place next to death with more and more colors and soon there were millions of pinholes of light. Believe me when I tell you, from my experience, just one pinhole can keep you alive. Grasp onto it.

Be brave. Use every color there is and then color over again. You can color your world happy.

10/12/08 ~

2:30 a.m.

I can't fail unless I quit. Grasping to hold on to now, you know, make it my present, while continuing to search for a future that will make a present I will love.

Taking care of Kerry Grant was unlike anything I have ever done. It really shows me the growth I have accomplished since moving from Pine Point.

I kicked methadone. Now that is something I never thought I'd say. I think it was "Pain Management" that prescribed that ugly drug to me. I now know that if something is making the pain go and stay away, it must be killing another part of the body.

Words. The words in songs. Have you ever felt like the hit song you hear is written for you at a particular time in your life? Steve Winwood's "Roll With It Baby" was the theme song for my business. I heard he wrote it for his wife, who was pregnant. Plant Pleasers was my baby that grew and soon became the identity by which I was known. It defined what I did and who I was.

I know I am a person that is honest. Tired maybe, even burnt out sometimes. But in the pile of ashes I hear that song and something beautiful, something good comes out. He understood.

All I have to offer is brokenness and strife. Please make something beautiful of my life.

I started with my living room. I rearranged it and am way more settled.

I decided my last chapter would be not about coming back but going forward. How far back am I? I know now the biggest things missing were self-worth, security, and confidence. Things that one should have, knowing God made and loves us.

I was very good-looking and had the means to spoil a partner. But I always wondered if anyone, with the exception of few, wanted to be with "me" just for me.

Well, maybe it turns out it wasn't just my looks or money. There was Diana.

Diana.

Diana told me she was abused by her father and her mother was mentally ill. So her mother sent her off instead of her husband. All I know is the situation was anything but your everyday family.

I heard Diana say, more than once, her plan was to wait until her daughter graduated high school and then leave her husband. Diana was invited to move back with her parents after she left Richard. They gave her the master bedroom with a bathroom, and she decorated it, especially the bathroom. She took on these projects with enthusiasm and well thought out decisions. Her bathroom was called the "India" bathroom. It was beautiful. It reflected her.

Although Diana was so quiet and shy and innocent, she was very much the instigator in our relationship. She made the first, second and all the moves. I noticed her clothes first, and then her pain. Then I noticed her love of my brutal being.

I did try to control my tone so her feelings didn't get hurt. My biggest "bitch" about her was when she lied about putting herself in a potentially bad situation with her dad or husband. She promised she wouldn't, but she did.

I couldn't let it go, and when I finally did, and told her so, she wasn't really convinced.

Okay—crazy school isn't the best place to meet and start a relationship with anyone. But that's what happened. She loved me. She took care of me. And I learned more things from her life after she died than I can comprehend.

I'm very unhappy with what's happening, or actually not happening, in my life. In bed now, off the couch, but doing much the same—not doing much. I am only taking two-thirds of the Oxycontin prescribed.

Let's look around the hood. There's my neighbor Jen, who just left her husband. I give her rides sometimes. She is a biker chick who is hard of hearing. There's Roxy and Jessie. She is mostly a walking chemical. Big

Jessie moved out, thank goodness. But most of the time I am all alone with Buckley and the chatterbox I call T.V.

Pine Point

I really believed that if, or when, I left there I would never look back.

Things that come to mind when I think about that place:

Sirens

Smell of death coming from the crematory/funeral home

Burning chimney

Lack of natural beauty

Traffic day and night Gun shots

Shouting Ambulances

Medical transportation vans

The smell as I walked in the main door to the elevator—kind of a cross between an elementary school cafeteria, an old folks home, a hospital, and the stairwells at downtown parking garages where homeless people relieve themselves

It's now a little after 5 a.m. I am going to pick up Esther and Sheila and go to church with them. I was supposed to go last Sunday but didn't make it. Esther said she'd keep waiting for me to show up. I didn't know her that well, so I was surprised when she told me I was missed at ol' Pine Needles. It meant a lot.

10/16/08 ~

I haven't slept, but it was okay. I wasn't getting "spun" (high) alone or with anyone. I accomplished a lot as far as getting unpacked and organized. I'm SO glad to have the plants I still have. They really do make me feel so much better. I love them.

Tammy is in my guest bedroom. Haven't seen her in a very long time. It's funny, because I was looking everywhere for her phone number.

Living here in the ghetto must be what people feel like when they visit a foreign country. They stick out. I stick out here. I've never lived any place like it. Despite this, I'm starting to feel settled. This is the first time I feel settled anywhere since I lost my house so many years ago.

I've been single these last three years. Except for that really brief time at Pine Point when I tried dating an old ex. Her drinking made her abusive, and I've seen that movie before. This is another first for the record book. I was always either dating or been with someone. I have always appreciated the great way sex can be a stress reliever. To have someone that close. And then drifting off into a much needed sleep, tangled around one another. There were people who seemed to like me even after I got hurt, and when I was in crazy school. Diana and I walked out of hell together.

Since moving here I haven't taken any steps toward meeting anyone. I keep to myself, and Buckley of course, most of the time. I really wonder what is in store for me. Anything great? Very good? Not bad? Nothing. Death.

PETE DAD BENSON PAMELA

PLANT PLEASERS INC.

DIANA

SHERRI

10/24/08 ~

My plan is to die on December 31, 2008. I don't want to die, but more than that I can't live like this any more. My new caregiver is a big meth dealer. I would save some of it so I could be up for church.

One Sunday at church it really hit me: I had to get high to find God. So I was crying, thinking it all seemed too far, impossible, and, if I did "get it," I figured I'd lose it anyway. I was about to leave early, when a very special lady named Hope came up to me. I looked at her, filled with anguish. I said, "You have no idea how many drugs it took to get me here."

Hope smiled and said, "God doesn't care about your drugs near as much as He cares about having a relationship with you." I just stood there, mouth open, head tilted a bit like a dog who hears a new sound. This was something I never thought I'd hear in church. Kindly, Hope looked into my eyes and said, "You just need more truth." Now, I had honestly felt I had had enough truth. The truths in my life left me raw. Maybe I needed different truths. This was a whole new God for sure.

11/4/08 ~

To Be Alive

Living isn't being full of life. Being alive doesn't mean one is lively. Living should mean growing—feeling the things that affect you. Sometimes being alive is feeling the presence of death. Acknowledging what is.

There are times when I feel too full of the death of life in me. Still, somehow I am still breathing, therefore, I'm alive. Life must be a process.

Without prior planning, or picking who or how it comes, I am more uncertain about life. I speak, I think . . . without spark. Am I detached so much from life yet more attached to who I am while detaching I become attached to being detached?

Same day

Way later

I feel wrapped up in those I loved so much who are gone. I can't let go. They are/were so important. How can I be, or go on, when the ones that were my "everyday people"—the ones who really knew me—are dead?

Then there are those who just decided not to be in my life. Oh, but only after they stomped my heart into the ground.

How did I end up so alone? I feel closer to those that are dead than anyone alive. Now I'm afraid to try again. It's like there's a war going on inside me.

My character, work ethic, optimism, are fighting against my completely broken heart and spirit.

11/8/08 ~

Today I went to church with Esther and Sheila. It's called Grace Foursquare. I had gone to this church over ten years ago when one of my very first Plant Pleaser customers invited me. It's funny that Esther is good friends with her. Anyway, after today the church will no longer be affiliated with Foursquare. The new name is City of Refuge. I visited a place on the Big Island of Hawaii, a very special place, called the City of Refuge. I loved it there. I believe this is my new church. It felt right. But, really, what do I know about right?

I do know time is ticking. I told Janna and Bub that my life has got to be so much better by December 31st or I will end it. I've moved, and I believe I've grown, but not enough. Esther testified to the fact that she is not the angry, sad person she was when she first came to this church. Good for her. I want that too, but don't know if I can make it there. I do know I am SO TIRED OF BAILING.

At the end of the service Pastor John asked if anyone wanted to come up and exchange any of their junk for God's good stuff. I went forward and when asked if I wanted to have a personal relationship with God, I answered "Well, what do I have to do?" He just simply said, "Be yourself," and I almost laughed, thinking about everything that comes along with being me. But I agreed, as I knew although I believed in God and, as you know, often wrote to Him in my journal, I didn't believe I would walk the walk as a "Christian" should. My experience with Christianity was as a child through my teen-age years. I believe the church I went to or 99% of all churches and people calling themselves Christians have not done God any favors in representing Him or His character. Back then the sermons were more likely than not very loud and filled with cries like: "Get saved or burn in hell for eternity." Cheery messages like that.

It was the Christian college I attended where I found my first gay relationship. This girl pursued me until I finally gave in, although I fought with feelings of guilt and shame. That was until I really started to love this girl. I remember my family more or less made me choose between them and her, as she was not allowed to come home with me. I pretty much stopped going home. About four years later, she faced something similar from her family. Only they made her choose between me and a very large inheritance. She told me she was leaving me for God. I was heart-broken plus mad that she brought me into the gay world and was leaving me there. Alone.

11/11/08 ~

Okay—

So it's time to start from the beginning and put all this together. Just in time for my awakening, or death. I will not stay like this.

I guess I believed somewhere inside I could get it together before the time limit I set for myself. OMG, what if I am wrong and December 31st is the day I say goodbye to life? Hopefully my farewell will really be a hello to a fulfilled life.

11/30/08 ~

I have always loved butterflies—ever since I was a young child. I found out that butterflies can fly only because they spend weeks strengthening their muscles, fighting to get out of their cocoon.

I must be in a cocoon. Only dreaming of flying.

12/5/08 ~

The top of the bottom. The ghetto. So here I am. July 4th was my last night as a resident of Pins & Needles, aka Pine Point. I swear, there were a couple of times during my stay there that the crematorium was cranked up too high or something and blew up. I watched the guy on the roof putting the top back on the chimney while talking to someone on the opposite side of the building. "Yeah, ya gotta be sure and remind everyone not to open that door! Especially with someone that big in there. Too many gases."

I am realizing and starting to think I could grasp the entirety of what is really happening. The spirit of God is. The letter "i" is the least noticeable letter in the name of His book: The Bible.

So it's time for this story to end. The best way, I guess, would be to start all over. But do I want to?

12/17/08 ~

Jessie told me today he had been looking everywhere for me. No one has looked for me for so long. He looked in my garage. Shit. I can't bear the thought of my best little buddy finding me and Buck dead.

God, if you are there, then send me a friend. Don't come yourself or you'll wig me out. So if you are there, send someone. A friend. I need to believe there are people left in this world that have the qualities of being a true friend.

My phone rings. It's Grace Richardson, one of the pastors at the City of Refuge. She simply asked, "Skye, would you like a friend to talk to about your new relationship with God?"

"Yyyy . . . eeesss," I stammered with difficulty. Was that more than a coincidence???

12/29/08 ~

I feel so lonely. It's not so much that I'm anti-social. Lots of time I think it's good for me to feel. Thinking of people in my life acting like flying broken glass which has torn me to pieces. Not just that, but some of them took away pieces of me. Pieces of the puzzle that is me.

For Christmas I got a carnival-like glass candy dish from a lady that lives a few doors down. I love it. She was drunk. I had to ask her husband to get her out. That was how I spent Christmas eve.

I got a Christmas card from Diana's parents and one from Esther and other friends from Pine Point. Marie made me a sweet little bird cage. Mom gave me money and a phone card. Jessie and Roxy came over for gifts. All I got from Roxy was a bad attitude, rude behavior, and a lot of negative talk. Jessie gave me smiles. That was the best.

Sometimes days go by and few words leave my mouth. Most of them go to Buckley. There is no human input. I'm sad that people don't want to hang with me. I spend the day in a cold, quiet place. Alone.

12/31/08 ~

Janna was aware of my plan. She also knew I wanted to see Kerry but didn't because she was in the same hospital Diana died in. So she suggested we go together. It is amazingly great to have such a good therapist who really cares whether I live or die. I believe in order to relate with the pain of others, one has to have lived through it themselves. I think that is why Janna is so good at her job. I remember when I first started going to see her, right after Diana died, I did not want to talk. She told me she didn't think I liked "feeling" so much. At first all I wanted to do is artwork while I was there. She kept all my art the entire five years I saw her. Of course Buckley was with me, sleeping on the couch in her office. The first and largest picture I drew was of Buckley.

After we saw Kerry, before Janna and I went our separate ways, she wished me a happy birthday and made me promise if I decided to end my life that night I would call her first. We made that deal when I first started therapy with her. I will always be honest with her as long as she promised not to put me back in the hospital. Somehow she knew I would keep my promise, and I knew she would keep hers.

When I got home I actually had some messages on my answering machine. A couple of people from City of Refuge called, wishing me a happy birthday and inviting me to a New Year's Eve party they were having in Battle Ground, Washington. Esther's message was I had to come because Hope made me a birthday cake. Someone else called from City of Refuge and said the birthday cake was a carrot cake . . . yummmmmm . . . that settles it. I am going to the party. Battle Ground instead of the grave yard.

Everyone in the ghetto was busy trying to get drugs. This was not much different than any other day actually.

This was supposed to be the day my last day.

1/09/09 ~

> I go to the store for food
> " " " " therapist for therapy
> " " " " bed for sleep
> " take pills so not to go too low
> " take pills so not to go too high
> Drugs wake me up
> Drugs make me sleep
> I'm: tired, fed up, sick, angry
> So many things to deal with
> How can I when I don't have a full deck to use?
> How can I have a winning hand?
> Not connected to Life!
> Don't stop my insanity unless it is replaced with life and love
> Unplugged to Life
> (the good part)

1/17/09 ~

All I have is the black heart of life. That is, except for my little friend Jessie. When his mom will allow him to talk to me. Usually when she wants a cig or something and I give it to her, then Jessie and I can hang out.

It snowed a lot, and we liked taking Buck to walk in it. Jessie loves when I bring my walkie talkies. I asked him what his handle was, and he told me, "John Bond, James Bond's secret good brother." I asked him what my handle is. He answered, without hesitation, "Straight arrow." Which is funny since I remember a while back I did some art and named it "broken arrow." This little guy is truly my friend. I'm not sure I'd be alive if it weren't for him. My plan was to sit in my Mustang in the garage and turn on the motor. Attached to the tailpipe was a hose—the other end was inside the car. I know this undoubtedly would have caused him more pain, and I started rethinking my plan.

Help me make what is broken dead in the dark.

1/22/09 ~

Facing faces. I have found through my many pieces of artwork (all have faces or the very least eyes) that they are all a part of me, or how I saw me.

Hurt, anger, bewilderment, destitute, lonely, sad—all of which I needed to deal with to have a full life and be a whole person.

2/20/09 ~

I read a book that was Diana's tonight. It was about a woman planning her death.

I'm angry she left me alone. She knew she was sick and that I was broken.

In spirit, heart, mind and body.

Why?

3/4/09 ~

Grace comes over every Tuesday. We started a class—renewing my mind and spirit.

I'm thinking it was only last year when I was dead girl walking. On methadone, lots of it, and so many other drugs. The doctors did a better job making me a drug addict than I even did. Living at Pine Point then . . . Oh God, thanks for so many blessings. There are many with less.

As I made a fire tonight I was thinking how wild it is. Fire burns are so painful. Satan lives in Hell, sinners will burn in Hell, all in agonizing pain. But then again, sitting by the fire warms us, which, in my humble opinion, is way better then being cold. Fire cooks our food, sterilizes our water—face it—fire is good and necessary for our livelihood. Like in the movie Castaway with Tom Hanks (love you, Tom). I bet it gets old Satan's goat that God made us and the universe we live in.

Isn't it horrible that evil exists? But, let's face it: the world we live in is more spiritual than anything. Good stuff makes more good stuff, as bad stuff makes more bad stuff.

Take my neighbor. The aunt who fosters the son of her sister since birth. He is my best friend here. Jessie turned eight yesterday. His birth mother didn't take him because she was an alcoholic drug addict and so bad off that the state said she shouldn't have kids. It's so hard to believe Jessie's birth mother is worse then Roxy. She is interested in nothing but herself and getting high. She's either trying to get drugs or doing drugs. She is the worst mother I have personally ever encountered. She beats him, yells like a big, mean, loud, rude, ruthless, loud, very loud, degrading, very loud bully.

Roxy says she believes only in the universe and herself and that there is no God. She's right. There is no God in her life. At least not the God I know. I'm pretty sure her God is drugs.

4/26/09 ~

City of Refuge

Water baptism—exchange your identity for Christ's identity.

If you don't like the fruit, the problem lies within the roots.

Baptism is more than what we think.

Competition and comparison = bitterness

5/1/09 ~

It's a long way down.

5/9/09 ~

Examine your life.

I need to continue allowing the Holy Spirit in all areas of my life.

6/9/09 ~

The way we think is the way we act. Learn new words. Acquire good vocabulary.

from drifting

to walking

from hating

to loving

from apathy

to caring

from wandering to

having direction

from running

to resting

from illusions

to reality

from eyes on me

to eyes on God

from outside

to inside

from me

to God

6/22/09 ~

I have looked with open eyes at my present address and caregiver. I decided a change, or at least my full attention to these issues, is necessary.

6/26/09 ~

Cari continues to come and go. She is constantly acting like my best friend . . . at first anyway. Last time she was here she broke my new drivel tool, and then, no matter how much I begged her to stop, she was yelling at me! I ended up in my room with my dresser in front of my door and strategically placed myself under my bed. I stayed there until I fell asleep.

The next day Janna called me, wondering why I didn't show for my appointment again. When I told her I was under my bed she came over. I told her about Kimberly (my not very good caregiver) and her side profession. She called Larry, my new caseworker and scheduled an appointment so I could get a new caregiver.

I like Kimberly, but I knew I would never stop doing meth with her as my caregiver. Kerry's caregiver, Jane, comes and visits me sometimes. She asked if I wanted her to replace Kimberly. Done.

Jane told me I could move out of the ghetto to a beautiful home and yard with her son. But first there was a ton of work to do cleaning and painting it. Hmmmm . . .

7/10/09 ~

Living here in the ghetto has taught me some hugely important lessons about having good or safe boundaries.

I was always a people person, pretty comfortable talking to anyone. I remember, way back, talking with some friends about naming my new business. Someone called me a people pleaser. My response was, "No, I'm a plant pleaser." Thus Plant Pleasers was born. But inside I knew what that person said had truth to it. I never liked being alone, with the exception of when I worked in my yard. Now I've had years of being alone. I choose being alone over being in bad relationships. Since Diana died.

There is so much pain and need and generally dark people here. I got myself into "situations" trying to be a good person that didn't pay off. Instead I felt pretty small and very used.

Roxy was a key player in the transformation of my heart, mind, and soul. Because Jessie, my best friend there, had to live with her, I tried to keep the peace. Even though many times I was just flat angry at her for the way she treated Jessie. Like when she figured out I liked spending time with Jessie and he with me, then wouldn't let him talk to me. This would end when she wanted something and sent him over to get it. There were times I had to call the cops when she was out of control and throwing large objects around. Being a cop-caller (which she yelled out loud at me when they came) didn't win me any brownie points here. I can never trust her, but I still am her friend. And I hope and pray she will know the truth I've found.

Through all these hard lessons, Jessie and I remain strong in our friendship.

I believe this little guy helped save my life.

7/12/09 ~

These last six months I've experienced a fresh taste of life with God. It's so good. I believe I got out of Pine Point because God heard my cries.

Nobody has inquired about what has been and is happening with me and my life. Except Cari, who leaves me lots of phone messages. Most of them say she's desperate and to please call. I called her back finally. She was jonesing to get high. I told her the truth. I had some, did some, and got rid of what I had. For today is the first day of a life free of street drugs. Forever.

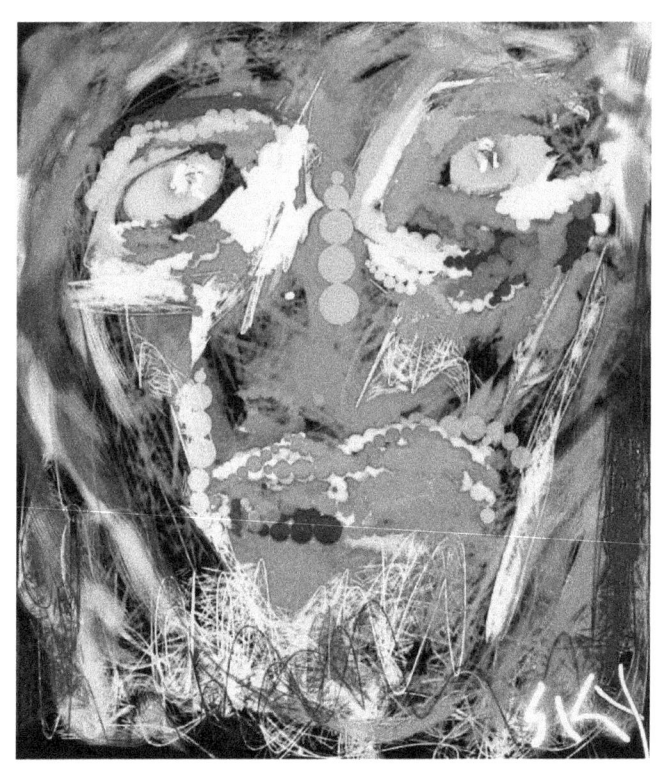

CHAPTER TWENTY-TWO
MY PAST, PRESENT AND FUTURE COLLIDE

8/09 ~

Spent a LOT of time working on and moving to Jane's son Trevor's home. I really should have thought more about Jane and the way she cares for Kerry before I agreed to have her as my caregiver. I did learn something new about her: she loves, more than anything, to go shopping. Especially with other people's money.

9/9/09 ~

The Finger of God
Live heart felt—not head first.
Let the Spirit FLOW!
Think with my head
Ponder with my heart.

10/19/09 ~

I have my service plan from the State of Oregon Department of Human Services for Seniors and People with Disabilities (that last one would be me). I had my assessment 9/29. It's really hard for me to read it, knowing it's about me. It says I need full assist from my caregiver in the following areas:

Adaptation Awareness Breakfast Dinner Housekeeping

Judgment Laundry Lunch Medication management

Memory Orientation Shopping Transportation

Sad, huh?

10/25/09 ~

City of Refuge—Good Morning!

God created my emotions. He is going to give me back the emotions I should have. Please God, lead me, guide me, fill me. I want to join my everything with your everything.

11/1/09 ~

The Jane and Trevor I was associating with are not the same Jane and Trevor that exist now. She tries to come across like the mother in Leave it to Beaver, but what I've seen is as far from the image of a mother as one could be. Which shows in her son, another alcoholic acting, let's say, very inappropriately to me.

I need to raise money to move so I am selling some of my things.

11/7/09 ~

I can't believe that I am still saying, "I can't believe how horribly I'm being treated." You'd think it would stop. Now it's my caregiver and her son, whose home I "live" in.

I'm SOOOOOO unhappy—and angry too—so don't get used to me taking your mean words and actions. I will not allow you to get away with it. Not this time.

I don't know how, but I will stand up for myself and guard myself and things from you. No matter how many times you can call the cops on me saying I threatened to kill you and your family and then me. Oh no. Fortunately the cops believed me and not you and Trevor.

11/11/09 ~

Great news! Yesterday, while on my way to Grace and Noah's for lunch, I saw this beautiful place for rent. They came with me today to look at the place, and we actually got to talk to the landlord.

TO: Potential New Landlord,

It was indeed a pleasure meeting you. I believe in my heart it was a divine appointment. I gained hope, if nothing else, that there are places out there where I could settle and be very content.

There are some things I would like for you to take in consideration concerning your decision to rent to me.

I have not been late on my rent ever. Since there are unusual circumstances at my present residence, I have no idea what you would hear from my landlord, Trevor.

I also paid my rent on time at the address on 183rd, where I rented prior to moving here, though I don't know what my landlord there would say as I am taking him to small claims for the return of my deposit. I paid a deposit of $799 with the promise of $400 returned. I took pictures of the place before I moved out. It was a lot better than when I moved in, as I painted and shampooed the carpet.

So what I was hoping for from you is the opportunity to show you my bank statements and/or cancelled checks proving my on-time rent payments. Before moving to 183rd I lived in an apartment building for handicapped people. It was called Pine Point, at 12025 SE Pine, #301, Portland OR 97232.

I understand it is important for you to know and believe you are renting to a credible person. Renting to me is more complicated. But I have faith that if you take the time to check my history and deal with Housing, I know you will be renting to someone who will care about and enjoy living in your rental.

11/15/09 ~

I get up, even feel good at times. But then I look around at the amount of work needed to get my stuff together. Again. I cannot wait to have a home where I will be able to have my things out of boxes and be settled. Did I mention that beside all the stuff stolen out from under my nose at the ghetto, my garage was broken into? What wasn't stolen was either damaged or completely broken. The car cover for my '89 Ford Mustang was thrown off and looked and smelled like a lot of cats lived in it. I bought the car on the ninth anniversary of my business. I always wanted a convertible, and this one was better than I hoped for. Then to have bankruptcy court let me keep it was awesome.

I just overheard Jane and Trevor talking about me. They were laughing at how easily I am tricked. And how they thought of me as their stupid, clumsy Cinderella. Okay, they didn't call me Cinderella, but what they did call me I would rather not write down. I hate it here as much as Pine Point, only for different reasons. I would much rather have stayed at the ghetto.

I don't understand how so many caregivers are in it for what they can take, and not for the giving care part. I've only had a couple that actually did their job. Kimberly was always on time and did the things I asked her to do. I really wish she didn't have that other side job.

11/16/09 ~

I am good at using my imagination from my landscape design work. I need to picture things in my mind. I need to have some deliverance.

How have I been using the eyes of my heart?

You know, God, your spirit and mine have been doing this for a long time. All good and true things come from God.

You wonder why you believed I was here or with you more times. Did you see a miracle out in the darkness? Because that is where the real need is.

Remember the darkest times. Then, instead of taking the road of destruction, I was drawn to nature, my dog, plants, and I remember all the good emotions. I'm so glad I have your attention now! Thank you, Lord.

11/17/09 ~

Jane and Trevor,

I decided to write a letter to both of you, as you'll share what I say anyway.

This is how I feel—you are NOT the same people I knew before and right after moving here.

I am the same! I try my best. It was bad enough reading the things I need help with from Aging and Disability Services, it didn't help adding the attitude both of you have after overhearing, more than once, the two of you talking about me.

I am ashamed of you Jane, you know my history. Morally, how could you bring me into a place and refuse to help me? Taking advantage of me so Trevor can keep the house and spending my money to fix this house.

Since I didn't get the total dollar amount I thought I would have from the insurance company, or couldn't do as much physically, not only did you not care about me or my life, but you showed me a very mean spirited side of you. Your words to me and the words I heard you both use when speaking about me were so far from what should come out of the mouth of a person getting paid to give care. Did you think the qualifications to be a caregiver are to be a two-faced uncaring person? In the job description you were given it states that you were supposed to help me make good and sensible judgment calls.

When I asked if you could look me in the eyes and tell me you felt no shame or remorse—and you did—it really hit me hard. It showed just how great you can pretend to act caring when you have an agenda or plan to get something you want.

It was wrong to take me shopping—allowing me to think you were doing good things for me—when really you were just using me and my money to buy stuff for your son's and your house. IF I was asked what I wanted, just as quickly you'd shrug them off.

I asked for receipts for the things you said I owed you. You never made any effort to go over anything with me. You were paid more money than I actually owed. And I willingly spent money for you, your son and your house.

I can't wait to move out of here and into my beautiful new place. I do not like it and never have felt like it was my home.

So believe me, I feel good about myself and know I am moving out into a better place. You will have to live with yourself.

THANKSGIVING ~

Like most holidays, Buck and I are alone. We slept, watched TV, and looked out the window at the pouring rain.

12/5/09 ~

I'm at my beautiful new place! My new caregiver, Greta, is someone recommended to me by a girl at church. I had taken a bad fall on my head, and was pretty out of it and not much help moving. Greta said not to worry, she'd take care of everything. And she did; only not everything got taken here. I woke up a few days later to find her and her son, who looks like some gang member, camping in my living room. And they were smoking the white stuff that makes the blue smoke. CRAP.

Doing the right thing is a lot harder than not. No more loss. I have the best ahead of me. It has to be . . .

1/7/10 ~

Today I told Greta I would not allow her son to continue living here, AND the guy I caught cooking meth in my kitchen last night is also not welcome. Before I could even finish, she went off on me like Mt. St. Helens. I just stood there while she yelled things like "I can take you down . . ." and "I know people who will kill you," etc. Her son was even trying to calm her down but couldn't.

My response was quiet and to the point: "That's fine; you will be doing me a favor. Would you like me to sign my car over to you first?"

I went into my bedroom and put on a CD I got from Grace. I started another conversation with God. This time I prayed for Him to come down and help me. I honestly felt the strong power and presence of God. I danced in delight while thanking Him for being faithful.

1/8/10 ~

I slept really well. I woke to find Greta & company getting their things together. Thank goodness they finally left! I believe God will help me if I ask. I still feel bad. Lonely and confused about what to do. If the person who referred Greta to me knew what she was really like, maybe this would not have happened. But I know better than to try and understand the past, especially when I have so much to do in the present.

Grace called, and I told her what happened. She sent Noah over to change my locks, just in case. I felt much better.

1/17/10 ~

Greta called and asked to be taken back as my caregiver. I declined her request.

2/20/10 ~

While Greta and her son were now among many on my list of people that needed to get out and stay out of my life, her other son, John Wayne, who I met a couple of times, was different. John came over with his best friend, Bruce Lee, today. Both these guys were young, I'd guess around 18-20, and seemed to have both a heart and conscience. They were also good at Rock Band on the Wii. We played this together often, and, I have to say, I am pretty good on the guitar.

John and Bruce asked what they could do to help me after I shared some of my experiences with them. At first I hesitated, as I'd been tricked pretty easily in the past and this was a habit I wanted to break. But they wound up helping me move a lot of furniture and boxes up and down the stairs. They made me laugh, and did A LOT of work around here.

I learned about John's childhood, which was pretty rough. He endured the consequences of his mother's poor and illegal choices his entire life. He renewed my belief that no matter how bad a person may be treated growing up, he or she can still be a good, honest asset to those around them and the world. He reminded me so much of Jessie. I hope Jessie can grow up to be as nice a person as John is. So many people blame or justify their bad actions toward those around them on lousy circumstances from their past. This is nothing more than a piss-poor excuse.

2/27/10 ~

After Greta, another person I thought was my friend became my caregiver. I haven't mentioned him because I hardly ever saw him. The person that did come over a few times a week to check on me was Grace. So the guy getting paid to be my caregiver said he'd pay Grace for the time she was doing his job. Then guess what? He disappeared for good.

Thankfully, Grace agreed to be my umpteenth caregiver. She cooks good stuff and leaves it in my refrigerator. We also talk about God.

3/6/10 ~

Grace took me to the DMV many times so I could replace my lost license, but I never seemed to have the right paperwork. Changing my name complicated matters a bit. We had to go downtown to the building of vital statistics to get a copy of my birth certificate or something. While waiting my turn, I saw someone that looked familiar. It turned out to be my fifth grade teacher from Kennewick, Washington! I will never forget her, as she was one person in my life (at that time) who gave me the positive attention and encouragement I needed. Not only did she remember me, but she told me I gave her a plant when I graduated elementary school. I told her how important plants turned out to be in my life. Thank God for good teachers.

3/14/10 ~

I have been sleeping quite a bit. I am having a lot of dental issues. My face was so swollen I was having a hard time breathing and ended up in the ol' ER again. So it looks like I will be seeing the dentist way too much this year.

I cannot say all my days have been good. But I can say all of my days are not bad.

Yesterday Marie came over and we walked up to where my street ends. There a path starts into a wonderful nature park that seems a million miles from any city. We collected moss for me to use in hanging flower baskets. As we were getting ready to go home, right in front of us appeared at least four or five deer. I was in awe. I loved seeing them, especially so close to my home.

This morning, when I let Buckley out, I saw a bunny sitting in the middle of my huge yard. Then I noticed new growth in my potted plants. Thinking about the deer and all this, I felt so amazed.

Then I remembered the deal I made with Grace a year ago. She made me promise not tot kill myself for a year, and said by then I'd see things differently. IT HAD COME TRUE!

4/12/10 ~

The huge pile of rubble I am standing on is what God will use to build my new life. All I have to do is unpack.

5/8/10 ~

2:00 a.m.

I spend most of my time alone. My spirit is on a rollercoaster. I love the God of my salvation and know that I am so weak. But through all my moods, bad choices, and situations, both good and bad, I will always in my heart want to do what honors God. I am thankful for the times I do feel good, but either way, every day of my life, I choose God.

5/11/10 ~

I actually feel pretty good today. Maybe it will be my first day I am feeling and doing a, hmmmm, six or a seven. I don't believe I have ever been feeling and doing the same. It is an absolutely beautiful day. Buckley is taking a nap. My windows and door are wide open. I love looking outside. Still to this day, I am so amazed when I look around where I live. It is so far from where I was a year ago.

I went to my back bedroom and was on my knees trying to put on some good God music when I hear something wildly strange above my head. Sounds curious, huh?

But first, let me tell you a short story. Many moons ago, I was in my office talking on the phone to Candy as we did almost every day. My window was open to the adjacent greenhouse I built. I recently found out Dad was diagnosed with lung cancer, and Benson just turned 16. I noticed a bird was in the greenhouse, and told Candy it seemed like it was heading for my office. Candy yelled, "Quick! Close the window! If the bird gets in someone will die!" I was used to her believing in superstitions, and recalled some predictions she made that came true.

"No kidding?" I replied. Just in case, I got up to close the window, but before I closed it the bird got in. And it wasn't too long before there were deaths near and dear.

As you probably figured out, the noise I heard was indeed a bird flying above my head in my bedroom. Without thinking, I grabbed my cell phone and ran outside. Frantically, I called Grace. "There's a bird in my house! Someone is going to die!" Grace did what she often did, she laughed at me. I had no idea I really believed this until that moment. It makes me realize how important it is to be careful what we allow into our heads.

"Why don't you go back in and ask God if he is trying to tell you something?" Grace advised. So I went back in. The bird was now in my living room, trying desperately to get out through my half-moon window. Finally I got enough gumption to try and chase it away from the window, which worked, except now the bird flew to the other side of the room and landed on a high shelf. While my heart was pounding I started drawing the bird. I also thought about what Grace said, and wrote down "Mark 11:22" on the same piece of paper.

Don't you see how much you are like this bird? Not knowing there is no one here who wants to do harm, the bird continues to bang against the window trying to get free and not giving up, as it is living out of fear. Getting yourself into bad situations due to fears, rational or not, during your everyday walk through life.

Not giving up things you know are not working and are causing you harm. Have faith in me, the God of your salvation, and know that I love you and will send many angels to guard, protect and guide you along your path to destiny.

I stopped writing and looked up at the bird, bowed my head, and thanked God for making Himself more real in my life. I heard something above my head move, and looked up just in time to see the bird fly outside to freedom.

Later I looked up Mark 11:22: HAVE FAITH IN GOD—WOW!

5/19/10 ~

When Grace came over today we just sat out on the deck and talked. I told her about all the help I got in crazy school. And as great as that turned out to be for me, it wasn't enough. The help I get from God is way different.

I am very thankful for my friendship with Grace, but I really need another friend. For someone who has always had many friends, it is hard to believe how many years I have had to endure being so alone. I asked God to please send me another friend, a good one this time.

Lately Janna, Bub, Scout, and Grace have brought up the fact that Buckley is old and I should start thinking that he will not always be here for me. My reply: "Buck is doing great! His hair isn't even gray yet." But I love him and will never let him suffer. When he cannot go up and down the stairs is when I will have to consider what to do.

5/28/10 ~

Mom told me she ran into an old school friend of mine, Lollie, at the mall. Lollie was my very best friend, and we spent almost every day together during high school. She even came to Portland a few times and stayed with me and Regina. We had such a good time going out dancing. Because I thought she already knew, I told her Regina was a lesbian and I was bi. She seemed fine with it. But then I never heard anything from her after that visit. I thought it was because of my lifestyle.

I found Lollie on Facebook, and we emailed each other at first. Then we started talking on the phone for hours almost every day. She said she missed me as much as I missed her. She knew the real Sherri Smith. The truth is, I lost Sherri Smith before my fall. Lollie told me one of her four sons lives in Portland, and she was coming to see him the following week-end. She asked if I wanted to go with them to see this band. I said sure, but didn't plan on going. After all, I do not go where there are a lot of people.

Lollie and her sons came here and stayed over. I cannot express in words how good it was to see her. I even went to see the band with them. It was great! She reminded me who I was growing up. I feel so much more whole as a person just having my friend back.

6/1/10 ~

Earlier this year I decided, without much thought, to quit pot. For my last hurrah, I smoked some and took Ativan. Both were prescribed. It felt good not to feel. However, the reality now is that it's truly amazing how much smarter I feel and probably have been since I stopped smoking. I also decided to stop taking Ativan.

6/23/10 ~

Five years ago Diana died. I will always place her highest on the list of top people I've ever known. In fact, the better I get, you know, being closer to a healthy, sound person, I realize so much more about her. The thing is, our relationship was more than anything a TRUE FRIENDSHIP.

I still miss you so very much, Diana, my best friend and love ever!

6/29/10 ~

Last Sunday, at City of Refuge, Esther told me she had a scripture specially for me. I just read it; it is Jeremiah 31:12-14. It speaks about the well-watered garden. Only plant people would really understand what a well-watered garden is. Not too much, not too little, but just enough.

I have learned that forgiveness is very important. Not only to ask for forgiveness for all my wrongs or sins, but equally important to forgive those people I am angry at, for whatever reason. And even forgive those who have hurt me. I will ask God to help me forgive.

7/1/10 ~

Although a bit rough at the start, my life in this beautiful place is good.

I talked to Mick when he was at Mom's. I told him I have been holding onto the hurt I felt when he didn't come to Portland after I called him way back in 2002 from double lock-down. Despite all these years of hurting and wondering why my big brother didn't come when I really needed him, I told him I forgive him. His response was he didn't know what I was talking about. Now, this gave me more reason to be upset. But, that is not how I chose to react to his comment. I forgave him. It felt really good to let it go. I should have years ago.

Now I will ask God to help me forgive Stormy and Sybil. If I can forgive them I will consider it a miracle from God Himself.

7/3/10 ~

Last night, after a rough day, Buckley had a really hard time getting up the stairs. He could not put any weight on one of his front legs. CRAP. I stayed up with him all night just holding him and crying. He has been my closest and, yes, many times, my only friend.

Grace came over today and drove Buck and me to the vet. I don't want him to have to suffer. Everyone agreed it was time. It was an agonizing decision, but it was the right one. He was licking my hand trying to comfort me when he died.

7/5/10 ~

I loved Buckley and am so thankful I got to be his best friend for the last fifteen years. I am so lost without him. One thing I am sure of: he would not have died if he wasn't certain I would be okay.

Mom wants me to come over and help her as she had gallbladder surgery the day Buck died. In the past she wouldn't allow me to bring him to her house. Which I found strange, since we usually had a dog when I was a kid. I have not even seen her new house, or have the address except for the city. But now Buckley is gone and Mom says she actually wants my help.

7/6/10 ~

Janna made a rare house-call when she found out Buckley died. She brought her two little cha-wow-wows she just got. They are brother and sister. I named them Dude and Lacey, and I am officially their godmother.

7/8/10 ~

I'm at Mom's. I did some cleaning and organized her closet. I bring a pan of warm water and Epson salt to Mom so she can soak her feet before I give her a massage. It feels good to be able to help her. Two of my nephews and one of my nieces live here, and it's good to spend time with them. Another nephew and his family live nearby, as does Aunt Harriet.

My cousin told me she might be able to get me a good deal on a standard poodle pup. I told this to Mom, who thought I shouldn't get another dog. Or at least wait until spring because then I can come here and help her over the fall and winter.

I love my mom, and am very thankful she is a God believer. I am pretty sure she isn't aware how much my feelings get hurt by some of the things she says to me. I tried to explain to her how most of the time I am alone and really feel I need a dog for companionship. She doesn't understand. And there are some things I don't understand about her. I honestly think she wishes her daughter was someone I am not and can never be. I finally asked her why it is that her dislike of my dog was so much greater than her love for me. Her words were not helping. I will believe it's the meds she's on. My niece and her husband came in, so I took this opportunity to take a walk.

I was sitting on the ground, watching the sunset, when I heard a sound I hadn't heard since I was a kid living here—rattle snakes! Just about then my phone rang. It was Lollie, who said my mom called her looking for me. I quickly made it back to Mom's, and asked why she called Lollie. She said she was worried about me. I thought of so many other times in the last several years when worrying about me would have been so much more appropriate.

7/14/10 ~

My aunt and cousin came to town and invited me to go the beach with them. They were going to visit my other cousin. I didn't know she lived there. So I went, and it was really good to spend time with them.

7/18/10 ~

I spent the week-end editing my book with Donna at her beach trailer. This was the first time I read beyond the first few chapters. There were a few times when she would look at me and ask, "Are you alright?"

After reading about Diana and the mustard seed necklace, I took a much needed break. As I was walking on the beach feeling pretty terrible, my long-lost-found friend Lollie texted me the story about the mustard seed. Then, right after that, I met a lady who has two dogs, one a standard poodle. I can't believe my constant companion is gone. This lady and I talked about our dogs and stuff. Turns out she's a singer/songwriter and wanted me to hear one of her songs. It is entitled "Mustard Seed" and it's on her CD she gave me!

It was pretty hard at times to read the book. But it was great to spend time with Donna, and, if I had to be somewhere to read the book, this place at this beautiful beach can't be matched.

8/10/10 ~

At Mom's. A hot summer night in the high desert. I just came inside after gazing outside at the star-studded sky. I go willingly to escape in the celestial world, and it swallows me up.

Tomorrow I will drive Mom and Aunt Harriet to Twin Falls, Idaho for a family reunion. Both my brothers and their families are coming, as well as assorted aunts, uncles, and cousins. It has been well over 20 years since I attended a family reunion. I am looking forward to seeing my relatives. I wonder who it is in me that they will see.

8/22/10 ~

I very much enjoyed seeing my relatives at the reunion. After all, I needed to inform everyone that I wanted back in the circle. I didn't have much interaction with my brothers, but that was okay. One thing I am sure of: each of us has to take responsibility for our actions. And I did not do a very good job staying connected to my family. But here I was, back in and around my family, and I was certain this time I was going to be the best daughter, sister, and relative I can be.

Although my heart was heavy with the loss of Buckley, I was glad I had such huge distractions. It was not always easy being around my mom and her grandkids, as I could see how strong all their relationships were. I do not doubt that they love me, but I do, however, see there just isn't much room in their full lives to get to know me again, or include me now. I did get to go down the river with my nieces and nephews a couple of times. It was fun, and I was happy to learn what's happening in their lives.

I was there to take care of my mom, and I know I stayed true to that and did a good job. I must continuously remind myself to be the best I can be. This was tough because many times my mom would say things in a subtle way that would hurt me. I'm not sure if she knows this, but I understand that she lost out on having the kind of daughter she wanted. So, with that and my new goals, I would dismiss the hurt. No sense in holding onto it. Wow—that's like making it through a tidal wave and coming out the other side upright!

After we got back to Mom's, Joe and his family stayed a day or two before heading back east. Joe's wife told me if I flew back east with Mom next month to see them, and if I could work in their yard, they would pay for my airline ticket. I said yes.

9/3/10 ~

I had a bike accident. I damaged some tendon I didn't know I had, and now have to wear a big, black, unfashionable, uncomfortable boot. Walking with it makes my whole body hurt.

9/12/10 ~

I guess I was blessed (we'll talk later, God) with this knack for adding insult to injury. While driving with the big, black boot I missed hitting the brake and wrecked my car. Now what?

9/26/10 ~

Up, Up, and Away . . . to Denver. Mom and I will meet at the airport there and fly to Baltimore to visit Joe and family. I know I've been there, but I have little to zero memory of it, as I'm sure at that time my meds included methadone.

I think of Buck and my mind and heart are smiling.

Leaving Denver now. Mom has a window seat with two empty seats next to her. I have a window seat with two empty seats next to me. So there are four seats and the middle aisle between us. She really shows so much dissatisfaction towards the person I am and the things I do. Maybe the things she sees me do remind her of things she does that she dislikes.

10/18/10 ~

It is really beautiful where my brother lives. I was more than happy to work on his massive yard.

Mom was still not feeling good. She had a lot of pain in her hip. While Joe and his wife were at work, Mom stayed in bed while I gardened. I really enjoyed the work, and being able to help both Mom and Joe. I wanted so much to be the best I could for my family. After all, Joe did fly across country just for me.

We traveled to Washington, D.C., Annapolis, and their vacation place in West Virginia. As much as I enjoyed all the sightseeing and great places to eat (especially enjoyed the crab cakes), I was just happy to be part of my family's life. The thing I enjoyed most during this trip was something Mom said to me: "I FEEL LIKE I AM GETTING MY DAUGHTER BACK."

10/29/10 ~

I stayed with Mom after we got back from our trip. She tried to talk me into NOT getting another dog, at least until spring. After all, she argued, she might need me to come back over the winter to help if she didn't get better. I was determined to both get a dog and make her understand the reason I wanted one. My life was so lonely that I really needed a dog. Another constant companion I could count on. I wanted Mom to accept the fact I liked having a dog in my life, and told her I accepted the fact that she did not.

I found a good deal on a van and bought it with Mom's help. Then I was off to meet my cousin halfway between Tri-Cities and Twin Falls. He was bringing my dogs. Yes, dogs. In addition to the five-month old male puppy, I agreed to take his mom, who was retiring after spending her life in a kennel breeding standard poodles.

10/31/10 ~

I could hardly believe my eyes when I saw them. The puppy was a little bigger than his mom at just five months. They were both sorely in need of a bath and haircut. My new car smell was replaced by ICK. I pulled over several times on the six-plus hour trip back to Portland so they could go to the bathroom. But they refused to budge and sat in the very back of the van, scared and confused. When we got home, and I was able to get a good look at them, I was amazed at how beautiful they are. They are not black, like Buck, but black and white. The puppy obviously hasn't been loved or around people much. His mom couldn't get enough petting. What did I get myself into?

11/5/10 ~

I named the puppy D.O.G., but this giant puppy wasn't catching on. It was around Halloween, so it seemed appropriate to yell "Boo!" at him, which got his attention. When I took them to meet Kerry, she suggested I change the name Boo Radley, from To Kill a Mockingbird. So I did. Boo's mom's name is Anyia, and though I had a hard time saying it, I kept it as she was so scared from all the changes.

11/16/10 ~

Anyia keeps jumping the fence and running away. So I get my exercise running after her. Then Boo caught on and now he goes running off with her. I don't like this game.

11/28/10 ~

Okay—I'm not sure if I should take this as a sign or not, but now the dogs are jumping out of my van windows, and, even worse, my second story bedroom window. The list of times I thought I've lost them is longer than I care to think about. I even prayed to God to find them another home to live in if He thought it best.

I love and take good care of them, but I don't feel like I've really bonded with them. And, of course, every time I talk to my mom she would ask if I've found them a home yet. It's like I'm hovering over this grand canyon between how I feel about having my dogs and knowing they'll never be welcome at Mom's. I don't know which side to jump to.

I came across a scripture in the Bible Proverbs 12:10 "The Godly care for their animals, but the wicked are always cruel." I'll tell Mom about it. She rarely argues with God.

1/17/11~

I've been attending this Apostolic Leadership and Ministry Institute and, have to say, I've really gained from it. Although my transformation had started before, I am convinced that what I learned about who God is, who I am with Him, and what I'm supposed to do with this information may never have been revealed to me so completely without attending. I had such wrong ideas about God and what was expected of me with Him in my life.

I looked at "reaping what you sow" differently; I never really imagined it to be something good. Except for the sowing and reaping of seeds, but even then the reaping part meant there's hard work to be done. Here's a transformation: instead, if we sow honor and respect for each other, that is what we will reap.

It hit me that what I was taught as a child, like accept God or go burn in hell, is NOT the way to represent Him. We should revere rather than fear God. It's His grace and love and forgiveness that allows someone like me, or anyone, to have a relationship with Him.

I definitely got a glimpse of my true identity for the first time during these classes. I am so much more equipped to not only handle my life now, but to also extend hope to those who feel hopeless. There is great excitement in the air as I have so much more good news to share now!

2/19/11 ~

Oh my God, poor Kerry! Hugging her good-bye, I happened to drop my lower bridge on her bed. Right after I left, somehow, a spark from her lighter hit her bed, started a fire, which ignited and blew up her oxygen, setting her, her bed and her room on fire. In fact, the plastic coating of the bed melted over her entire back and neck. One would think this would have killed her, but not my friend. After being put on hold TWICE from her "Help me I fell" button, she amazingly found her landline and called 911. It is a miracle she is still alive.

2/26/11 ~

For years now I have been telling my caseworkers I don't need them. And now they may believe it. The county called and now wants to interview me along with my caregiver, Grace. Hmmmm . . .

3/8/11 ~

Grace and I sat through three or more interviews with different people asking me very embarrassing questions. Usually I would just want them to look at my plants or artwork. Anything but what they were there for. This time, though, it was I, rather than my caregiver, who actually, matter-of-factly, answered their questions.

3/15/11 ~

Well, they finally agreed with me. The county said I will no longer have a caregiver or my appointments with Janna. That's all that would change, they said. So, you can imagine my surprise to find my medical insurance had been cancelled. Thank God I went to member services the very last day I had to reinstate my health insurance and somehow pay for it myself. They even extended my coverage for a couple of months.

3/20/11 ~

The last day Grace was my caregiver she assured me she would still put my meds in the weekly holders for me. When she left, my feelings flew from one spectrum to the other. I was scared to death. I was free. I was alone. I graduated to adulthood all over again. I was excited with anticipation of the future, yet unsure if I could stay afloat on my own again.

I do believe they could have given me more time to adjust. And correct information about my health coverage.

3/29/11 ~

The time of my life is fast approaching that all the dots will be connected and my true identity and purpose will be aligned at the time planned. Making the most out of the knowledge of the truth.

My life's aim is being the best me I can be. I want to speak to those who will listen (and read) to prevent them from making the same mistakes I did. I want to give hope to the hopeless and help put a smile on people's faces. Thank you, God, for not giving up on me!

4/3/11 ~

Looking back ten years ago . . . the absolute worst storm slammed into my life and steered it into an eddy of torment. Surprisingly, I do have some good memories from those years since my fall. I think about them often. The "groups" for example. Watching people, learning from their experiences. Caring for and feeling close to absolute strangers. I think it's because we are all the same. Nobody judges but encourages instead.

The therapists. Doing their job obviously not for the money, but to help others. I made it through those times more whole and complete because of their help and guidance.

I'm not thankful for my fall, I'm not that crazy, but I am grateful for all the people and all the tools I've been given to rebuild myself. I am a better person today because of this.

4/12/11 ~

Kerry was coming home after about two months in the hospital. She had to have dead people's skin stapled on her entire back. I told her I'd try to find her a good caregiver. And I did.

I first met Olga a couple of years back at church. It was one of many places she gave her ministry services. She told me that she was particularly called to help gays, or "them" as she put it. I told her it would help more if she stopped calling them "them." Olga was the perfect choice to help take care of Kerry.

4/17/11 ~

Surprise of surprises! Stormy calls and, laughing, says she thought I'd be dead. I told her I had forgiven her. She blamed everything on Sybil, and I let her. She came over. It was nice to see her. I always liked so many things about her as an artist and friend. But there was no way I would let her pass the huge boundaries I set in stone around me.

We worked on art projects for a while when Kerry called, asking me to come over. Stormy decided to come with me to Pine Point. Kerry was happy with Olga, which made me really happy. Then she says she has stage four cancer. I felt as though someone hit me in the stomach.

5/3/11~

After taking my latest round of meds for about a year as prescribed, I wanted to get off them. At least what I could. My doctor said he would take me off Remeron and Ativan and cut the Neurontin in half. Instead of three Cymbalta a day, I'll start taking two. Slowly I WILL get off these things.

5/7/11 ~

I feel so good about my future. I have hope. And less pills!

5/16/11 ~

Grace called me. I couldn't believe my ears when she told me Olga died. She had walking pneumonia. I knew she had been fighting a cold, but . . . WHAT???!!!

I remember her as a good, caring person. She once told me that my mess is my message, and my tests are my testimony. Grace said I was good for Olga, that I helped show her things were not simply black and white.

5/20/11 ~

Mom had hip surgery and asked me to come help her again. I couldn't say no, but I did have to ask Lollie's son to dog-sit. Stormy promised she would check in on Kerry for me. We both knew that Kerry needed 24 hour care, but the state would not pay for it. I felt good that Stormy was offering to help Kerry.

When I got back from Mom's, Stormy had more or less moved into Kerry's living room. Kerry liked her, and I did say I forgave her, but knew not to let my guard down.

6/9/11 ~

Stormy was up to her usual tricks. Despite my telling Kerry it was not a good idea, Stormy slithered her way to become Kerry's new caregiver. Stormy was trying to move Kerry into where she and her unemployed drug addict alcoholic friends could live with Kerry paying for everything. After giving Kerry my opinion, I had to stand back and let her decide. And I prayed she would make the right decision. Kerry had to move as she was evicted from Pine Point for smoking in bed. Time was running out. I knew I couldn't bring her here since I live up a long flight of stairs. It is definitely not ADA here. Maybe ADHD, but not ADA.

6/16/11 ~

Kerry did see Stormy for what she is and kicked her out. A couple of days later Kerry was moved into the best assisted living facility I've ever seen. Luckily it's close to me, and everyone there is excited to see my dogs when I visit.

CHAPTER TWENTY-THREE
THE END . . . OR IS IT THE BEGINNING?

SUMMER 2011

I often wondered how I would end this book. Like the beginning, I had various takes. I was going to rant about how we the poor people need to change the system where people buy pop with food stamps, go outside, dump the pop, recycle their cans to get cash for cigarettes.

I could definitely speak to the proliferation of doctors over-prescribing and combining way too many drugs to the masses, convincing us we need them despite the myriad of harmful side effects.

But I want to move forward. Noah and Grace speak at prisons as part of their ministry. They asked me to speak at two of the prisons, so I summoned the courage and did it. I talked about the pinhole of light that led me out of the darkness. And how things have changed since I brought God into my life. I also spoke at the City of Refuge at Grace's request. I am taking chances now . . . allowing myself to be me. I have come to believe that most things, if not all, come full circle. We would not genuinely know and appreciate the sunshine without weathering the storm.

I guess happily ever after is only in fairy tales. But, I do not live in the darkness any more. How we react to life's storms is what really matters. We all have choices, though sometimes we get so caught up in the whirlwind we can't see beyond it.

With or without drastic events, life is a messy adventure. With each of us in the leading role, the key is whether the script is written by others or us. When it's all said and done, it's the same for everyone: when we take a glimpse in the mirror, the looking glass, we must face ourselves.

Facing Face is not as easy as just looking in the mirror. You have to really see who is looking back and face the facts. Doing so with a loving heart, although hard, is better than going to battle with them.

So that's my story and I'm stuck to it. I've bailed myself out of the storms and, I believe, am a better person for it. You can do it, too. Thanks for coming along on my journey!

Proverbs 27:19

As in water, face reflects face, so will our hearts reflect our lives.

CHAPTER TWENTY-FOUR
CELEBRATE YOUR SCARS

March 21 2023

Twelve years since Facing Face was published I tried ignoring it. I couldn't believe such private matters were public. I never would have agreed to having my journals published if i had not had a brain injury. I didnt market my book. In fact, Donna has not spoken to me in years because I hindered, not helped marketing this book.

A couple of years ago, a very good salesman from Page Turner publishing called me and convinced me to edit the book myself and write another chapter then relaunch. I thought the last sentence (Proverb) of the original book was a perfect ending, but at the same time the part about my heart reflecting my life really bothered me. I thought to myself "is my heart bad? Why did so many bad things happen to me? Why dosent my family want me in their lives?"

After going through the book and considering my life events, then doing much soul searching, I realized that my heart was not bad, it was broken. I had spent my life with a heart that did not feel whole. I had many trust issues. There are many reasons I could never give myself wholely to anyone. My grandma used to tell me good relationships are not a 50/50 they are a 100/100 and I'm definitely not100%.

At a very young age, I closed down especially against the male gender. Being taken advantage of as a small child sexually was detrimental to my life. I lost my virginity when I was 12 years old, not by choice. My dad didnt abuse me in this manner, but he damagedme in other ways. The way he spoke to me and my mother caused a lot of self worth issues. He verbally abused my mother calling her names and giving her no respect. When my dad was angry with me he would tell me I was just like my mother and my mother would tell me I was just like my father.

I thought to myself growing up that I didn't want to have a life like either my mom or dad. Neither were perfect but cannot stress enough that I wouldn't trade them for anyone else. They were not perfect people but they did the best they could and I realize that life could have been much worse with different parents.

My first memory of my eldest brother Mick, was holding me down and farting or offering me a quarter to touch the electric fence. He once gave me and my cousin a whole box of Ex-Lax telling us it was chocolate candy resulting in my cousin having to have his stomach pumped. My first memory of my other brother Joe is singing "Carpenter "songs with him. He and I would invite all the neighbor kids over and we would make a carnival for everyone. My brothers are about as opposite as two people could be. I cannot think of many things, if any things, that they actually have in common, yet they are very close.

I know my brothers are good people, which maybe is why I thought I wasn't. When Mick told me they did not want me in their lives because I wasnt a very nice person, this honestly just about did me in. In retrospect, maybe I should thank them because it triggered me to do a deep dive into my soul and heart to fix what seemed broken in me. What I came to know as true is that I am a nice person. Ive always been a nice person. In fact, I'm one of the nicest people I know. There was a time in my life when I disliked myself. During that time, I was too nice, go figure.

During the bulk of my recovery, I seldom left my home, it seemed my life exploded socially, considering I was alone 99% of the time for 10 years. Pretty much everyone I interacted with was a paid professional... doctors, nurses, therapists, etc, etc. Now the world seemed different and unfamiliar than I remembered it. It was darker and more scary. My existence was starting to look like I had a life…different than any I'd had before.

I have a friend I hang out with named Cooper. I met him through Cari. When Cari stopped by, he was with her. Once Cooper and I connected he just kept coming by to see me without Cari.

Cooper made me laugh or he would sit and write poetry while I painted. We had a lot in common. He calls me "Wifey" because I cleaned his house and did his laundry sometimes. He was also a hairdresser that changed my hair to every color of the rainbow. He pushed me to go out in public. For that I ill always be thankful. I had spent many years just surviving, mostly alone along side my medical team.

In 2011 I moved to a one level so mom could come visit me. Infact, it was two weeks after I moved, Mick and his wife brought mom to stay with me. They stopped by my place for maybe five minutes. Micks wife stayed in their truck while Mick brought moms suitcase in and set it down and left. I was excited to have her for more than one night. I was also thinking that maybe I could get some answers as to why she was so unhappy. That was a fleeting thought and I quickly changed my mind about approaching her about this when I saw her.

Mom had recently been diagnosed with Parkinsons. She seemed like she was miserable most of the time. I decided to be the best daughter I could be. It wasn't easy, but I treasure this time I had with her.

With my mom being in the fragile state that she was, I tried to keep my two poodles Boo Radley and Repo Sauve' out of her sight as much as possible. The first week she was here she renamed them to "Get Back" and " Get Down".

One night while cooking her dinner I burned my finger. Right about the same time I heardmy mom say, "Sis will you come here." I answered, " I'll be right there." It sounded a bit frustrated. When I took the tray with her dinner she said she wasn't hungry. This was her way of showing me she thought I was mad at her.

I asked her, "is this about my tone?" We both know I have tone issues. Many times I have been mistaken for being angry when when I wasnt.

"But mother, did't you tell me that actions speak louder than words?" She said, "yes."

"Have I done anything that says anything different than I love and respect you and want you to feel comfotable and cared for?" She said "no." I told her to eat her dinner and she did.

Later that night she called me to my bedroom where she slept. She was sitting on the edge of the bed and she asked me how to get into bed. I took her seriously, walked over to her, and sat down on the side of the bed next to her. I grabbed my knees and rolled back I did this over and over and she just looked at me. I said you are not even trying and I grabbed her, pushed her back, and started tickeling her. We both layed on my bed laughing.

Mom and me laughed about me yelling at Siri in the car giving me bad directions. I said, "Siri you are so dumb," then Siri answered saying "I'm doing the best I can." We laughed about a guy that was on Undercover Boss that night. We belly laughed and it never felt so good to laugh before or after that night laughing with my mom.

Cooper came over almost daily. I did't tell my mom that Cooper was gay or why Cooper calls me Wifey. Almost daily mom would ask me, "is he gay? Are you going to marry him?" She was confused. I told her if she wanted to know she should ask Cooper.

Many friends came around and visited my mom. Resy, one of my best friends who is s park ranger, offered to sit with my mom on Wednesdays for four hours while I went and worked. I was afraid my mom wouldn't like Resy since she likely would think she looks gay.

Anyway, I am so pleased that I was wrong about mom and Resy. Infact, Resy turned out to be my mom's favorite of my friends. She said Resy reminded her of a christian singer she listened to.

My mom insisted on going for mutiple drives every day. She would say, "take me for a drive before I lose my mind." During those drives we started to get to know each other, but she still was calling my aunt and telling her I was yelling at her… not true, but she told me things about my brothers I would bet weren't true either.

Dementia was setting in. She always told me she didnt want to die alone in a care facility. She told me what songs and who she wants to sing them at her funeral. My brother texted me and asked if I would take mom to Idaho to look at a care faciliy one of my cousins runs. So I did. Mom was not herself the whole trip. She complained of her legs cramping. I suggested we sing some hymns. Even that didnt console her for long.

For several months she had been keeping her eyes closed most of time. After we got back to Tri-Cities I texted both of my brothers, Mick and Joe. My honest account of the care facility in Idaho was that I didn't think it would work for for mom. It was very dark. Mom cannot stand dark rooms. I also told them it was three times further for me to drive and that mom can be a bit demanding so we should consider our relatives. I said the three of us should talk about what would be best for mom.

I heard back from both brothers. It was one of the saddest days in my life. They told me that they were sick of my lies and hidden agendas.

My mind started racing I was just driving out of Tri-Cities going back to Portland . I had no idea what they could be talking about. I pulled over and called my lifelong best friend Lollie. She always makes me feel better. She is super good at being my bestie. I texted my brothers back asking what I did wrong but they never responded.

The following summer, my cousin Shirley, my mom, and I, drove to Idaho for a family reunion. I had not missed one since I started going way back when I was still part of the family circle. My brothers and their kids and families didnt come to this family reunion. It was my aunts, uncles, and cousins. My mom said she needed to go home earlier than we planned. So we packed up and went home.

Later, I found out my brothers, their kids, grandkids, and mom had a family reunion planned only I was not invited. Ouch right? I knew I didnt want any more regrets in my life because they suck big time!

Despite the heartache of our torn family, I continued to be the best daughter I could be. I would show up early in the morning with her favorite McDonald's breakfast. We would watch Cash Cab, Jeopardy, and Wheel of Fortune. I took her on picnics and lots of drives. I truly just liked spending time with her. Sometimes I would just sit and watch her sleep in her chair. For almost two years I would call my mom and my aunt near daily on a three-way call so we could sing together. I cannot believe how many songs I didnt even know I knew.

As mom progressed with her illness there were times she would just set the phone down and walk away. I remember sitting in my 1989 Mustang 5.0 convertible I've owned forover 25 years with my mom and aunt on speaker phone singing I'lll FLY AWAY while at a light. People were giving me some stange looks, but we didn't care!

I learned that people with Parkinsons sometimes hallcinate. My mom would say she was seeing scary monsters.

I asked her if she trusts me and she said "yes" without hesitation. I told her that her illness was causing her to see things that are not real. I told her I would pray they go away which I would do right then.

The next week she told me she has a real nice family sharing her apartment. She said they were quiet and stayed to themselves. Since she seemed happy about the family being there I didnt tell her they were not real. I just wanted her to be at peace. I knew she was lonely and I knew how that felt which is one of the worse feelings to have. It is right up there with the feeling of regret.

So I was informed by text from Mick that mom would be moving to Rathdrum Idaho to a facility named Generations, located an hour from where he lived. This was over twice as far for me to drive, on top of the fact that neither mom nor myself knew a single soul in this town. Unlike where she was in Tri-Cities, I had many places I could stay. I had reconnected with the three people that I spent nearly everyday with in highschool. It was great for the four of us to be together again.

So instead of seeing my mom 3-4 times a month I got to see her only for a couple of hours 3-4 times during the 2 plus years she was there. I did call her everyday but more and more she was just silent. Sometimes someone that worked there would hold the phone up to moms ear and I would sing to her. I don't have a good voice by a long shot, but I love my mom and wanted her to feel better so I had no shame. I could feel how lonely she was and it killed me inside. Loneliness might be one of the worse things to feel and I don't wish it for anyone.

I got to go see my mom about a month before she died. I got to stay two days but due to the pandemic I only got to see her about 30-minutes twice a day. The day I was leaving I was in telling my mom goodbye. She told me that I'd better just go before she starts crying like a baby. Those turned out to be the last words my mom ever spoke to me.

A woman came in to tell me they were locking down again due to the pandemic as I was leaving. I happened to visit the only two days they were not locked down during the pandemic,,..I'M BLESSED!

Then August 2020 I called her and was told she wasnt doing well and it wouldnt be long until she passed. I left Portland that night and picked up my cousin Shirley in Yakima Washington. She knew she couldnt go in to the facility, but didnt want me to have to drive alone. "Thanks Shirley."

When I walked into moms room she was moaning and talking jibberish waving both arms in the air. I ran to her and told her it was her daughter and she was ok. I called my aunt and put her on speaker and we sang and prayed for my mom.

In 2013 when mom lived with me for four months I started an app on my phone that sent me random bible verses daily. I would forward these to my mom and my aunts.

On August 21st I had been there two days. I was sitting on a chair next to moms bed with my back to the door. I kept feeling like someone was walking in but when I turned around no one was there. Besides the nurses I was the only one with my mom the last two days of her life. About 10:00 AM that morning I said to my mom lets see what todays verse is and opened the app on my phone. I began reading the scripture which was Phillipanians 3:7,

It said "For your citizenship is in heaven..exchange your body of humiliation for the crown of glory." I looked at my mom and knew she had passed.

I called Mick and my aunt. Mick called Joe. I stayed with my mom for the next hour or so until Mick got there. When he walked in I went up to him and gave him a hug. He didn't hug back, but said," mom is gone not in pain so I was crying for myself." He then said that we grieve very differently. Im still unsure what he meant by that, but I didnt get a chance to ask because hospice came in and said they needed to prepare moms body for the coroner so I dropped the subject.

Mick suggested we go get coffee and I agreed. With tears in my eyes I asked Mick to please tell me why him and Joe were so upset with me and didnt want me in their lives so I could fix the problem. He just shrugged his shoulders and told me they just didn't think I was a very nice person. I asked for examples but he couldnt give me any. I was in shock and disbelief. How could he be so cold especially two hours after Mom died. He told me not to have a funeral because he wanted it done right. Don't worry I won't. I respect that is your call since you are the oldest. It's been 4 and a half years since then, and still she has not had a funeral. I have not talked to any of my immediate family at all.

No one has ever stood up for me. My brothers didnt care I had been raped or that I almost died. This was how it was and I had to accept it without knowing why. It took a lot of work but I was willing to go through what was needed to fix what felt broken.

It turned out I am not who my brothers think I am. I am more at home in this body that has many scars and has not aged all that well. When I was young It should've been easy to feel good about my outward looks, but inside I was incomplete and broken. But I learned to act at an early age. In highschool I was in drama production class, We wrote a kids play and performed in elementary schools. I was a very popular toy at the time... I was a Weeble. My only lines were "Weebles wobble but they don't fall down. Then in highschool I actually won an award for most promising new coming actress playing Sleeping beauty in"Bumping jump steps into legend" It is when Sleeping Beauty wakes up and falls for the scallion instead of the prince, Then in church I played a girl who is trying to decide which way to go in "Give me your dreams" I guess all of these were showing me about my future in different ways. I found acting was much easier than reality. So I spent my life always trying to hide that deep seeded anger and disappointment for not feeling safe as a child to being a people pleaser. In 1988 when I started my business, some friends were over and someone said I was always going to be a people pleaser... I said no I am not ; I'm going to be a Plant Pleaser. This was how I named my business The Plant Pleasers Inc. I loved that business and it was very successful. These years were the happiest times of my life.I got into my first gay relationship in college. I begged God to change me although there was no question I truly did love her.I am not here to judge anyone. I've had many relationships with both genders, I didn't like calling myself bi because I thought that meant I would have sex with anyone. It was around this time it was just starting to be cool to be gay at least in Portland Oregon.

There was a time that Webster's dictionary said gay meant happy or cheerful.. I googled what gay means today and it means sexually attracted to the same sex as well as a bunch of stuff mostly pertaining to men.

God said besides blasphemy there are no sins greater than another. Why is it that most churches will not make the gay population welcome?

I feel churches in general give the gay population no hope for salvation. If they do welcome them , people might think they are ok with it. So it's welcome to our church where God thinks how you are living is an abomination to Him.. but it clearly says judge not lest you be judged. I have known many gay women and I can safely say 90% of them have been sexually abused as children. Many gay men have as well. I have always thought and told my guy gay friends I thought they were just perverted as most will have sex with anyone. I now feel gay relationships are a counterfeit to what God wants for us.But I also believe it's God's job to judge and the churches job to accept everyone with the love of God. The Bible says clearly that it's the kindness of God that leads to repentance, I don't believe it is the judgment of people that makes anyone want to know God. When I spent 3 years in all day treatment five days a week there were several trans people there. Their stories are the saddest of all.

They thought having a sex change would fix the brokenness in them. When it didn't but only added more problems and pain it was too much. I will never agree to tell anyone I agree with them that they were just born in the wrong body. God doesn't make mistakes. The facts are that more trans people kill themselves after surgery than before.. I know 2 that were my friends in the hospital that committed suicide. The pain and daily things they have to do and they will never enjoy sex ever again isn't talked about much from the medical staff. It's just a way to make money for them.

I have always been somewhat of a tomboy but never wanted to be a boy. I would rather go outside and garden rather than learn to sew. But I am still 100% girl.

I lost my virginity around 11 or 12 by a family member. Not my immediate family. But I was molested and or raped by 6 different guys or men from as early as 5 until 13. The way my dad talked to my mom was so disrespectful and called us all free loading SOB's. My brothers never cared about me. even after I told them what happened to me or that I almost died in the hospital. In general I didn't have a lot of trust for the male gender. I definitely felt safer with girls. I still liked guys but had huge trust issues.

I couldn't take the chance. So Although I did love my boyfriend in college I chose the girl. I thought I was sick and for sure going to hell. I was accused by her family that I was dragging her to hell. I barely knew what gay meant then, Besides I can honestly say I have never made the first move on anyone. Her mom called my mom and my oldest brother and their pastor (that I'm pretty sure ended up leaving the church for a gay lifestyle.) and told them I was a gay drug dealer when I was 21. My mom made my brothers come to Portland to not take me home but put me on a plane for South Carolina to some weird jim jones place for runaway teens. It took me 3 days to learn where my return plane ticket was and to pick a lock. I was then on my way back to Portland, I didn't talk to my family for several years. I truly loved my 1st girlfriend. Webster's dictionary says to love someone is to want their highest good. So when her family gave her a choice of me or them after almost 4.5 years I was devastated but told her I wanted her to go to heaven more than I wanted to be with her. However, I thought we would be friends. She along with many after her told me they loved me and would always be my friend are not. I have never understood how anyone that truly cared could just stop caring and never talk to me again.

Recently I left a facebook group of friends that I truly believed would always be in my life. The reason I left is I kept getting very disrespectful posts. Flipping me off and other things friends don't do to friends. I've known them for years even though many said I was their best friend. They were not my friends as I haven't heard from them for years. The interesting thing is my family don't want me around because they say I'm not a nice person and my friends are not my friends because I'm now a conservative. My door has always and will always be open to my brothers and their families. My self worth is no longer affected by what they think of me. The fact is I don't know why they feel this way makes it much worse. I've cried many many times about this. I love my brothers and their families . But I refuse to allow them or anyone else to be in charge of how I feel about myself. I know I'm a nice person and have done nothing wrong to them.

After many prayers to God and lots of time alone crying and screaming and wondering why I wasn't getting answers. I realized I was doing all the talking I needed to listen for my answers.

I started going to a bible study. It was at Thomas and Mazzie's. Not long after I was told I no longer needed a caregiver. I applied to be Mazzie's dad's caregiver for weekends and the graveyard shift. He had MS . Well, I got the job. It was my first job in a long time. . On my way out I said to Mazzie's dad "you're a gambling man aren't you' Myrie was a great man. I loved talking to him and taking care of him. I first met Thomas when I sold him some tools. I loved going to visit them. They lived up close to Mt. Hood. I took them plants as I needed to downsize. I truly enjoyed being around both of them. Thomas had a quick wit and sense of humor that made me laugh. Something I had not done for a long time. He would usually make me very strong drinks. When I asked what was in them , he would say everything. I think he was telling me the truth considering how I felt after drinking them. Mazzie's dad passed away and I didn't see Thomas for several years. I had lunch with Mazzie and another caregiver named Terri of Myrie's. Then Mazzie called me and asked if I would be a caregiver for her grandpa, John as he had a stroke. I said yes. Mazzie and her two brothers would take turns to have John live at their house 4 months each for the first year or so. The first time I saw Thomas I said well don't you look shiny and new.

He then told me about a dream he had about how much God loves us. He had tears in his eyes and I could tell it affected him greatly as it did me, I will never forget... He was a better version of himself. I got to visit with him quite a lot when John was there. He was my friend. He treated me how I wished my brothers would. So when I started going to bible study the first night we read from the book of Genesis.

It was a part where this wife of this guy sent her servants to have sex with her husband, I was in shock. Afterwards they asked how I liked bible study that night and all I could say was " I thought this was a holy book." That was a couple of years ago and I still attend. There are lots of people in the bible that were used by God. I now know why God always uses imperfect people. IT'S BECAUSE THAT IS ALL THERE IS. So often I felt I needed to stop this or change that to go to God.

Until I finally learned God wants us to come as we are. I know this because it took several months to stop shooting drugs and allowing God in all aspects of my life. Choosing to believe He loves me. Not only did I stop shooting drugs, I also quit all my prescription drugs' That was 15 years ago. This last year in 2023 Thomas had a heart attack and went to be with Jesus as did Grace's husband. Two guys that were too young and loved to die. We still have bible study…the group has gotten smaller but it's always good to learn more about the bible. Trenton and Robin, his wife, and Mazzie and I usually have dinner together first.. I actually feel I'm part of a group of people that want me there and care. I love having these new friends. I feel accepted and cared about. The same goes for Mazzie's two brothers and their wives. Mitch and Cassie and Travis and Nicci.

I really care about these people. I'm blessed to have them in my life.

I actually had a good relationship with my mom before she died . This makes me very happy as I had been so angry at her for not keeping me safe.

After all these things had happened to me in life, I had faced faced and it wasnt easy. I found that I had waited for someone else to tell me my worth, but it was my opinion of myself that mattered. I looked in the mirror and saw myself and made some changes. I realized that life is messy and sometimes painful. The downs makes the ups so much better.

So what advise would I give to anyone that finds themselves in hell?…Don't stop, keep going. God gives us all a map out of hell. It's up to us whether we use it or not. It's good to know that light shines brightest in the dark.

I am thankful for the road Ive traveled with all the detours and challenges. I know, had I not been broken, I would not have learned how to be whole. My scars say where I have been but do not get to dictate where Im going.

Obviously, my life didn't turn out as expected, but I learned through this journey that I don't have to walk alone. None of us do. I'm not only thankful that God gave me a map out of hell, but He was with me every step of the way. So now I'm promised a better ending than a happily ever after. I will be happy for eternity..

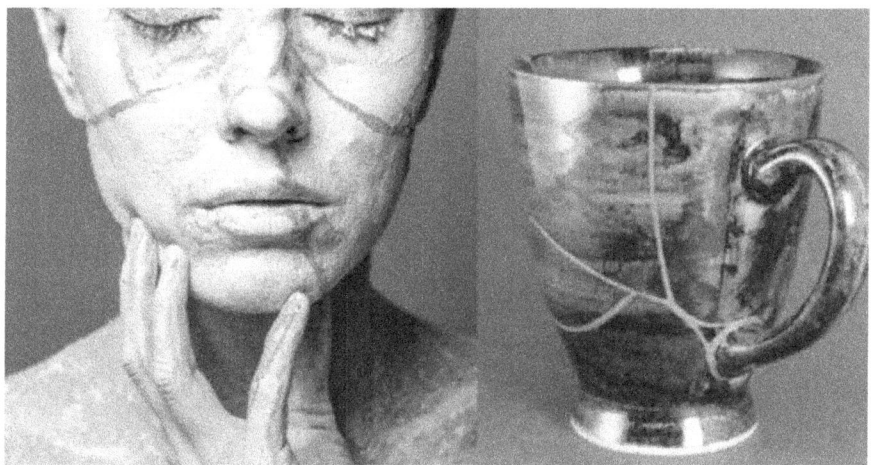

Photo: Shutterstock.

Celebrate Your Scars

Kintsugi is Japenese art that is created from broken pottery and put back together using a metal powder lacquer to repair the broken pieces to make whole again. The finished product becomes a new piece of beautiful art. Kintsugi inspires us to look for the potential in things and people.

These lines are like my scars that are from the pain that caused me to feel broken into pieces so many times in my life. I have taken all of the solid pieces of me and put myself back together again.

Read more at: https://www.onmanorama.com/lifestyle/news/2019/12/04/japanese-art-kintsugi-philosophy.html